UNSHOT COLUMBO

CRACKING THE CASES THAT NEVER GOT FILMED

By David Koenig

For Akeo Machida,
for his immense support and generosity.
Duomo arigatou gozaimasu.

Unshot Columbo: Cracking the Cases That Never Got Filmed

Published by
BONAVENTURE PRESS
Aliso Viejo, CA
USA
www.bonaventurepress.com

All rights reserved. No part of this book may be reproduced or transmitted in any form or by any means, electronic or mechanical, including scanning, photocopying, recording or by any information storage and retrieval system without written permission from the author, except for the inclusion of brief quotations in a review.

Cover art by Kevin Jakubowski
Edited by Hugh Allison

Copyright 2024 by David Koenig

Publisher's Cataloging in Publication Data
Koenig, David G., 1962-
    Unshot Columbo: Cracking the Cases That Never Got Filmed
        p. cm.
    Includes annotated references and index.

       1. Columbo (Television Program) [1. Columbo (Television Program)
       2. Mystery and detective television programs. 3. Television programs] 1. Title.
       791.4572

Library of Congress Control Number: 2024933483

ISBN 978-1-937878-23-8 (Paperback)
ISBN 978-1-937878-24-5 (Hardcover)
ISBN 978-1-937878-25-2 (Kindle ebook)

Contents

Prelude	5
1. Make Us a Perfect Murder	7
2. Season 3: The Murder Consultant	11
Murder Out of Tune *Death Do Us Part*	
Shooting Script	
3. Season 4: Psychological Problems	48
Dead as a Duck	
Sugar and Spice and Everything Nice	
4. Season 5: Lethal Athletes	72
Roar of the Crowd *Murder in B Flat*	
5. Season 6: Old-Fashioned Murders	103
In Deadly Hate *The Lesser of Two Evils*	
6. Season 8: The Return of the Raincoat	130
Untitled Courtroom Story *Last of the Redcoats*	
7. Season 9: The Last of Link	143
The Bride of Frankenstein *Double Vision*	
Stunt Girl *Shooting Star*	
8. The First Specials: A New Sheriff in Town	169
Killer's Choice *Critic's Choice: Murder*	
9. The Final Specials: Petering Out	181
Murder by Suicide	
Hear No Evil/Columbo's Last Case	
Index	196

Books by David Koenig

Mouse Tales:
A Behind-the-Ears Look at Disneyland

Mouse Under Glass:
Secrets of Disney Animation & Theme Parks

More Mouse Tales:
A Closer Peek Backstage at Disneyland

Realityland:
True-Life Adventures at Walt Disney World

Danny Kaye:
King of Jesters

The People v. Disneyland:
How Lawsuits & Lawyers Transformed the Magic

The 55ers:
The Pioneers Who Settled Disneyland

Shooting Columbo:
The Lives & Deaths of TV's Rumpled Detective

Unshot Columbo:
Cracking the Cases That Never Got Filmed

Prelude

While researching my previous book, *Shooting Columbo: The Lives and Deaths of TV's Rumpled Detective*, I became particularly intrigued with the episodes that Peter Falk *almost* filmed, but never did. For all of the complaining by him, his producers, and his story editors that the show never had enough quality scripts, I uncovered numerous tales that read as though they would have made terrific *Columbos*. (Granted, a great script does not guarantee a great show.)

I became determined to track down as many of the missing mysteries as possible. Many were revelations. Most needed more work. A couple seemed beyond saving. And several remain lost (although my search will continue).

But truly, the hunt was as exciting as the discovery. And such a great many wonderful people assisted in that hunt—and in helping to piece together the backstories. No one was more vital to this project than Akeo Machida, the leading authority on *Columbo* in Japan—if not the world. His knowledge, insight and collection of *Columbo* materials pale only in comparison to his generosity.

Jim and Melody Rondeau supplied copies of several rare scripts.

Archivists held even more. I thank Hilary Swett and her team at the Writers Guild Foundation, as well as the research staffs at Boston University's Howard Gotlieb Archival Research Center, the University of Iowa, UCLA Library Special Collections, and the Academy of Motion Picture Arts and Sciences' Margaret Herrick Library.

Dene Kernohan was ever-helpful. He graciously shared transcripts of his interviews with Stanley Kallis, Nancy Meyer, and Francesca Redwine.

I am equally indebted to those who personally shared their memories with me: Peter Berk, Paul Robert Coyle, Frank D'Angeli, Peter S. Fischer, Philip

Gerson, Candida Gillis, Barry Glasser, Dean Hargrove, Jack Horger, Chris Manheim, and Mark Bruce Rosin.

I am ever-thankful for and inspired by fellow *Columbo* aficionados Mark Dawidziak, author of the landmark *The Columbo Phile*, for suggesting the title *Unshot Columbo*, and to blogger The Columbophile, author of *The Columbo Companion*, for encouragement and support.

I am beyond grateful for editor extraordinaire Hugh Allison. Every project is made a thousand times better because of Hugh. You could not find a finer partner for your editing needs. Reach him at contactTYPE@gmail.com.

The superb cover illustration and design were created by absurdly talented artist Kevin Jakubowski (www.kevinjakubowski.com). Thank you, Kevin.

I am blessed with the most wonderful, supportive family imaginable—Laura, Zach, Sofia and Rebecca Koenig, as well as Joe, Paul, Maryanne and Anne Koenig, who was my first link to the Lieutenant, 50+ years ago.

Above all, I give thanks to Jesus Christ, my leader and rescuer, who gets me out of jams on a daily basis and has promised a literal eternity of joy.

1
Make Us a Perfect Murder

Ever since the show's premiere, audiences have been starved for more *Columbos*. They would practically kill for "just one more" episode. No matter how many were produced in a season, there never seemed to be enough.

The decision to ration the output over three and a half decades was star Peter Falk's. He preferred to make movies rather than toil in the less glamorous world of series television. Originally, Falk only agreed to turn his movie-of-the-week character into a series lead for the money—and a once-every-three-or-four-week series at that, rotating with other detective shows as part of *The NBC Mystery Movie* "wheel." Falk kept at it, in large part, because he knew just how much the audience loved the character. He truly felt he owed it to the fans around the world.

In total, counting the two pilots, he appeared in 69 mysteries. That might sound like a lot, but they were spread out over 35 years. The most episodes ever filmed in a calendar year was eight, which was in 1972—a time when the typical television drama aired three times that number.

Asked why they made so few episodes, Falk and his producers customarily cited a shortage of quality scripts. The explanation does hold some water, in that the quality of the show grew spottier as the years went on.

According to longtime Universal Television executive vice president of creative Charlie Engel, "Of all the shows I have been involved with over 40 years at Universal, the hardest television script to write is *Columbo*. It was very difficult to write. Many tried, not a lot succeeded. Somebody wealthy commits a murder that's so difficult to solve that the police department can't do it. It takes Columbo to solve it. That was the key to *Columbo* in that you have a really crafty antagonist. It's very difficult to write a perfect crime and yet still leave it so it can be solved by a guy who appears to be completely inept and gets in the way. Who makes the murderer feel that they are so lucky that the LAPD has assigned this doofus to solve the crime, because he'll never figure it out."

Indeed, in an ideal episode, the crime should seem unsolvable not just to the perpetrator, but to the audience as well… until our unassuming hero uncovers one easily overlooked inconsistency after another, which culminates in a dramatic reveal of actual proof. The murderer's alibi should unravel one insignificant thread at a time. Falk loved how associate producer Jack Horger's young son described the murderer's plight—like being "nibbled to death by a duck."

Even in the best episodes, there's a minimum of action. By nature, the program is talky, like a verbal chess match. In great measure, the show rides on the quirkiness and lovability of Columbo, and the ingenuity of the solving of the mystery.

The prolific Peter S. Fischer, who wrote nine *Columbos* and—as executive story consultant—oversaw nine more, was amazed that so few outsiders could pull it off. Executive producer Dean Hargrove said that, until he hired Fischer, "usually we used freelance writers, almost exclusively. Guys would come in and they'd have an idea. If you liked the idea, you'd bring them back. If you brought someone back after they pitched an idea, that was a story commitment as prescribed by the Writers Guild. And you'd bring them in and many times you'd sit and work with them to work out all the plotting on them. Then you'd get a draft. If you liked their writing, you'd get a rewrite. And at a certain point the script came back to you. It went through, in those days, your typewriter, and you did the final work on the script. You did the production changes. You did a lot of writing on the show as a writer/producer, for which you were never credited. There's only been once or twice in my career where I've put in for credit because I just felt the writer really hadn't done anything, and I felt that it was fair for me to have that. Other than that, you say that's part of the job, that's what you have to do."

Over the years, *Columbo's* executive producers purchased several dozen scripts that were never filmed. Peter Falk's assistant, Francesca Redwine, noted, "It's true that quite a few scripts were bought that never made it to production, but it isn't true that the series developed four or five scripts for every episode. During a series, while one episode is being shot (about three weeks for a two-hour show), producers and writing staff are working on the script for the next episode and reading/writing scripts for future episodes;

the pace is fast on a series, hectic. Promising scripts are bought for future production, but some don't pan out from paper to camera-ready for one reason or another, or maybe a better script happens along."

Some scripts were ultimately deemed too similar to what the series had done before. Others were bypassed for stories that seemed more exciting or marketable. Some simply didn't appeal to Falk or to the new producer who inherited them from his predecessor. A few were considered too flawed to be fixed. But all of them are fascinating to look back on and imagine what if.

Seasons 1 and 2 (1971-1973)

The original writing team for *Columbo* consisted of executive producers Richard Levinson and William Link, their story editor Steven Bochco, and—unofficially—anyone they could pull out of the halls of Universal's Producers Building to bounce ideas off of. As time went on, they'd receive input on their scripts and treatments from their overseers at NBC and Universal, as well as from other storymen working in nearby offices, including Doug Benton, Roland Kibbee, and others.

Levinson and Link encouraged regular Universal freelancers to submit story ideas and spec scripts. Yet their show's formula was so unique, its inverted mystery style so difficult to write, its drama so difficult to sustain, that most of the frequent contributors to other series avoided *Columbo*.

Consequently, most of the ideas for the seven shows of Season 1 (1971-72) originated with Levinson and Link themselves. And they were so consumed with completing their commitment before star Peter Falk ran off to Broadway, there was little time to develop stories that weren't assured of being produced. Generating a surplus of scripts was impossible. In fact, the season's last-filmed episode—Jackson Gillis' *Short Fuse*—was rushed from story idea to filming in mere weeks, without any of the months of rewriting that usually went into crafting a satisfying mystery (and, some would say, it shows).

Levinson and Link knew they would be overseeing the series for just the inaugural season so, before leaving the program, they began stockpiling story ideas and scripts for their Season 2 successor, Dean Hargrove. By this time, with the show finally airing on television—and garnering increasingly stellar ratings—more freelancers started pitching to the producers. *Columbo* now had a growing stable of professionals interested in writing for the show.

Hargrove didn't have the luxury of an excess of scripts to choose from until after filming was completed on Season 2. He began looking toward Season

3, with the intention of doing the same favor as Levinson and Link did for him, handing the reins over to new producer Doug Benton with a reserve of ideas… including several fascinating teleplays that would never be filmed.

2
Season 3 (1973-1974)
The Murder Consultant

To help amass a large quantity of workable story ideas, *Columbo* needed a productive storyman with a vivid imagination and an innate understanding of the show. Peter Falk pushed for Larry Cohen, the offbeat writer/director who years before had cast him in an early TV role that had led to his Oscar-nominated part in *Murder, Inc.*

Cohen was certainly prolific—over the previous decade, he'd cranked out dozens upon dozens of scripts for TV shows, created several series (*Branded, Blue Light, Coronet Blue, The Invaders,* and *Cool Million*), and written and directed a number of horror and blaxploitation movies.

Cohen also claimed that the previous summer, while Levinson and Link were brainstorming the first season of *Columbo*, they sought his input, and it was he who had proposed the idea of a bestselling author getting bumped off when he tries to break up with his coattail-riding partner. The suggestion inspired the series premiere, *Murder by the Book*.

His capacity for dreaming up original, devious murder plots seemed limitless. Cohen just didn't have the time to write a bunch of full scripts. He was leaving for a year's sabbatical in England. So he agreed to be a "murder consultant." For $100,000, he'd provide more than a dozen plots—ranging from two-page story ideas to 20-plus-page treatments.

Cohen turned in the first five in December of 1972. Two of them would be filmed for Season 3 as *Any Old Port in a Storm* and *Candidate for Crime*, and another as the season opener for Season 4, *An Exercise in Fatality*. The other two had shorter lifespans.

Murder Out of Tune

Cohen's 15-page treatment for *Murder Out of Tune* centered on award-winning film composer Gloria Taylor. An "ultrasophisticated dame," Gloria has a terrific sense of humor, knows everyone, and owns palatial homes in Beverly Hills, Palm Springs, and Big Bear. Her walls are lined with gold records and she's constantly on the move, jetting from one coast to the other for the latest party, where she's invariably begged to sit at the piano and play a medley of her hits.

— ⌒ —

Gloria's been married for years, though few think of her as a married woman. She's had numerous lovers and does whatever she pleases; she doesn't care what anyone else thinks. She sees little of her husband, Dr. Harold Taylor, a pediatrician who spends most of his time at work. The couple have neither children nor common interests. Yet they're both so busy, there's no thought of divorce. Gloria, in a way, feels her marriage protects her from other relationships. She doesn't want to get serious with any of her flings, and her understanding with Dr. Harold has made her life comfortable.

Currently, Gloria is composing the score for a big-budget movie that's almost ready to shoot. Unfortunately, she's having trouble getting started because of her latest lover, a "beach bum" named Jim Temple. Jim's a starving, talentless actor who doesn't want to give up Gloria. With all her money, he'd love to marry her. For the first time, Gloria just can't ditch a used boyfriend. She impresses upon Jim that she already has a husband and will never divorce. Jim offers to get her "un-married," very quickly. Such talk rattles Gloria. She's seen Jim's violent side; he once beat up a drunk at a bar who accidentally bumped into him.

Yet she can't shake him. Jim shows up at restaurants where she's dining with friends and forces himself into the party. He takes the wheel of her sportscar and drives up to 100 mph along the hairpin turns of Pacific Coast Highway. She changes her phone number, but he breaks into her home after dark and threatens her. All the while, Jim keeps talking about knocking off her husband and "giving her freedom." Gloria grows increasingly worried for Harold's safety. He's always been kind to her—and willing to take her back whenever she decides to return home. He's almost like the father she never had.

One night, Gloria returns home to discover Jim hiding in her garage. He

"MURDER CONSULTANT" Larry Cohen was a veritable treasure trove of story ideas for *Columbo* leading into its third season.

resumes his crazy talk about committing a perfect murder. Gloria despairs; she realizes that there's nothing the police can do for her. They can only become involved after a crime—when it would be too late for Harold. Any complaint she has would be disregarded as coming from an unfaithful wife. Gloria knows she'll have to take matters into her own hands. If Jim wants a murder, he'll have one—his own. She takes Jim inside the house and pours him a drink. She says she's up for getting rid of Harold, but they must plan it out carefully. Because of their obvious shared motive, they'd be the prime suspects. First, they must stop seeing each other. Jim must buy a plane ticket, leave town, and return on another flight, under an assumed name. He then must purchase the necessary equipment to carry out the murder—rope, canvas, chains, and weights—from a hardware store. A used gun from a pawn shop. A fake beard and glasses for a disguise. On the appointed day, Gloria will convince Harold to join her for a weekend at their ski lodge in Big Bear. The cabin next door sits unoccupied during the winter. Its swimming pool, however, remains filled and is frozen over. Jim will kill Harold, wrap his body in the canvas and then in the chains, weigh him down, and drop him through the ice into the pool. The body will remain hidden for months beneath the frozen surface. By the time it thaws, it'll be impossible to determine the time of death. Gloria will leave immediately for Europe to be on location for her new movie and, soon after, Jim will join her. They'll both establish alibis abroad and stay there until the body has been recovered.

Over the ensuing days, Gloria works feverishly on her musical score, while Jim leaves L.A. He returns with a growth of beard, bleached hair, dark glasses, and even a phony limp. As Cohen writes, "He flatters himself that he's playing the performance of his life, but actually he's simply playing into Gloria's hands."

Jim purchases the supplies, including buying an old car using an assumed name. He calls Gloria to tell her he's done his part. She visits her husband, who's consumed with his hospital work. She shares that she finally realizes how much she loves him and wants to move back home. Harold says he can't promise he'll give up his work and doesn't expect Gloria to give up hers, but he's been patient this long and is open to reconciling.

That night, Jim calls Gloria at her studio to report that everything's set. He's in Big Bear, waiting. He has all the gear and no qualms about going through with murder.

Gloria informs her male secretary that she's going to be working alone trying to compose the title song for the picture. It's past due, the movie producer's upset, and she's stuck. She's not to be disturbed all night. She locks herself in her soundproof studio. She knows her secretary sneaks out for a drink every night at 8:00. So, she uses this opportunity to slip out of the studio and make the two-hour drive to Big Bear, alone.

It's snowing. She parks a few hundred feet from the lodge and walks the rest of the way. Jim, who's been hiding behind the frozen-over swimming pool, emerges from the darkness. He is back to his normal appearance again, having shaved his beard and ditched the glasses and his dye job. Jim wants to know where Harold is. Gloria claims that their car is stuck in the snow a few hundred yards away and Harold is busy putting chains on the tires. She asks if he brought the gear. Jim shows her everything, including the gun. She takes the weapon to make sure it's loaded, then, before Jim realizes what's happening, she fires. Two quick shots kill Jim. Hurriedly, she wraps his body in the canvas, secures it with the rope, chain and weights, then slides him into the pool. But the ice is so thick, the body doesn't break the surface. In desperation, Gloria pounds at the ice with a hunk of firewood. It finally cracks. The body vanishes into the frosty water below.

Gloria rushes to her car and speeds back to L.A. She slips back into her studio unseen as her secretary chatters away on the phone. A few minutes later, she emerges from the studio, score in hand, proclaiming that she's finally "licked the title song." She plays the tune for her secretary and again for her husband, who drops by on his way back from the hospital. What she didn't know was that her neighbor's lodge in Big Bear was in escrow, and inspecting the property, the new owners would soon uncover the corpse at the bottom of the pool.

Soon after, Columbo and the police discover the gun on the pool floor, and the canvas, chain and old car abandoned nearby. He then learns that the vehicle had been purchased for $100 at a used car lot by a man with a beard, glasses and limp who went by the name "Joe Fletcher."

Gloria figured the police would ask about her relationship with Jim. So she's not surprised when Columbo shows up. She is startled by his familiarity with her songs. He's just crazy about her music and has a million questions—none of which has anything to do with the unfortunate demise of a bit actor. Columbo asks if her friend ever mentioned someone meeting the suspect's description, possibly an enemy. Gloria doesn't recall.

She insists she hasn't seen or spoken with Jim since he left Hollywood months ago and conveniently produces a postcard he sent her from back East.

But Columbo is disturbed by the fact that the body was found dead back in Southern California, in a pool not far from the Taylors' cabin.

Columbo checks the stores where the mystery man made his purchases.

Everyone seems to remember the guy, since he did a lot of talking and had an exaggerated limp—though some witnesses recalled he limped with his right foot and others with his left. Columbo reasons that most killers who are buying implements for a future crime would remain silent and inconspicuous, while this murderer seemed to be "hamming it up." Columbo will learn from Jim's former agent and ex-roommate that he was not a good actor; he overplayed everything. The agent pulls out a stack of 8x10s picturing Jim in all sorts of different costumes. Jim would spend most of his unemployment checks printing up publicity shots of himself that invariably ended up in the wastebins of casting directors.

Columbo visits Dr. Harold, who's busy making his rounds at the hospital. The detective pesters him with questions—as well as solicits free medical advice about his bad back. He learns that Harold and Gloria have reconciled, and are living together for the first time in years. Columbo says, "I guess you would've been upset if you knew her ex-boyfriend was back." Harold is not easily excited and reacts patiently to Columbo's insinuation. He doesn't have an alibi for the day of the murder. He was home alone reading medical journals until he decided to stop by his wife's studio.

Gloria grows concerned that Columbo is beginning to suspect her husband. She demands that Columbo leave the doctor alone and go look for the mysterious Fletcher.

Columbo returns to Big Bear to speak with the local sheriff. "Sure, Fletcher drove his car up here with the canvas, rope and the chains, but how did he leave?" Columbo asks. "I mean, his car was still here abandoned a few hundred yards away in the woods days later when the body was found." The sheriff posits that Fletcher probably left in Jim's car. Columbo isn't buying it: "You mean he murdered him for his car? That doesn't make sense. He has all this prepared. He was planning it way in advance. And after murdering the man why would he be foolish enough to drive around in his car? Besides which, the car never turned up. And also besides which, there is no proof that Temple ever had a car."

The Lieutenant is coming to realize that there was only one man, who was playing two roles—the alleged murderer was, in fact, the actual victim. Columbo seems intent on pinning the murder on Harold. Not even Gloria is buying her husband's weak alibi. She knows he never has a free moment to himself; he'd never just sit around the house reading. She deduces correctly that he had seen her leave the studio that night and followed her. He'd reached Big Bear just in time to hear the gunshots, then followed her back to L.A. He was hoping that she would confess to him. Gloria tells Harold not to worry about Columbo; they're much too smart for him.

Meanwhile, Columbo has another idea. He figures that, because Jim was so conceited, if he and Fletcher were the same person, he wouldn't have been able to resist having himself photographed in the getup. After contacting every photo studio in town, Columbo finds one that took 8x10s of Jim with a beard and his hair dyed blond.

Instead of going after Gloria, Columbo has her husband arrested. There's nothing Gloria can do to cover for him, since her alibi was that she was locked in her soundproof studio composing the song.

The next afternoon, Columbo visits Gloria's studio. He diverts the secretary's attention and sneaks inside a large storage room that houses all the music Gloria has written over the years. He apparently finds what he's looking for and slips out, just as the office phone rings. It's the San Diego Police, notifying Columbo that they've just arrested a man that fits Fletcher's description.

Gloria arrives home that evening only to find that her servants have let

Columbo in. He's seated behind her piano, tapping out a tune with two fingers. Columbo asks if she's been able to recall the limping blond man named Fletcher. Gloria says she's thought it over, and does remember once when she and Jim spotted such a man across the street and had to duck into a cocktail lounge to avoid running into him. Columbo is pleased; perhaps she'll be able to identify this man when he's brought in from San Diego. Gloria explains the incident was a long time ago; she definitely saw him, but the details are hazy. To jog her memory, Columbo flashes several 8x10s of Jim, including one of him disguised as Fletcher.

Gloria is unperturbed. "Well, isn't that wonderful," she says. "They're both the same man. Perhaps he had a split personality. But what an elaborate way to commit suicide."

Columbo disagrees. A man can't commit suicide then tie himself up in a canvas bag and throw himself in a pool. "No, somebody set Jim Temple up. He thought he was going to be an accomplice to somebody else's murder, not his own."

Gloria reiterates that she couldn't be the real murderer, since she was busy the entire night composing a song.

"You know, Mrs. Taylor, I admire your talent so much," Columbo says. "You're a brilliant woman, but I just never thought you were cold-blooded enough to murder a man and then come right back and write a song, particularly a love song. So I figured if you wrote that song, it wasn't written that night. So while you were out, I went into your files. Like I told you, I read music. My mother gave me piano lessons as a kid. Well, it took me all night long and going all the way back to 1944 before I found that same melody and most of those same lyrics. You took that song out of the trunk, like they say."

Columbo pulls out an old manuscript, dated nearly 30 years earlier and written in Gloria's own handwriting. On the night of the murder, she didn't compose anything; she'd just copied the music onto a new page. "I feel much better now knowing I was right," Columbo says, smiling. "All those wonderful songs you wrote. That wonderful sentiment. I just knew you couldn't have written one after committing a murder. It just wouldn't be like you. It would've changed my whole opinion of your work."

For the first time in her life, Gloria is at a loss for words. The doorbell rings. It's Dr. Harold, released from custody. He had never really been a suspect. Gloria tells him he can tell the police everything. Trying to be conciliatory, Columbo reminds Gloria that she can continue writing songs—just behind prison bars.

Harold watches as his wife is taken away by the police. Once again, he's lost her. "Well, Doc, she really must've loved you," Columbo says. "She went to a hell of a lot of trouble for you." Encouraged, Harold exits. Columbo sits back down behind the grand piano and starts fooling with the keys—until the help turns off the lights, as a not-too-subtle hint. Columbo closes the piano and takes one last look around. He lights his cigar as he steps outside into the night, humming Gloria's "latest" tune to himself.

Second-season producer Dean Hargrove liked the story enough to assign a production number to it. Then he passed it on to others to get their input, including story editor Jackson Gillis and Hargrove's frequent writing partner, Roland Kibbee, who was simultaneously co-producing the series *Madigan* with him. Kibbee identified a litany of story problems, which he enumerated in a memo dated December 19, 1972.

First, Kibbee was concerned that Gloria's propensity for carrying on with young studs and her relationship with Jim the beach bum was too similar to the setup for another, more promising story under development by a writer named Goldschmidt. (Although in that story, the older woman ends up the victim, not the murderer.)

Next, Kibbee disputed Cohen's contention that, when Gloria started to fear Jim, she couldn't run to the police, because they "can only become involved after a crime." Surely, she could have filed a complaint with the police over Jim's threats. "For a woman of this caliber to feel that murder is her only way out—indeed, the very first remedy she tries—seems to weaken her character," Kibbee wrote. "As set up by the author in his outline, one doesn't feel that she is driven to such a desperate act. Indeed, it is indicated that the relationship with her husband is such that she doesn't conceal her affairs from him, and that he is sophisticated enough to tolerate them. What is to prevent her from telling him that his life is in danger so that he can take steps to protect himself? This motivation for murder would have to be substantially strengthened to be made convincing."

Kibbee also found it hard to believe that Jim is a "schmuck," but doesn't think twice when Gloria, after trying so hard to shake him, suddenly does an about-face and joins in on the plan to knock off her husband. He'd need convincing reasons ("convincing enough, at least, for a schmuck") to fall for her ploy.

Kibbee didn't believe that anyone could be counted on, as Gloria counts on her secretary, to "always slip out for a drink at 8:00." He even always leaves the phone off the hook for a few minutes. "This is an author's convenience of staggering proportions," Kibbee complained. "I'm not even clear, from the outline, why it's needed for Gloria to 'slip out' unobserved. According to the outline, she slips right back in hours later, when the secretary is on the job, and is not seen by him. And would the secretary really go to the trouble of providing Gloria with an alibi by claiming he knew her to be in the study at work all the time? I presume that's why the author set up that 8:00 drink device. Merely in order to cover such a minor lapse of duty as slipping out for a drink? For a woman as hip as Gloria, she's counting on an awfully precarious alibi."

Kibbee pointed out that a murder in an ice-encrusted swimming pool seemed uncomfortably similar to the killing in Season 2's recently aired *The Most Crucial Game*, in which Robert Culp brains his victim in a swimming pool with a shard of ice. "I realize it is by no means the same thing, but cinematically it could be quite reminiscent," he noted.

Similarly, Kibbee felt Columbo's tactic of pursuing the husband he knows is innocent to prompt Gloria to confess was too much like another story in development, Steven Bochco's *Mind Over Mayhem*, in which Columbo goes after an innocent son to prompt his guilty father to come clean.

Kibbee also thought Gloria's alibi was particularly weak. Perhaps her husband, who was familiar with her work habit, might be astonished that Gloria wrote the song "all in one evening." Certainly songwriters, especially lyricists, have labored for months over one tune. But much of the general public believe songs are written in one evening—or less. Of course, many songs have been composed ridiculously quickly. Celebrated lyricist Sammy Cahn once told Kibbee that he and composer Gene De Paul wrote their big hit "Teach Me Tonight" at a piano in an office at Warner Bros. in 11 minutes. "Gloria isn't in an operating room doing a heart transplant," Kibbee noted. "She's only writing a song!"

There was also the coincidence of someone buying the house with the corpse-containing pool; it should have been something Gloria might reasonably have feared would happen. And if her plan was to hide the body in the frozen pool so the time of death couldn't be determined, why did she go to the trouble of setting up an alibi for her whereabouts the night of the murder? Doesn't she believe in her own perfect crime plan?

As for how the body gets discovered, Kibbee wondered, "Wouldn't it be theoretically more effective to have one of those 'unusual' California weather eccentricities—a hot spell that melted the ice, or something of that nature?" (Little did he know that one of the next scripts that he'd be reading would be Cohen's outline about a winemaker whose plan is foiled by an unexpected hot spell.)

Along the same lines, although Kibbee didn't point it out, Columbo unearthing the killer's old writing is reminiscent of the final, dead-to-rights "gotcha" clue in *Murder by the Book*.

Most importantly, Kibbee felt that since Gloria was just trying to protect her nice-guy husband from the lunatic Jim, audiences might not have a rooting interest in Columbo trapping her.

With better story options on the table, Kibbee advised, "I don't think we ought to go any further on this one." Hargrove agreed. Columbo would have to wait a little longer to go toe to toe with a philandering singer/songwriter, in Season 3's *Swan Song* starring Johnny Cash.

Death Do Us Part

Cohen had even higher hopes for the divorce-lawyer yarn *Death Do Us Part*. In late 1972, he submitted an initial 26-page story. Then, after receiving notes from Hargrove's team, he expanded the treatment to 30 pages. Satisfied the storyline was solid, Cohen began fleshing it out into a full 90-minute teleplay. He must have been fully confident his script would get a green light, since this would be the only formal screenplay he would write for the series.

— 📖 —

Fifty and looking fabulous, Scott Phillips is Beverly Hills' preeminent divorce lawyer. Most of his clients are gorgeous young women anxious to shed wealthy husbands. Attorney Phillips lands massive settlements, while keeping a sizable chunk for himself, and then consoles his clients sexually, taking advantage of their vulnerable state. His high-profile cases have made him a household name, boosted by his bestselling book on divorce and marriage.

Phillips has just delivered his closing arguments in the case of Devlon v. Devlon. He, naturally, represents the beautiful Sarah Devlon, who demands her "just share" from ex-husband Howard Devlon, a highly successful restauranteur. The judge is swayed by Phillips' accusation that Howard is a serial wife beater. Sarah will receive their Bel Air home, most of their liquid assets, and monthly support checks. Howard is left cash poor with just his chain of restaurants, which he'll now have to sell just to meet the massive alimony payments. As the judge hands down his ruling, we behold the perfectly coiffed Phillips seated next to his lovely client. The camera drops beneath the table and we see his hand slide onto hers and caress it gently.

Phillips praises the court for its wisdom and asks for a restraining order to protect his client from her abusive ex-husband. Howard explodes and must be censured by the judge. Once court is adjourned, Phillips and Sarah walk out together into the corridor, where they are accosted by an enraged Howard. Howard suspects Sarah has been having an affair with her attorney. Surrounded by witnesses, he threatens to kill both of them. Phillips is amused. If he wants to kill him, "Take a number. There are about 250 other husbands ahead of you."

Howard persists. Phillips has ruined him. He now has to sell everything. He's going to kill the cheat.

"Are you going to run me over with your Maserati?" Phillips cracks. "Oh, you don't have the Maserati anymore, do you? She has it."

Phillips gets a kick out of provoking poor Howard, just like he incites opposing attorneys to lose their temper in court. Raving, Howard must be restrained by the courthouse police.

Phillips heads for his opulent Beverly Hills office, to meet with Constance, a similarly statuesque blonde who's been married to Phillips since law school. She has endured the endless parade of affairs because he always comes home. But this time, Phillips has a different story for his wife. He confesses that Sarah Devlon is not just a fling. For the first time in his life, he's fallen in love. He wants a divorce, so he can marry Sarah.

Constance laughs. Her husband has never talked about love before. He's never even pretended to care about anyone before—including her. She thinks he looks ridiculous acting like a lovesick schoolboy. Yet, she's still attracted to him—physically and financially. After putting him through law school and enduring a loveless marriage, now the great divorce lawyer wants a divorce? Ha! She flatly refuses. She knows all his tricks, his angles, the dirty deals and the dark secrets the bar association and the IRS would be anxious to hear about. She shares that she recently discovered that he's been misappropriating funds from the trust accounts of an elderly female client. Constance has enough dirt to bury him. "Believe me, the entire legal community will love what happens to you if you ever try to divorce me," she smirks.

Phillips is sharp enough to recognize that he's lost. So, suppressing his emotions, he throws his arms around Constance and kisses her. He says he's flattered that she cares so much about him. And now that he knows how tough she is, he respects her even more.

Constance says they should go away for the weekend, to patch up their relationship. How about what used to be their favorite place together, the Beachfront Cottages? Phillips rolls his eyes. The cottages were popular in the

'50s and '60s, but nobody goes there anymore. Plus, it's off season and the place will soon shut down for the winter. But he's in no position to argue. He tells Constance to reserve a room.

The following morning, Phillips visits the Bel Air mansion Sarah got to keep in her divorce. Sarah is waiting eagerly, adorned in a stunning black-lace negligee. Phillips enjoys knowing that Howard purchased the skimpy outfit for Sarah, but he's the one who's getting all the pleasure from it.

Unfortunately for the couple, there will be no sexual escapades this morning. Phillips has come to tell her he can't see her anymore. But before he can break it off, the doorbell rings. It's Howard's longtime secretary, the "mannish" Kathleen Tompkins. She's alarmed. She tells Sarah that Howard has purchased a gun and she's afraid he's going to commit suicide. Sarah, though, is more concerned that Howard may carry out on his threat to kill her and her lover. Phillips welcomes the news. He begins formulating a plan that could solve all his problems.

He asks Miss Tompkins to wait downstairs while he speaks with his "client." Privately, he reminds Sarah that anything she tells the secretary will get back to Howard. He encourages her to get out of town. But what if Howard follows her?

Phillips suggests that Sarah tell Tompkins that she's going away for the weekend to the beach all by herself—someplace quiet like the old Beachfront Cottages. In reality, Sarah will fly to Tucson and spend a few days riding. Phillips will stay behind, because he can't stand horses, and will call her when it's safe to come home.

But what about *his* safety? Phillips assures her that he'll be fine; he has a license to carry a gun. Phillips leaves, and Sarah mentions to Tompkins that she'll be spending the weekend at the beach.

Back at his office, Phillips makes sure to let everyone know that he, too, is going to the Beachfront Cottages. He heads out early and drives to a lingerie shop in the Valley, where he purchases a black-lace negligee that looks exactly like the one Sarah was wearing. He pays cash.

Soon after, he picks up his wife, and they head for the beach. They check into the same cabin they stayed at more than 20 years ago. The cottages are spread out and mostly vacant. Constance is thrilled to have her husband back and wants to relive the past. She uncorks a bottle of wine. She's just had her blonde hair touched up and, in the dim light from the fireplace, looks spectacular. Phillips presents her with a gift—the sexy black nightie. He pleads for her to try it on for him. We've already seen him tear the price tag off and flush it down the drain.

Meanwhile, Howard has phoned Phillips' office and, using a pseudonym, learns that the lawyer will be at the Beachfront Cottages until Monday. He's now certain of the tip he got from his secretary. Howard drives to the beach, his gun resting on the passenger seat.

At the cottage, Phillips and Constance have finished their dinner and wine, and have retired to the bedroom. He appears on edge, and keeps glancing out the window. A few minutes later, Howard drives up. He spots Phillips' Jaguar parked next to one of the few occupied bungalows. He's certain Phillips is in there with his ex-wife. Visibly trembling, Howard makes his way to the back door. It's unlocked. Howard enters, and edges down the hallway to the bedroom, gun in hand. Phillips isn't taking any chances. He excuses himself for a quick trip to the bathroom.

The bedroom door is open a crack. Through it, Howard sees a leggy blonde in a familiar negligee. It must be Sarah. He flings open the door and bursts in. But instead of firing, Howard hesitates. Constance screams. Even in the darkness, Howard can tell she's not his ex-wife. Phillips quickly shifts to Plan B. He fires his own gun—equipped with a silencer—at Howard, taking him down with a single shot to the chest. Phillips turns on the light. Constance sobs. "Who was he? What did he want?"

Phillips walks over to retrieve the gun dropped by Howard. He points it directly at his wife. Constance notices that he's wearing a transparent cellophane glove that he must have slipped on while he was in the bathroom. It finally hits her—she's been set up, as part of an elaborate murder plot. Phillips pulls the trigger. But it clicks empty. The gun wasn't loaded. Furious, Phillips begins yelling at Howard's corpse that he didn't even have the guts to load the gun.

Constance tries to flee, but Phillips strikes her, knocking her onto the bed. He now moves to Plan C. He kneels down and starts searching Howard's pockets, until he finds a half-dozen loose cartridges. He loads the gun and again points it at Constance. She's reaching for the phone, and Phillips' deadly shot hits her in the back.

Phillips quickly places the gun in Howard's hand and presses his finger against the trigger. The shot goes wild, hitting the wall just above the bed. Howard's hand now has traces of nitrate and antimony, and his fingerprints will be on the cartridges fished from his pocket. Finally, for the benefit of witnesses, Phillips removes the silencer from his own gun, opens a window, and fires a bullet toward the field outside. The shots have aroused several guests in adjoining cabins.

Phillips quickly removes his gloves and flushes them down the toilet. He then runs out the front door screaming for help. Upon reaching the cliffside, he discreetly tosses the silencer into the raging waters below.

The other residents have already called the police. Phillips tells the authorities that he and his wife were celebrating a "second honeymoon" when Howard suddenly burst into their bedroom and, with no warning, shot poor Constance. The crazed intruder then tried to shoot Phillips, but the attorney had had time to grab his own gun and fire back. It all happened so fast, in a matter of seconds. But Phillips is sure he fired once and Howard fired twice. Three shots, just as the witnesses reported. It wasn't until the shooting was over that Phillips realized the intruder was Howard Devlon.

Phillips pretends to break down weeping in front of the police. It's all my fault. Everyone knew I was seeing the man's wife. The nutjob must have mistaken my wife for his.

The camera pans to the doorway, where Columbo stands. We're not sure how long he's been there, or how much he's heard, but he ambles in, identifies himself, and tries to console the anguished attorney. Columbo notes Phillips was fortunate he reacted so quickly or he, too, would be dead.

Other witnesses are brought in to Columbo. They all agree that three shots were fired in rapid succession. Two shots, then a considerably louder third shot. Columbo wonders why the last one was louder, but we know the answer—the final shot was fired out the window. Phillips suggests that maybe, since the first two shots woke people from their sleep, the last shot sounded louder to them because they were now fully awake. Columbo's impressed. But one thing puzzles him. Why would Phillips bring his gun to a romantic weekend? Phillips explains that, because of the many threats on his life, he obtained a gun license 12 years ago and takes the weapon with him everywhere he goes, for self-defense.

Medical personnel remove the bodies from the premises. Phillips doesn't want to spend the night at the scene of his wife's murder, so he's going to drive home. Columbo asks if he can hitch a ride. The car that brought him has already left for town. Phillips consents, but—explaining that he's in no condition to drive—asks if Columbo will take the wheel.

Columbo gladly takes control of the souped-up Jag—and makes Phillips instantly regret his request. The detective swerves around the narrow curves of Pacific Coast Highway, while trying to disarm the lawyer with conversation. Columbo, it seems, is suddenly fascinated with the subject of divorce. Phillips wonders if it's because the detective is having marital problems. No, Columbo says, he and Mrs. Columbo are doing fine, but Phillips advises him to check the balance of his bank accounts and safety deposit box. Nah, Mrs. Columbo handles all their finances. Phillips calls it a very dangerous practice, and claims a "little checking up on the wife never hurts." Columbo says he could never do anything like that, but his expression betrays a hint of doubt.

As soon as they reach Phillips' manor, the attorney just wants to get to bed, but must wait for a cab to pick up Columbo—a cab that seems to take forever to arrive. In the meantime, the detective keeps rambling. Accidentally, he brushes against a lamp, knocking it to the floor with a clatter. Columbo is very apologetic as he places the lamp back on the table—fortunately, it's not broken. But he does note how when the lamp crashed, Phillips whirled around. "Whenever you hear a noise like that, the natural thing is to turn around to see what happened," Columbo muses. Phillips agrees that's normal, prompting the Lieutenant to wonder why Constance was shot in the back. Wouldn't she have spun around as soon as she heard the intruder? Phillips posits that perhaps the first bullet was the one that hit the wall over the bed, and she was killed by the second bullet. In any event, she was reaching for the phone on the nightstand, to call for help.

"Oh, is that what happened?" Columbo sighs. "I don't know why it's so hard for me to figure these things out for myself."

Phillips explains that that's his specialty—helping a judge and jury to focus on what really happened and disregard the extraneous.

The taxi finally arrives to take Columbo away, but not before Phillips again encourages checking up on Mrs. Columbo. "Take my advice, I know a troubled man when I see one," he advises. The Lieutenant mulls it over: "Maybe you've got something there."

Columbo, however, doesn't go to bed. Instead, he retrieves his own car and returns to the Beachfront Cottages. He pores over the scene of the crime. He checks the bullet hole in the wall. He finds a fragment of plastic string that used to hold a price tag to a garment. And he discovers a miniscule tear in the negligee where a tag appears to have been hastily torn off. What he doesn't find is a price tag. Someone must have torn it off and disposed of it, but it's not in the wastebasket. Why would anyone go to that much trouble to dispose of a tag?

Columbo then asks the forensics technicians to check Howard's hands for any residue. He also wants the police to track down charge receipts for any recent credit card purchases by Phillips and Constance.

In the morning, Columbo visits an exotic lingerie shop on Sunset Boulevard, where he uncomfortably explores the displays of sexy undergarments. The saleswomen look on curiously. One finally asks how she can help him. He shows the clerk Constance's black nightie and asks where one would purchase one like it. She replies that this particular garment was produced in limited quantities. She'd have to special order it from one of their other locations. Columbo orders one, as a gift for his wife. "We're having a little trouble at home," he says. "This might help."

Using credit card records, Columbo notes that Phillips and Constance put almost everything they purchased, including all their clothing, on their Mastercard—everything, except the nightie.

At dawn, Phillips heads out to the beach. Not to watch the sunrise, but to run a metal detector through the field at the now-deserted Beachfront Cottages. After just a few minutes, he locks in on the bullet that he fired out the window. He tosses it off the cliff into the ocean. Nobody sees him. He returns to Beverly Hills confident that he's committed two perfect murders.

Later that day, Phillips is back in court. He's in the middle of cross-examining a witness when he spies Columbo in the gallery. Distracted, Phillips loses his line of attack. The judge admonishes him for repeating a question. When Phillips returns to the plaintiff's table, Columbo slides into the front row of the audience, right behind Phillips. He leans over the rail and makes clear he urgently needs to speak with the lawyer.

During the brief recess, Phillips would prefer to consult with his client, but Columbo corners him, looking troubled. The detective explains that he hasn't been able to sleep. He finally went down to the bank to check his accounts and, boy, was he in for a surprise. Mrs. Columbo has secretly been sending money to her sister and brother-in-law—not to mention making out a slew of checks to "Cash."

Columbo wants to know what he should do. He needs advice, but can't afford Phillips' rates. So the lawyer suggests he buy a copy of his book; it's only $19.95. Columbo, though, has already bought a copy—at a discount store for $12. He finished it in one night. Couldn't put it down. And he now carries it around with him—he doesn't want his wife to see it and become suspicious.

The next day, Columbo returns to watch the continuing divorce trial, but sits in the back, leafing through Phillips' book. He gets excited any time he sees the lawyer use one of the courtroom tactics he's just read about. Columbo gets a special kick out of Phillips' strategy of being adaptable and always having backup plans.

When the trial breaks for lunch, Phillips slips off to a phonebooth to call Sarah in Tucson. She has remained in Arizona to avoid reporters. She asks if he thinks it's safe for her to return. "We have things to talk about," she says, in a tone that troubles Phillips.

Phillips steps out of the phonebooth, where Columbo is waiting, still reading the book. Phillips says he really doesn't have time to help him with his personal problems. But Columbo says this isn't personal; it's business. Police business. Miss Tompkins had told him that she'd warned Phillips and Sarah that Howard had purchased a gun. Phillips calmly replies that the secretary feared that Howard might commit suicide.

Yet Tompkins had also told Columbo that Howard was deathly afraid of guns. That he was even scared it might go off in his pocket. That gave Columbo the idea that if Howard was so scared of guns, maybe he wouldn't load his. So Columbo had the lab analyze the bullets to see if they had been handled by someone who had already fired a gun. Sure enough, there were traces of nitrate and antimony on the bullets.

Phillips plays dumb: "I don't follow you."

Columbo explains that whoever loaded Howard's gun had recently fired one. Again, Phillips thinks fast. He says that if someone had just bought a gun to use to murder someone, he'd logically want to take it somewhere to practice firing it. "Only a damn fool would walk into a dark room and try to use a gun he never fired before."

Columbo agrees, appreciating the help. He begins to walk away, but is stopped by Phillips. "One more thing, Lieutenant. Tell me the truth: have you ever been unfaithful to Mrs. Columbo?"

"Never."

If so, Phillips reasons, she must be the one who is cheating. He walks away smiling, as doubts continue to grow in Columbo's mind.

In Tucson, Sarah grows increasingly restless. She wants to fly home, collect her huge divorce settlement, sell the Bel Air estate, and wed Phillips. But who should arrive but Phillips, who wants to profess his love—and to be certain Sarah has her story straight before Columbo gets to her. Unfortunately for him, she is beginning to piece together what really happened: Phillips instructed her to tell everyone she was going to the Beachfront Cottages. He knew Howard would find out. He wanted Howard to think she was out there with him. So, she asks Phillips straight out: did he want Howard to go to the cottages so he'd have an excuse to kill him?

Phillips dismisses the notion, but Sarah knows better. Finally, he pretends to tell the truth. He knew that Howard would hound them for the rest of their lives. Howard was crazy and sadistic, and Phillips couldn't take the chance that he'd follow through on his threats and harm Sarah. "I did it for you, Sarah, for your safety, so that we could have our life together," Phillips says. "I wasn't sure he'd show up, but if he did, I had every intention of defending myself. It all just happened too quick. He shot poor Connie before I could do anything."

Sarah believes his story, but wants assurances. She asks if it's true that a wife can't be forced to testify against her husband. He says she's correct. So Sarah insists they get married as soon as possible to ensure she can't ever be used as a witness against him. It would be a small, private ceremony, held at Phillips' mansion. Phillips resists; it's too soon and would look bad.

Just then, there's another knock on the hotel door. It's Columbo, who's flown to Tucson to question Sarah. Unruffled, Sarah holds her own, twisting the truth to protect her man. Impressed, Phillips blurts out that he and Sarah are very much in love, and will be getting married next week. Columbo is taken aback. He can't reveal that he suspects they're a couple if they freely admit it.

The wedding takes place the following weekend. Several family friends refuse to show up out of respect for Constance. But there is one uninvited guest—in a rumpled raincoat, bearing a gift. Columbo explains that after all the free legal advice Phillips gave him, the least he could do was bring a gift. He spends most of his time following the wedding party, raiding the buffet, and pestering the new Mrs. Phillips to open her present. Finally, to shut him up, she unwraps the package and lifts the lid. Phillips is aghast. Inside is an exact duplicate of the black negligee. Sarah, unaware of what Constance was wearing when she was murdered, is about to exclaim that she had one just like it. Phillips stops her in the nick of time. Columbo notices the looks they exchange and apologizes. "I'm afraid the gift is a bit personal," Phillips remarks. Columbo offers to return the nightie for something more tasteful, but Phillips suggests he instead give it to Mrs. Columbo. It might help their marriage. Phillips then shows his party crasher out, noting, "Columbo, you're a devious fellow; you would have made a great lawyer."

Columbo responds, "Mr. Phillips, you would've made a great murderer."

Once all the guests have left, Phillips remains troubled by the black negligee. He tears through Sarah's closets and drawers looking for hers. No luck. She asks what he's doing. He wants to know what happened to her black nightie. Sarah says she gave it away to a maid once the divorce was final, because it reminded her of her ex. But why is it so important to him? She doesn't buy that Phillips is jealous of Howard, especially since the garment never bothered him when they were married. Now's different, he explains, considering Howard killed his wife. "Everything about his memory makes me sick. I'm glad you got rid of it." It's obvious that Phillips doesn't want Sarah to learn the full truth, because he's afraid of losing her.

Come Monday morning, Columbo is back in court, where Phillips is arguing yet another celebrated divorce case. The detective again starts signaling to get Phillips' attention, annoying the humorless judge. Apparently Mrs. Columbo didn't come home last night and he suspects another man. Phillips does his best to ignore Columbo. The judge repeatedly admonishes Columbo to stay in his seat and stop whispering to the plaintiff's attorney. The interruptions also irk Phillips' lovely young client, who fears this shabby-looking fellow is harming her case. Finally, Phillips steps up to the bench and whispers that he's being harassed by a disgruntled stalker. The judge promises to take care of the matter. He calls up Columbo, who identifies himself as a detective. Unimpressed, the judge demands to know how Columbo is involved with the trial at hand. Hearing the answer is not at all, the judge has Columbo thrown out of the courtroom and barred from returning. If Columbo bothers Phillips again, he'll be held in contempt of court. The trial goes on, with Columbo's face peering through the glass panel in the door.

At home that night, Sarah tells Phillips that Columbo paid her a visit earlier in the day. Phillips is furious. What precisely did she tell him? She can't recall her exact words. He begins cross-examining her as if she were on the stand. Sarah does not like it one bit. She's never seen him afraid of anyone before. He bristles at the thought. She then shares how surprised she was to learn what poor Constance was wearing when she was shot. "No wonder you were worried about my negligee turning up." She's figured it out.

Phillips grabs Sarah and slaps her violently. She had better not suggest anything like that ever again. Sarah is stunned. Phillips apologizes. He's just overwhelmed with Columbo's attempts to destroy their marriage.

Desperate to close the book on the killings and on Columbo, Phillips contacts his friends at the district attorney's office to arrange a hearing to, once and for all, establish the cause of the murders. It will be held in open court—Phillips' home turf. He'll put Columbo on the stand and make sure he never bothers him again. First, witnesses from the cottages testify on the shots they heard. Next comes the coroner. And finally Columbo. The DA interrogates him first, then Phillips asks if he can ask a few questions. He cleverly twists Columbo's answers to make him sound silly.

Finally, Columbo offers to share the latest development in the case. He reminds everyone how residue gets on the hands of someone when they fire a gun. Phillips asks him to get to the point. Columbo says that the coroner found traces of nitrate and antimony on Constance's cheek. Yet Phillips never said anything about Howard touching her.

Phillips confirms that Howard was halfway across the room when he walked in and shot her. Columbo adds that Constance's cheek was also bruised, as if she'd been hit. Phillips postulates that perhaps Constance struck her face on the bedpost after she was shot. But how did the nitrate and antimony particles get on her cheek?

The judge leans in, anxious to hear more. Phillips offers a deal: "Detective Columbo, if I tell you, will you go away forever?" Columbo is agreeable. Phillips reveals that after the exchange of gunfire, it was he who embraced the dead woman and caressed her cheek. Columbo feigns total embarrassment and continues apologizing as the judge asks him to step down.

Phillips' victory seems complete. Columbo is discredited. No charges will be filed. The hearing adjourns with the record showing that Howard killed Constance. The investigation has concluded.

Phillips hurries home to break the news to his wife, only to learn from the servants that she's left for the Beachfront Cottages. But they've been closed for weeks. Why would Sarah go there of all places? It must be Columbo.

Phillips speeds to the beach, where just one cabin is occupied—the scene of the murders. Inside are Sarah and Columbo. Phillips is enraged. The case was declared closed. Columbo should be brought up on charges of harassment. Columbo, in fact, is trying to recreate different ways the murders could have taken place. He tries popping out of bed. He tries bursting out of the bathroom. He pretends to fire one shot. He pretends to fire a series of shots. Sarah looks on, fascinated. Phillips demands he stop and she leave. She won't budge. She wants to know the truth. She knows Phillips killed Howard and is good with that; he was an abuser who deserved what came to him. But Constance?

By now, Columbo is back to wondering how many shots were fired, in what succession, and why the last one was louder. He already knows that, since there was antimony on the shells, Howard must have arrived with an empty gun. It took time for Phillips to load Devlon's gun and shoot his wife with it. Howard must have already been dead. So how could all three shots have been heard one right after another? Phillips must have used a silencer on his own gun when shooting Howard, then later fired out the window to ensure three audible shots were heard.

Phillips is amused. A theory's one thing, but where's the proof? Columbo yanks open the drapes. Outside, the police have dug up the entire field, searching for a spent bullet.

"You think it's easy finding a single bullet in a field?" Columbo says. "We been digging for weeks. Oh, sure, you found a bullet out there in a few minutes, didn't you? But that's only because we made it easy for you. We put

NEARLY 20 YEARS later, *Columbo and the Murder of a Rock Star* (1991) would tread similar ground to *Death Do Us Part*, with Dabney Coleman as the hotheaded lawyer. *[Credit: NBCUniversal]*

40 spent bullets out there, figuring you'd find one pretty quick. But we didn't come up with yours till early today."

Columbo holds out the slug. "It fits the grooves of your gun. Now is that evidence or what?"

Phillips reaches for Sarah, but she's now repulsed by him. She tells Columbo she's ready to make a statement about a certain black negligee, a trip to Tucson, "and a few other things." Phillips starts shouting at her to be quiet, but Columbo smiles and requests that he stop badgering the witness. Phillips is cooked. He slumps down on the couch in defeat. Columbo does offer a word of consolation, explaining that there's no need to worry anymore about Mrs. Columbo. "We patched things up, thanks to you."

Cohen completed the first 29 pages of the screenplay, sticking closely to his revised treatment. He wrote as far as the scene of the Beachfront Cottages murder, when he was informed that the episode wouldn't be moving forward.

There are likely a few reasons why the project was killed in its tracks. At the time, its motive was unique—a loveless womanizer who kills out of true love. Yet, *Columbo* had already had a hardcore lawyer as a murderer (*Ransom for a Dead Man*, 1971), albeit a female insurance litigator who kills because she's bored with her husband.

More problematic, though fixable, were the far-fetched assumptions that the characters rely on to advance the story. Phillips seems extremely confident that a man who presumably has never murdered before will kill at a preordained place and time. Admittedly, Howard seems primed to do so, but taking for granted that he would proceed seems a stretch.

Phillips also makes sure to have Sarah tell everyone she's going to the Beachfront Cottages that night. Certainly, she would have been able to figure out why he wanted her to do this.

Columbo makes similarly broad leaps of logic, particularly in focusing on the black negligee just because he linked it to a stray shred of plastic. A giftbox or giftwrap must have been at the cottage; wouldn't it be likelier that the price tag was removed before the nightie was wrapped and the plastic fragment went along for the ride?

But the likeliest obstacle to the episode getting made was its raciness. *Columbo* had never before focused on sex, let alone shown lovers in bed, or used underwear as the central clue. Early 1970s audiences may not have been ready for it. It would take until 1989's *Sex and the Married Detective* before the show was comfortable enough with building sex into the plot. Like *Death Do Us Part*, women's panties become the key clue in a later beach-house-murder plot, *Murder in Malibu* (1990). But that episode is so awkward, particularly Columbo's strange preoccupation with the underwear, that maybe it's for the best that the earlier tale was never filmed.

Not so coincidentally, *Murder in Malibu* was written on spec by Jackson Gillis, who had been *Columbo's* story editor 18 years earlier, when Larry Cohen submitted this tale.

Death Do Us Part, however, most foreshadows *Columbo and the Murder of a Rock Star* (1991), in which a hot-tempered superstar attorney (Dabney Coleman) tries to leave his two-timing lover. When she threatens to blackmail him, he plots to kill her while she beds her lover in his beach house. The attorney even calls in favors with the DA to try to get Columbo off his back.

Cohen contributed 10 more story ideas that were seriously considered for Season 4:

- *Murder by a Thoroughbred*
- *No Tax on Murder*
- *Murder with a Feminine Touch*
- *An Aria for Murder*
- *A+ for Murder*
- *Murder Is a Star Vehicle*
- *Death Is a Lonely Dance*
- *Murder Is the Eighth Lively Art*
- *An Aptitude for Murder*
- *Murder Is a Sport of Honor*

The last one inspired Season 5's *A Matter of Honor*, though Brad Radnitz rewrote it so extensively, Cohen received no billing. None of the others was produced, although the first four did appear promising enough to be assigned production numbers.

Cohen's contributions to *Columbo*, however, were finished. He returned to the United States to write, produce and direct the horror film *It's Alive* in the summer of 1973, with a slew of low-budget horror films to follow.

Shooting Script

In March 1973, just as *Any Old Port in a Storm*, the second episode of Season 3, was about to go before the cameras, the Writers Guild went on strike. Development of future *Columbo* episodes stopped. When the production team reconvened that summer, producer Doug Benton and story editor Jackson Gillis were gone, and Hargrove and Kibbee returned as executive producers.

Peter Falk, of course, was back as well. But whereas during the previous season he had no interest in seeing the scripts until he was ready to shoot them, he now wanted to read them beforehand. Of the stories Hargrove had to choose from, the producer was most interested in a change-of-pace, which was referred to him by Steven Spielberg. As Hargrove recalled: "The only time I ever had an issue with Peter (Falk) was that Steven Spielberg had called me and said, 'There's a director named Brian De Palma who's been out of work. He needs a job. Would you hire him to do *Columbo*?' I had known Steven because I'd hired him on *The Name of the Game*, and recommended him for the truck show (*Duel*), so he was a friend of mine. I knew Brian De Palma's work, because he'd done a couple of films in New York called *Greetings* and *Hi, Mom!*, very off the wall and low budget, with a very young Robert De Niro in them. They were very amusing, very droll."

De Palma met with Hargrove and Kibbee to pitch his idea: an eccentric writer—modeled after *In Cold Blood* author Truman Capote—films himself murdering a vapid TV talk-show host, inspired by Johnny Carson. De Palma wanted to both write the script and direct it. He shared some of his ideas, such as filming the first scenes from a height of 4-foot-9, as if they were being photographed by the diminutive Capote character. (He had opened *Hi, Mom!* similarly.) In fact, any time the villain was using his handheld camera, the scene would be filmed from his vantage point.

Hargrove was intrigued. De Palma said he was already writing the script, in partnership with Jay Cocks, the movie critic for *Time* magazine. The producers invited him to come back when he finished the script.

Cocks, who wrote under the pseudonym Joseph P. Gillis (named after the struggling screenwriter character in *Sunset Boulevard*), and De Palma submitted their teleplay, *Shooting Script*, on July 26, 1973.

— 🕮 —

It's nighttime in the study of novelist Quentin Lee. We see nothing—the room is pitch black—and hear only the voice of Lee, described as having "wisps of a Southern accent. It is not really effeminate, just oddly pitched, as if the speaker is perennially bemused." He is introducing a video "diary of a perfect crime" by paraphrasing *Crime and Punishment*: "Of what is man most afraid? Is it taking an untried step? Can I do that? That might be amusing. Murder? Maybe a fantasy thing. Yet something to satisfy a curiosity, not serious at all." Dostoevsky, Quentin points out, restricted himself to fiction.

Through the lens of Lee's camera we see his hand switch on a videotape recorder. San Quentin State Prison appears on a TV screen. The scene slowly tracks past the cells as the opening credits appear: "Conversations on Death Row," then "With Quentin Lee."

As he fast-forwards the tape, Quentin explains that he got the inspiration for his latest project while filming this documentary on Death Row. He freezes on the face of inmate Frank Mathis, whom Quentin interviewed shortly before his execution. Quentin asks if the prisoner thought it not terribly bright to discard the murder weapon in a vacant lot next to his apartment building. Mathis admits it was a mistake. Quentin pushes the issue: it could have been the "perfect murder—except for one horrendous and obvious blunder." Mathis snaps: who is Lee to judge him? The writer lectures everyone about crime, Mathis snarls, but what does he really know about it? About the moment when you look at someone who's alive and then pull the trigger. "You don't know what it's like and you never will—because you've never killed anyone."

Quentin now speaks over the videotape: "He was right, of course. One writes, after all, only from what one knows."

Quentin reasons that the perfect crime is one that is motiveless—of which there is no such thing. What confounds the police is subtlety of motive. Unlike him, the police have no taste. And his exquisite taste will be his motive. What Quentin finds most distasteful is the "cult of pseudo-celebrities"—television personalities. He will kill a TV star. And since his chic apartment building is filled with them, he will kill one of those.

We see his hand pick up a dart and throw it at a typed list of tenants that's he's pinned to a bulletin board. The dart settles on the name of talk-show host Duane Downs. Quentin is ecstatic.

Late that evening, after he's finished taping his talk show, Downs returns to the Sunset Chalet Apartments, a young lovely on each arm. Quentin is waiting for them on the elevator, still filming. Downs wants to know what's up with the camera. Quentin confesses that he's been inconspicuously filming him; he thought it would be fun to show the tapes on his program. Downs likes the idea. "We can play it like I'm caught off guard by the idea," Downs says. "I'll get some good ad-libs ready."

Downs and his dates step out of the elevator on the sixth floor. Quentin volunteers to come by the next night to show him the footage he's taken thus far—so long as Downs is alone. Downs agrees, and the elevator doors shut, closing the scene and Act I like a curtain.

The following evening, we continue from the point of view of Lee's handheld camera. His hand takes a screwdriver, which he uses to make scratches on the basement door of the apartment building. Quentin informs us that the marks will lead the police to believe an intruder jimmied the door to gain access, since Security is stationed at the lobby entrance. He moves along the corridor and takes the service elevator to Downs' floor. Quentin waits in the hallway until he sees his "blandly unsuspecting victim" approaching. Before Quentin can make his presence known, a man springs from behind a stairwell and startles Downs. The man, starving actor Lynn Loring, plays it off as "a marvelous coincidence. I was just leaving a party at your neighbor's here…"

"It must have been a small party," Downs replies. "My neighbors have been in the Bahamas since January."

Loring introduces himself and is shocked that Downs has never heard of him, considering his 20 years in theater, television and film. He specializes in one-man shows, performing passages of Shakespeare, O'Neill and Chekhov. "I'm famous for my Treplev."

Downs has also never heard of Konstantin Treplev, the central character of Chekhov's *The Seagull*. Whatever he's famous for, Downs tells him, put it in writing, send it to his secretary, and she'll make him an appointment.

Loring has tried that, several times. Arriving at his apartment door, Downs pleads exhaustion. If Loring tells his secretary that he's spoken to him, she will give him an appointment. Pleased, Loring leaves Downs with a few 8x10 glossies. Downs slips inside his apartment. A moment later, there's a knock on his door. Downs angrily yanks open the door, expecting to see Loring. He's relieved to find Quentin, with his camera rolling. Downs invites the author in for a drink and tosses the headshots onto the mantelpiece.

"Would you believe that some creep of an actor named Lynn Loring just snuck in from my balcony looking for a spot on the show? Wanted to show me his Treplev," Downs laughs. "I should have sent him over to Carson." Downs invites Quentin to appear on his show the following week.

Lee agrees, but could Downs move over a bit, so he can get a side angle? Downs moves over, to in front of a mirror, but he's tiring of the camera schtick.

It won't last much longer. Quentin raises an antique twin-barreled derringer, both hammers cocked. Downs grins, assuming it's some sort of joke. "That's right," Quentin says. "Smile for the camera."

Quentin squeezes the trigger. Both hammers drop with a thunderous discharge. Downs falls backwards, sporting two neatly spaced holes in his dinner jacket. Quentin finally sets down the camera. A faint pinkish ring remains around his right eye, where he had been holding the eyepiece. He begins ransacking the apartment.

Some hours later, Columbo arrives on the scene, where the police and a news crew have already set up camp. He apologizes to Officer Hernandez for being late—his TV set's busted so he and his wife went to their neighbor's house to watch Duane Downs' show. The program was interrupted by a news report of the killing—which briefly threw Columbo for a loop, since he was unaware Downs prerecorded his shows.

Downs' apartment is a mess. His corpse lies where it fell, covered with a sheet. Quentin sits on a sofa across the room, chatting on the phone. Quentin now wears a voluptuous bathrobe, slippers and a towel muffler—along with a trace of that pinkish ring around his right eye.

Hernandez points out the apparent signs of a struggle, and of forced entry: the door's safety chain and part of the moulding have been ripped off. The body had been discovered earlier that morning by a delivery boy from the liquor store. Columbo is more curious, though, about the unusual-looking gentleman on the couch. Quentin's finishing up a call with Downs' producer, consenting to host a tribute show about his fallen friend. Before Quentin can dial another number, Columbo interrupts. Lee's already given his statement—he lives upstairs, in 9C. He was in his bath and heard the shots at exactly 10 p.m. Lee returns to the phone.

While Columbo's waiting, three college film majors arrive and ask to be allowed in. They say they're "field assignment," authorized by the department. It takes a second, but Columbo remembers—he had agreed to guest-lecture on police methodology, but kept forgetting.

Among the students, Chapman handles the tape recorder and does most of the talking. Spielberg works the still camera. And the female, Brooks, takes copious notes.

When Quentin finally hangs up, Columbo asks him to identify the body. Quentin wants to know who the kids are. "What is this—*Meet the Press?*" Told they're students conducting research, Quentin mocks, "Obviously, a real trio of crime stoppers."

After Quentin IDs the body, he turns to leave. Columbo says that if he's upset, the police can station an officer near his door. Lee scoffs at the suggestion. "Boy, that's a crime writer for you," enthuses Columbo. "Cool as a cucumber. Most people would be a nervous wreck if a guy were killed right next door."

Quentin corrects him. He may analyze crime in his writing, but he's not a crime writer. He leaves that to "the paperback hacks." He's only interested in crimes that probe great philosophical questions, which require complete emotional detachment—just as he'd expect Columbo to investigate the case.

He closes the door behind him and goes out. Columbo stands there thinking for a second, then turns to go back into the room, but the students have cornered him against the door. Chapman and Brooks pepper Columbo with questions about the investigation. How did the killer get in the building? What's the motive—does this look like a Charles Manson-type murder? Columbo stops them. It's getting late. But he does have a question for Spielberg: why doesn't *he* ask any questions? "I'm into electronics," Spielberg replies. "Surveillance devices. Photographic equipment."

Columbo agrees to meet them in the morning at the police lab. They should have some results by then.

Alone, Columbo heads for 9C. Quentin answers the door, the pink ring now gone from around his eye. The author invites him in, but just for a moment. Immediately, Columbo is distracted by the view and wanders out onto the balcony. Columbo guesses Quentin had been out on the balcony when he heard the shots. No, Quentin corrects him, he repeats that he was taking a bath. But the terrace door was open, so he could hear the gunfire. He only closed the door a moment ago, because he was feeling chilly.

In the bathroom, Columbo searches around the large sunken tub. There's no clock in the room and Quentin wouldn't have been wearing a watch. How did he know it was 10:00 exactly? Quentin says there's a grandfather clock in the living room that strikes the hour. He'll show it to Columbo… on his way out. Columbo admires the antique grandfather clock and tries to confirm that it's telling the correct time by comparing it to his wristwatch—which has stopped.

Columbo looks up to discover Lee aiming the videotape camera at him. Being filmed makes Columbo nervous and uncomfortable. He's so self-conscious, he doesn't even let his wife take home movies of him. Lee says he commits his daily diary to film—and Columbo has become an "inescapable part" of his day. Quentin asks him to make a statement on the murder. But Columbo's making for the exit. "Sir, if you don't mind, I'll just say good night."

Thinking Columbo's gone, Quentin lowers the camera, but Columbo turns back for one more thing—to take note of the ring around Quentin's eye. Quentin quickly resumes filming Columbo as he walks down the hall, occasionally glancing back.

The next morning, Quentin is viewing the Downs murder on a playback set in his study. A camera is also filming Quentin, to get his reaction to watching his crime. Quentin is pleased, in fact proud, that his plan seems flawless. The derringer he used has been in his family for a century and would be impossible to trace. But then he catches something odd on the screen. He hits rewind and anxiously replays the sequence. "Holy Mother." There, right behind the victim, is a face. Someone else was in the house, watching. Near hysterical, Quentin zooms in closer and closer, trying to make out the face through the blurriness and swirling traces of gunpowder in the air. Quentin can now see it's a reflection in the mirror behind Downs. A man, "watching the killing as coolly as if it were a television show." But if the uninvited guest had already gone to the police, they would have been at the door by now.

Suddenly, the face registers—it's that idiot actor who surprised Downs in the hallway. Lee rewinds the tape and freezes on their earlier encounter. Definitely the same person. Lynn Loring.

"An actor with negligible prospects," Quentin muses, "and probably a taste for blackmail. Well, come ahead and make your move, my friend. I could use a subplot."

Our next stop is an electronic store, as shakily viewed through a handheld video camera—by the unsteady hand of Columbo. He confirms with the store manager that such a camera could film at night, with available light. Their conversation is interrupted by the arrival of Chapman, Brooks and Spielberg. When Columbo lowers the camera, he spots his reflection on a glass case—there's a ring around his eye. The students show Columbo a photo Spielberg took last night at the murder scene. There appears to be a man on Downs' balcony. Spielberg hands him an enlargement. Loring's face is clear as day. But Columbo tells them that the face is a photograph reflected in the glass door. He points to a photo of the other side of the room, showing the photo on the mantelpiece. Spielberg and Brooks are impressed, Chapman discouraged. Columbo tries to cheer him up: "Don't feel bad. I made the same mistake once. Put out an APB and a description. I got halfway through the description before I realized I was talking about Rock Hudson."

Quentin Lee arrives at the television studio, and takes just a few steps out of his car before he's confronted by Loring. Loring is stunned that Quentin recognizes him. Quentin says he knows he was at Downs' apartment last night—"at a rather embarrassing time." Loring says he didn't want to go to the police. "I mean, being the last one to see Mr. Downs alive, suspicion might fall on me. The last one, that is, except for the murderer. You understand."

Quentin nods, "Completely." He says he has a show to do and suggests they meet later, privately, in the parking lot. As Quentin walks away, Loring ponders what to make of the invitation—but, with a career on the line, he's not about to ask.

During the taping of Downs' memorial show, Columbo stands backstage peering out from behind a curtain. As host, Lee sits near Downs' desk, although Downs' own chair is empty, "draped in funeral black for this mournful occasion." At the other side of the desk sit a shocked Roy Edwards (Downs' announcer and "loyal laughing machine") and a young actress, trying very hard to look subdued. Quentin introduces one of Downs' great discoveries, warbly voiced ukulelist Tiny Tim. Stricken with emotion, Tiny Tim tries to sing and play a song, but has trouble finishing. During the performance, Quentin notices Columbo. As soon as he cuts to commercial,

Quentin heads behind the curtain to greet Columbo and agrees to answer his "routine questions"—"the only kind I would expect." Suddenly, the lights go down and the music swells. Columbo is disconcerted: "What's going on?"

"*You* are!" Lee answers.

The curtain parts to reveal an energetic studio audience. Columbo shields his eyes from the sudden harsh light. A television camera dollies in for a closeup. Lee introduces viewers to his next guest, the police lieutenant in charge of investigating Downs' murder. Columbo is paralyzed. Quentin leads him across the stage to the couch. Lee asks if he'd be more comfortable if he took his jacket. Columbo unconsciously clings a little tighter to his raincoat. Quentin opines that many celebrity murders are crimes specifically *designed* for public consumption. In fact, he suspects Downs' killer is one such child of the media, and announces that his next project will be a detailed study of the murder. He asks Columbo what he thinks of his speculation. Columbo hasn't worked out his own theory quite yet, he's just asking a lot of questions. Quentin tries his best to mock Columbo's simple approach. As soon as they break for commercial, Columbo excuses himself. "What about those questions you were so eager to ask me?" Lee inquires.

Columbo says he didn't feel they were appropriate to ask with the cameras rolling, but he is curious about the ring he saw around his eye on the night of the murder. Quentin wonders if that means Columbo thinks he was filming himself in the tub. "You're surely not suggesting that I'd murder Duane Downs and tape myself doing it. That would take a supreme egotist, and I'm known for my modesty."

Before Columbo can ask another question, the five-second call goes out for the end of the break. "I'll see you later," Columbo says.

"Yes, you probably will."

After the taping, Quentin finds Loring sitting in his car, reading *Variety*. Quentin slips into the passenger seat and dons a "precautionary pair of sunglasses." Quentin wants to get right to the point. What does Loring want?

Loring heard Lee was guest-hosting for Downs and was hoping he'd allow him to appear. Some of the readings from his one-man show might make for a nice memorial, like Marc Antony's eulogy from *Julius Caesar*.

No, what does he really want? "Just a chance, Mr. Lee."

Quentin is incredulous. All he's asking for is one appearance on the Duane Downs show? Absolutely, Loring says. He thinks it would make him. But then wouldn't he soon want more? Oh, no. Loring promises never to bother him again. Quentin doesn't believe him. "Let's start with a payoff worthy of your capabilities," Quentin says. "I want our relationship to be brief and conclusive." What if he backed him in a one-man show on Broadway?

Loring is over the moon. Of course, Quentin first would need to see his repertoire—especially his Treplev. Loring suggests they meet tomorrow morning at his small studio workshop; it's very private.

Later that day, Columbo returns to Quentin's apartment, carrying a stack of books his wife wants him to get autographed for various members of the family. As Quentin signs, Columbo roams off to admire the remarkable bathtub and its intricate Venetian fixtures. Columbo turns a handle and a torrent of water spews from the tap. Columbo jumps back before he gets fully drenched.

"Now I see why you wear the raincoat," Quentin says. He adjusts the fixture to a lighter flow and states that, at the time of the murder, the water was coming out at just about that rate. Consequently, he continues, Columbo can safely signal his accomplice to fire a shot in Downs' apartment. A second later, there's a gunshot. Quentin turns off the water. Columbo sheepishly apologizes for having to check out his story. Quentin confirms that's the same sound he heard last night. But that was only one shot, Columbo notes. Didn't he say he heard *shots*? And Ballistics has since established that there was only one shot fired—the murder weapon was a derringer that fired two bullets simultaneously, eliciting a single report.

The next morning, Quentin enters Loring's tiny studio, as viewed through the lens of his handheld camera. The walls are covered with posters of past Lynn Loring triumphs. There are a few rows of folding chairs, a riser for a stage, and, in the corner, a card table with a typewriter. A moment later, Loring arrives, startled to find Lee inside. He's sure he locked up last night. Obviously he didn't, Quentin reasons. Loring wants to know what's up with the camera. Quentin says it's for his backers, so they'll know what they're investing in.

Quentin's camera follows Loring as he steps onstage to look over the props. He's puzzled by the presence of a gun. Loring assumes they'll be doing the final scene, but in the play the gunshot is offstage. Not for this performance, Quentin says. Treplev's suicide will take place in full view of the audience. An interesting touch, Loring admits. Loring picks up a hat; he likes it. But he doesn't want to use the scarf. Too constraining. Quentin grants him his wish; only the gun is important.

Before they go on, Quentin insists on Loring signing a release; his backers won't look at a foot of film unless they have legal protection. Quentin extends a pen and a thick contract, folding back the first pages. Loring—now wearing the Treplev hat—signs without hesitancy. Quentin chatters on about the posters to further distract Loring from scrutinizing the contract.

Quentin sets the scene and feeds Loring his first lines. With each word, Loring sounds hammier and more pompous. The script instructs Treplev to tear up the room, but Quentin directs him to "mime the destruction, then finally discover the gun on the table and… use it."

Loring launches into a preposterously embarrassing mad scene. Quentin can barely hide his laughter. Loring finally "discovers" the gun on the table. He seizes it, presses the weapon against his temple, and fires. He's in complete shock, as he falls backwards. He's just blown his brains out.

After a moment of complete silence, Quentin applauds. He sets the camera down on a chair to film himself walking up to the table. From the contract, he pulls out a suicide note which Loring unwittingly signed.

Some hours later, the police and the college trio are on the scene. Columbo reads the suicide note: an admission that Loring killed Downs because he humiliated him, and now would take his own life due to feelings of hopelessness and guilt. It includes a Treplev quote for good measure. Columbo's confused.

Quentin shows up to lend a hand, pointing his ever-present camera. Columbo is delighted to see him, since the death might fit Quentin's theory about a "media murder." But there's a suicide note, Quentin points out. Shouldn't that answer all of his questions? Columbo's not entirely convinced that Loring killed himself. First of all, who's Treplev?

Lee explains, "A young and rather impetuous poet in Chekhov's play *The Seagull*… who kills himself in the course of the play." So what would that have to do with it *not* being a suicide?

Columbo admits it's definitely meant to look like one. But most suicide notes are handwritten rather than typed. Loring signed it, but maybe he was tricked into it. And then there was the silly hat—why would someone put that on before killing himself?

Quentin chalks it up to the eccentricities of being an actor. Lee calls the students over, as Columbo has to take a call. Quentin hands Spielberg his camera and asks Chapman to turn on his tape recorder and Brooks to take notes. Quentin then walks around the room, explaining how the investigation should be conducted. First, investigators must determine if there was a relationship between the dead actor and Downs. Then, since no murder weapon was found, Loring's gun should be examined to see if it's one and the same. Finally, despite Columbo stalking him for the last 48 hours, he's failed to turn up any motive on Lee's part. No motive, no case.

Columbo returns. He's learned that, for some time, Loring had been spotted hanging around Downs' office, studio and apartment in an effort to get booked on his show.

Satisfied, Lee invites the students to a small soiree that night at his place. He'll be running some of his tapes on penal reform. With that, he declares the end of the interview and, he presumes, the case. Quentin takes his camera back from Spielberg.

Columbo mentions that Spielberg is terrific with a camera, and asks the student to show Quentin some of his shots from the night of the murder. Columbo stops on one enlargement and points out the photo on the mantel that reflected to make it seem like Loring was in the room. Quentin turns momentarily ashen, but recovers. He *really* has to go—to get ready for the party.

Columbo visits the diner. Bert brings him his usual—a bowl of chili. The college kids soon join him at the counter. He thought they were going to Lee's party. They say it sounded like a bore. Instead, they each order a bowl of chili. Bert turns on a TV set that's behind the counter. A talk show is on with guest Quentin Lee.

Columbo now thinks Lee is following *him*. Chapman says it could be worse—it could be a rerun of Columbo's appearance on Downs' show. Why, that's it, Columbo realizes. That's when Lee gave away his game, when he suggested that he might've filmed himself committing the murder. He had such a huge ego and has written so many books about crime, he had to prove that he would be good at it.

Chapman is convinced, and ready to round up Lee's videotapes. But they can't just break in and grab his tapes. They'd have to request a search warrant, and a judge would think Columbo was crazy for suspecting someone filmed himself committing murder.

Chapman says they wouldn't have to break in. After all, they were invited to his screening party. Brooks suggests Columbo distract Lee while they go through his tapes. But Quentin's library contains hundreds of tapes and they don't even know if the incriminating tape is among them.

Chapman agrees that it would be far-fetched. But Spielberg thinks that's exactly what he'd do. The others are astonished as Spielberg, who heretofore has said very little, expertly analyzes Lee: he's a megalomaniac, so he wouldn't let the tape get too far from his sight. Second, he's an egomaniac, who would go for a stunt like in Edgar Allan Poe's *The Purloined Letter*, in which the incriminating letter was placed in a card rack in plain view—among a number of other letters. Spielberg suggests they trick Lee into leading them to the tape.

The party at Lee's apartment is in full swing. Columbo ambles down the

DIMINUTIVE Paul Williams was approached to play Quentin Lee, the Truman Capote-esque killer in *Shooting Script*. When the *Columbo* episode fell through, Brian De Palma cast Williams as the unscrupulous record producer in *Phantom of the Paradise* (1974). *[Credit: 20th Century Fox]*

corridor. He stops at Quentin's door and quickly polishes his shoes on the back of his pant legs. He rings the bell. A butler answers and sizes up Columbo, disapprovingly. Columbo must show his badge to gain entry. Quentin is disappointed to see his uninvited guest. "What a surprise, Lieutenant," he says. "Is this an official call or do I have to be charming?"

Columbo asks Quentin if he can speak with him privately—no stunts. They head for the balcony. The instant the balcony door closes behind them, Chapman and Brooks head in one direction, Spielberg in another.

Columbo shares that, while he was having dinner, he received a call from the lab. Loring's gun checked out as the one that shot Downs. Ballistics determined the derringer was a presentation model, special issue, 1884. Lee demands to know if it was traced to him. No, Columbo says. It has no registration number. The gun's untraceable. But, pulling out his notebook, Columbo reveals that there were 50 such guns presented to the survivors of a Confederate outfit after the Civil War—Seventh Artillery Regiment, Brundidge, Alabama.

Quentin grows increasingly impatient. Columbo says he was thumbing through one of Lee's books in which he writes that he was born in Brundidge, Alabama. Quentin rolls his eyes and turns to leave. Columbo, seemingly angry, takes Quentin by the arm. He demands an explanation. Quentin refuses and starts to slide open the door. Columbo slams it shut. With Quentin's brilliant mind, he should be able to calculate the odds of Loring owning an antique pistol from Lee's hometown. What, 10 million to one? Loring must have ended up with the gun because it was Lee's. Lee killed Downs. And then Lee killed Loring.

Quentin stares at him for a long moment, then laughs. He can't believe Columbo staged this pitiful scene, trying to unnerve him by claiming he found something connecting him to the murder weapon. Did Columbo have such a low opinion of him that he thinks he'd use a gun that could be traced back to him? Or that he was dumb enough to be bluffed into admitting it?

Columbo shrugs, half smiling. He crumples up the report and tosses it aside. He had to give it a shot. What did he have to lose?

Quentin says there are no hard feelings. Columbo's welcome to stay and have a drink. But it's getting late. Columbo says he'd better get going. Quentin requests that if Columbo ever sees him again, it should only be on TV. As Columbo heads for the exit, Quentin gathers his guests for "movie time." He puts on a tape from one of two boxes, expecting it to be a documentary he made at Folsom Prison. Instead, his Death Row program begins to play. Quentin is confused. He apologizes for the little mix-up and says he'll play his Alcatraz show instead. He puts in that tape, but it, too, is the wrong show.

He stares at the mislabeled video sleeve. Slight panic begins to set in. He takes the two boxes and excuses himself to the library. He locks the door behind him and moves to the wall of tapes. He stops and looks at a slightly ajar closet door. He flings it open, but no one is hiding behind it. Now certain he's alone, he takes one of the tapes from the wall and inserts it into his playback machine. It's the Downs murder. Lee quickly turns the tape off and returns it to its place on the shelf. Relieved, he opens the library door—to discover Columbo standing there, with the three students behind him.

Columbo says he decided to hang around after all. He didn't want to miss the world premiere. He'd said that Spielberg was a talented photographer, but forgot to mention that he was also great with electronics. The kid equipped Quentin's door with a "photoelectric gizmo." As soon as anyone opened the door, Lee's own camera switched on. While Spielberg was rigging the door, Chapman and Brooks went to work mixing up the tapes that Lee had planned to show.

Spielberg takes the tape from Quentin's camera and puts it in the playback machine. There's Quentin taking the murder tape off the shelf and watching it. Lee is irritated, but impressed. Columbo has spoiled his plans to release

FILMMAKING FRIEND: Martin Scorsese (*left*) was suggested by Brian De Palma (*right*) to take his place as director of *Shooting Script* after De Palma received a movie offer.

the tape posthumously.

The Lieutenant asks if Quentin is ready to leave. But doesn't Columbo want to watch the rest of the picture? "No, thanks," he says. "I know how it comes out."

De Palma had named the film students after his fellow aspiring filmmaker friends (Steven) Spielberg, (Albert) Brooks, and (Michael) Chapman. He resurrected Bert the counterman at Barney's Beanery, who hadn't been spotted since *Dead Weight,* the third episode of Season 1. He notated a range of unusual camera angles that, in time, would become his hallmark. But his story, as exciting as it was, was a huge departure from the series' formula. There were very few clues. Little time was spent with Columbo and Lee volleying on Lee's home turf. And the villain had such a big personality, Columbo became sort of an afterthought. Our hero needed to exhibit more Columbo-ish behavior, to endear him to the audience (as, three years later, he would when playing off William Shatner's flamboyant Ward Fowler in Season 6's *Fade In to Murder*).

Hargrove was keenly aware of the script's shortcomings and figured they could be ironed out in the coming weeks. Hargrove pushed forward, meeting with pint-sized singer/songwriter/actor Paul Williams, who agreed to star as Quentin Lee. Hargrove had De Palma and Cocks write at least two more revised scripts. He assigned it a production number, intending to film it in the fall. At the last minute, De Palma had to step away when he received an offer to make his dream film, *Phantom of the Paradise*, but he referred his friend, Martin Scorsese, to direct. The one obstacle Hargrove couldn't overcome was Falk, who didn't care for the script.

Hargrove admitted the story was unusual, but that was the exciting part of it. He promised that the writing team would tweak it to better conform to the *Columbo* format. But that wasn't what was bothering Falk—it was the character of Quentin Lee. He was just too colorful. He thought the Lieutenant was himself so idiosyncratic, he'd be diminished by squaring up with someone equally eccentric. Falk thought his character played better off of someone straight, serious, rich and successful—not an oddball like Lee. Hargrove enumerated all of the plusses and assured him he would address any specific elements, but Falk wasn't having any of it. The episode wouldn't work if Lee lost his outrageousness.

Shooting Script was officially scrapped—a shame, because it could have been one of the most memorable *Columbos* ever made. Remnants did survive. A similar ending—in which the killer panics and leads Columbo to the evidence—was used later in Season 3, in *Double Exposure*. De Palma cast Paul Williams as the unscrupulous record producer in *Phantom of the Paradise*. In 1980's *Dressed to Kill*, De Palma reused the idea of IDing the killer through a hidden camera (though it was a time-lapse, not a motion-sensitive camera). In 1986, Hargrove co-wrote a vaguely reminiscent TV movie, *Perry Mason: The Case of the Shooting Star*, about an actor accused of killing a talk-show host live on TV. And the dynamic of a team of students assisting Columbo with his investigation foreshadows Season 10's *Columbo Goes to College*.

Cocks' and De Palma's careers suffered no ill effects. Cocks became a frequent collaborator of Scorsese, writing such screenplays as the Academy Award-nominated films *The Age of Innocence* and *Gangs of New York*. And De Palma would direct *Carrie, Blow Out, Scarface, The Untouchables, Casualties of War, Carlito's Way, Mission: Impossible*, and more than a dozen other big-budget films.

3
Season 4 (1974-1975)
Psychological Problems

After retaking charge of the series, executive producers Hargrove and Kibbee began furiously compiling scripts and story ideas. Season 4 would feature just six episodes yet, by the time filming restarted in the summer of 1974, they already had 20 story possibilities in various stages of development. Four of those would be held over for later seasons, but most would never see the light of day, including two that would have been huge departures for the series.

Dead as a Duck

The first was a cast-off from *McMillan & Wife* penned by Theodore J. Flicker, a primarily satirical writer who moonlighted on detective series. In the 1950s, Flicker, along with Elaine May, was a member of the pioneering improv group the Compass Theater in Chicago. In 1959, he wrote and directed the Broadway musical *The Nervous Set*—the first "beat musical." A year later, he co-founded *The Premise*, a satirical revue in New York, with the likes of Buck Henry, Gene Hackman and George Segal. In 1964, Flicker moved into movies, co-writing *The Troublemaker* with Henry, breaking out with Elvis Presley's *Spinout*, and making his biggest mark with *The President's Analyst* (1967). Along the way, he started submitting spec scripts for series such as *I Dream of Jeannie*, *Night Gallery*, and—in the early 1970s—for detective shows like *Banyon*, *The Mod Squad*, and *The Streets of San Francisco*.

After selling a script for *Banacek*, Flicker decided to write for another *NBC*

Mystery Movie, McMillan & Wife. On August 12, 1973, he completed a 34-page treatment for *The Dead Swan*, a whodunit involving the reunion of a Mr. Rogers-type puppeteer and his eccentric troupe of performers. Flicker was undoubtedly influenced by his background in comedy troupes and his penchant for weaving psychoanalysis into his work.

McMillan & Wife producer Paul Mason didn't think the script was right for his show, but suggested it might be an intriguing change of pace for *Columbo*. Instead of Mac's wife (played by Susan Saint James) becoming fond of the puppeteer, Flicker had the performer romanced by a wealthy young widow named Gloria, whose awkward son Columbo takes a shine to. Flicker's 102-page *Columbo*, finished December 2, still needed work. Mason suggested the script lose at least 10 pages—ideally coming in at 85 pages to fill a 90-minute episode. Mason advised there was too much time spent on the comedians and dancers performing at the Hollywood Bowl—with too many silly antics that had nothing to do with Columbo. For a true whodunit, the story could also use one or two more suspects. How about the propmaster? He could live on a boat, which Columbo visits—and ends up getting seasick on. And, in place of Columbo simply driving up to the murderer's house at the end to make the arrest, the story should have a "Charlie Chan ending," in which all of the suspects are present and the solution is revealed dramatically.

Flicker incorporated all of Mason's suggestions into his final 83-page script, submitted two weeks later and renamed *Dead as a Duck*.

The Hollywood Bowl is packed for the annual Police Benefit Gala to help children's charities. The show has already gotten underway. Acrobats and clowns are in mid-act, as Columbo hurries toward the box office.

Backstage is equally frantic. A blur of stagehands scampers about. Two of the performers are arguing intensely. Bobby Mellon, an elegant ballet dancer partially dressed in a Fairy Prince outfit, hisses at the cruel, morbidly obese Ding-Ding, not yet in his Swan costume.

"You swine—you filthy, greedy swine!" Bobby snaps. "You'll pay for it. I swear you will." Ding-Ding laughs insolently.

In another corner, young, pint-sized Monica, adorned in her Princess makeup, is being manhandled by the brutish Mickey. "This is the last time, sweetheart," he snarls, grabbing her by the arm. "You're gonna do it 'cause I told you to." Monica wails that he's hurting her arm. Mickey threatens to hurt a lot more than that.

Further backstage, kiddie TV personality Sam Smith is holding hands with wealthy, 30-something-year-old widow Gloria Van Nelson. She tells Sam that she hopes everything goes well for him. From the look she gives him, it's obvious that she's deeply in love.

Andy Shephard, the aged propman, looks on, smirking. He is carrying the head, wings and other parts of the Swan costume to the prop table.

In the audience, Columbo has finally found his row. An usher points out his seat. Columbo crouches and shimmies to his seat, trying unsuccessfully to not block anyone's view and apologizing the whole way. He ends up in a front-row box, seated next to Gloria's priggish son, William Van Nelson IV, age 9 going on 60. William explains that his mother will return in a moment. Oh, and that police work is his hobby. "You must be just coming off the Jimson case," William notes. "My guess was the uncle killed her."

Backstage, the prop table is covered with the various components of Ding-Ding's Swan costume: a papier-mâché head, wings, tail and huge, flappy webbed feet. Suddenly, gloved hands enter the frame. The hands remove the Swan head from the table, and set it on a chair. They quickly slide a small, bomb-like canister up into the head and tape it securely inside.

In the audience, William looks bored with the show, despite Columbo's continued efforts to spread his enthusiasm—and other guests' constant shushes for the Lieutenant to be quiet. The boy claims he saw better acrobats at his fourth birthday party. His mother arrives at the box, just as Sam and Bobby are helping Ding-Ding strap on his costume and slip into the Swan head.

Columbo is delighted to learn that Ding-Ding and the other "Crazy Clowns" will be up next. Back when he first got married, he and Mrs. Columbo used to love watching them on TV.

A puppet theater has been set up center stage. Out walks Sam Smith, wearing a comfortable cardigan sweater. The audience cheers wildly. Sam smiles shyly, waiting for the applause to settle before moving to the microphone. He's warm, humble, irresistibly likable. Flicker likened him to Will Rogers, but he reads more like Mr. Rogers.

Sam is both gratified and embarrassed by the warm reception. It's been so long since "we stopped doing this foolish act," he says. "To tell you the truth, it's been 20 years since Bobby and Ding-Ding and I have been together on a stage. So, before we start, I'd like to say thank you to the lady who put this benefit together and who brought us together again… Mrs. Gloria Van Nelson!"

After Gloria acknowledges the applause, Sam signals the orchestra to begin playing the Crazy Clown theme and he slips into the puppet theater. The footlights of the little theater come up, the curtains open, and up pops Furry. The hand puppet is a ball of fur, with two big eyes and a mouth that keeps disappearing behind the shag. He's sunny, though not bright, always acting before he thinks. The audience startles him. Furry calls for his friend, Mr. Snip. "Hey, Mr. Snip! Mr. Snip! Snip? Snippie! Hey, Snippie!" Furry moves about the stage, searching and now calling out in silly sing-song: "Snippie boy! Yo, Snip!" Mr. Snip, the "anal-compulsive stork," finally appears behind Furry, looking on with his perpetual grimace of disapproval. Mr. Snip wears glasses, has a sharp voice, and insists that everything be in its proper place—usually resulting in Furry driving him crazy. Columbo and the rest of the audience—minus William—adore their antics.

The two puppets decide to tell a story, as out dance Bobby as the Prince and Monica as the Princess, to the music of Tchaikovsky's *Swan Lake*. As Furry and Mr. Snip narrate, Bobby and Monica's serious love duet is interrupted by a huge flash of smoke. When it clears, the ballerina has been "transformed" into Ding-Ding as the comic Swan. The prissy Prince attempts to dance with the ungainly fowl, as the audience howls with laughter. As the Swan flops around, we hear a faint pop and hissing sound. A foam-like substance begins oozing out of the Swan's meshed eyeholes and around the bottom edges of the mask. Ding-Ding reaches up to pull off the head, but can't because of the wings strapped to his arms. His muffled screams are inaudible over the music and laughter. He staggers about the stage, knocking over scenery. The Swan crashes into Bobby, in mid-pirouette, sending the dancer reeling. Even William is laughing now, in spite of himself.

Bobby is in a rage as he rises to his feet. He starts for Ding-Ding, who's staggering off in another direction. The Prince dances over to the Swan, arriving just as the Swan collapses to the stage floor and begins to thrash about.

Bobby's face contorts in horror. Styrofoam has extruded from the openings in the mask and hardened over the Swan's eyes and neck. Bobby drops to his knees and pulls at Ding-Ding's mask. It won't come off. He frantically calls to drop the curtain.

Columbo rushes to the stage, with Gloria and William following. Behind the curtain, a ring of cast and crew surrounds the prone form of Ding-Ding. A policeman cuts the mask away from the clown's face. The onlookers gasp. The man's head is completely encased in Styrofoam.

At the police lab, the technician shows Columbo the foam canister that had been placed inside the Swan head. "Essentially, it is a foamed plastic bomb," the tech says. Columbo doesn't understand how so much foam could come out of such a little can. "Easy," he's told. "It's a chemical process. The can is divided into two separate sections. In one side there is the polystyrene... in this case a chemical product called Insta-Foam. The other side contains a catalyst. A simple timing device breaks the separating wall at the desired time and, in less than a second, the mask is filled with Insta-Foam. And within three seconds it has set."

Columbo learns that the Swan head was also made from an Insta-Foam mold, hardened on the surfaces by a resin-gel coat.

Additionally, the technician discovered a single strand of nonhuman hair, snagged in the timing device inside the canister. With more time, he'll get a better idea of what type of hair it is.

Columbo drives to Sam Smith's home—a large mansion with rolling lawns, but no high walls or foreboding gates. Columbo parks his Peugeot at the end of the driveway, next to a fashionably aged Rolls-Royce.

Inside the house, Columbo finds Smith in the sunroom with Gloria. Sam is happy to see Columbo—he was just about to call the police, to turn himself in. "But you didn't do it, Sam!" Gloria protests. Sam says it doesn't make a difference, since he sees himself as the likeliest one to be charged and wants to be arrested "as quietly as possible to protect those children, and all the others who believe in the things I say."

Sam takes Columbo to his studio, which Flicker describes as "Santa's workshop. Wonderful puppets of all sizes hang or lounge about. There are fanciful animals, fearsome dragons, goblins and beautiful princes and princesses. There are drawings and paintings of dolls and kingdoms to come, and completed set pieces."

Sitting on a workbench is Exhibit A—the mold for the Swan head. Next to it, Exhibit B—cans of Insta-Foam. Yes, Columbo asks, but what about motive?

Sam shares something that happened 20 years ago, back when he, Ding-Ding, and Bobby were about 20. They came to New York, separately, to make their fortune in the theater. With no other options, they formed the Crazy Clowns. At first, they performed for free in the park. Practically overnight, the act was a hit. They tried out various dancers to play the Princess, but each one soon left because of the lecherous Ding-Ding... until they hired Elaine.

In dreamy flashback, we meet Elaine Harris, a true fairy-tale princess. Sam joins her. They stroll and frolic as lovers. "Elaine and I fell in love," Sam narrates. "For the first time in my life, I had a girl. Those months together, New York, then on the road, were the first truly happy moments of my life.

And then—"

Elaine disappears. Sam stands alone, bewildered. They were supposed to meet after a performance, but she didn't show up. We flash to the dark, evil prop room. The propman enters and walks to a large iron-bound trunk. He opens the trunk and is horrified at the sight. Inside is Elaine's lifeless, suffocated body.

Columbo and Gloria are moved by Sam's story. Elaine's death is still listed as an unsolved murder. And, the tragedy spelled the end of the Crazy Clowns. The members went their separate ways. Then, Sam says, while the group was rehearsing for its return to the stage, he discovered who was responsible for Elaine being locked in the trunk. Ding-Ding was making moves on Elaine. She broke free just as Sam and the propman walked in. Thinking Sam might misunderstand, Elaine climbed into the trunk and closed the lid, accidentally locking herself in.

"And Ding?" Sam narrates. "He just went out and got drunk. He never thought about her again… that poor, exquisite creature struggling in the airless horror of that trunk…"

The parts of the story Sam didn't witness had been recently relayed to him by Ding-Ding. "We were having dinner. He got drunk and told me… like it was just another show business anecdote."

Sam, though, says he didn't kill Ding-Ding. So while things look bad for Sam, Columbo won't be arresting anyone just yet.

Columbo heads to the Mellon Ballet-de-Californa, where Bobby—dressed in a black leotard, silver ballet slippers, and a flowing white shirt—is putting a line of dancers through their paces. He holds a long ballet master's stick, which he uses to beat time on the floor and to jab the ballerinas, calling them "elephants" and screaming for them to move faster and stretch higher.

Columbo slips in and watches the beautiful dancers. Bobby notices and, furious, stops the rehearsal. He berates Columbo for interrupting… unless, of course, he's a dancer, in which case he should "hurry into your leotard and join us." Blushing, Columbo pulls out his ID. Bobby changes his tune. He commands the girls to do 20 minutes of exercises while he talks to the detective in his office.

Bobby's office "is pretty spectacular in a 19th-century chic sort of way. It's all overdone. Framed posters show that the Mellon Ballet-de-Californa is a world-famous success. Pictures of dancers adorn the walls. Every inch of surface is either hung with some objet d'art or carved. Even Bobby's ornate desk is theatrically set on a large platform, to give him some imagined psychological advantage over his guests. While Columbo stares in wonder at all of this, Bobby moves to his throne-like desk chair and seats himself grandly."

Columbo wants to know about Bobby's friend, Ding-Ding. Bobby corrects him. He detested Ding-Ding. Columbo relates Sam's belief that he's the likeliest suspect. Bobby finds the idea absurd, but he isn't surprised that Sam—in his usual pathetic way—would presume such a thing. Bobby says everyone hated Ding-Ding. "Delightfully funny clown, if one likes low humor, but with the greasepaint off, he was a swine," Bobby snarls. "To know him was to desire his slow and painful death."

When asked about Elaine, Bobby narrates his recollections of her, only his flashbacks are depicted realistically. His Elaine is not pure, but rather a tawdry, peroxide blonde, vulgar in dress and movement. She's affectionate toward the blushing Sam, knowing he's the biggest reason for the act's success. Sam falls for her play. Then, one night while Sam is working late, Bobby discovers Elaine making out with Ding-Ding. Bobby's enraged and stalks off, knowing that Sam had trusted them to look after his girl. "When she was found dead in that trunk," confesses Bobby, "my first reaction was one of joy. She was hurting Sam, and I was glad she was gone."

Bobby suspects Ding-Ding was killed by his wife, Monica, who only married him for his money. Yet she soon discovered that he was a miser who stashed every cent he ever made in shoeboxes.

Columbo returns to his car. As he slides behind the wheel, William pops up in the back seat, giving Columbo a scare. William has decided to help out on the investigation. He's checked up on Columbo and has learned the detective solves a very high percentage of his cases. Columbo tells him he's going to take him home. William responds by offering to buy him a new car. "You trying to bribe me, kid?" Columbo asks. Columbo starts heading for the Van Nelson home, when he sees William sink into his seat, gloomy and painfully lonely. He realizes the boy needs some paternal companionship. So he changes course. The Lieutenant says he has to question another witness downtown, but is afraid that in such a sketchy neighborhood someone might try to hotwire the ignition. Columbo offers to let William come along, if he stays put to keep an eye on his car. William lights up.

The Peugeot drives down a seedy street and "pulls up to a hotel that is just a degree or two better than sleeping in the park." Columbo gets out and turns back to the car: "Okay, Willie, you stay here. Anybody tries to steal my car, you flip on the siren. Be right back."

In the hotel, the clerk lets Columbo into Ding-Ding's apartment, explaining that the widow "left with her boyfriend." Inside, the room's a mess, littered with Ding-Ding's clothing, opened drawers, and empty shoeboxes. As Columbo combs through the debris, William walks in. Columbo is perturbed. What if somebody steals his car? William says there's no chance of that. Some big kids came by and he gave them each a dollar to guard the vehicle. Columbo has a sinking feeling. He grabs a few shoeboxes and they head to the street to find his car picked clean—wheels, engine parts, the works.

They take a cab to the Van Nelson estate in Bel Air. William pays the fare. Sam's Rolls is parked out front. As they start for the front door, we glimpse a shadowy figure hiding behind a cypress tree. As they pass, Furry pops out from behind the tree, followed by Mr. Snip. Columbo engages with the puppets; William rolls his eyes. Mr. Snip thinks William should be put to bed without supper for frightening his mother half to death; Furry is more forgiving. Gloria opens the door and is relieved to find William safe. She invites Columbo to join them for dinner.

Over dinner, Columbo updates Gloria, Sam, Furry and Mr. Snip on the case. Gloria is encouraged to hear that Columbo has uncovered additional suspects and motives. Sam invites Columbo to the free puppet show he stages on his front lawn every Sunday.

Later that evening, Columbo tracks down Ding-Ding's widow in a ritzy $125-a-night suite at the Beverly Wilshire Hotel. The room's a mess, cluttered with champagne bottles and newly purchased furs, clothing and accessories. Monica wears a sexy nightie as she simultaneously smokes, sips champagne, and holds up new clothes in front of the mirror. Her brainless weightlifter boyfriend, Mickey, is in the shower. Columbo begins questioning her when Mickey, wrapped only in a towel, bolts into the room. Columbo informs them that the lab has analyzed Ding-Ding's shoeboxes and can tell what used to be inside of them. Mickey tells Monica to keep her trap shut, but she can't help herself. She says Mickey used to run a popcorn machine in Ding-Ding's clown act. Giant balls of popcorn would fly out of the contraption and bury Ding-Ding. Balls made of Insta-Foam.

The next morning, Columbo goes to pick up his car at the police department garage. The Peugeot's been restored to pristine condition, with a tuned-up engine, new tires, new everything, except for its decomposing body. The mechanic's even given it a wax job—even though there's no paint left on the car; it's all primer.

The mechanic asks why the Lieutenant doesn't use one of the cars out of the motor pool. "This baby's got 10 years yet," Columbo says, proudly.

Driving out of the garage, he notices William standing outside, waiting for him. Columbo goes to a phonebooth to call Gloria. She hopes Columbo doesn't mind her son tagging along; yesterday was the happiest the boy's been since before his father passed away. Columbo reluctantly allows William to tag along, if he stays in the car.

They first stop at Bobby's dance studio. As Columbo nears the door, he hears a loud argument breaking out between Bobby and Mickey. Mickey advances on Bobby, who backs away. Mickey takes a swing. Bobby, however, is an expert at the French martial art of savate. One kick sends Mickey reeling. The brute rises, swings again, and is once more kicked to the floor. Columbo bursts in to stop the fight. Columbo asks Bobby if he wants to press charges. "No, I don't think so," Bobby replies, with a mean smile. "He's been punished enough. Must be absolutely humiliating for such a big, strong weightlifter to be beaten up by a wisp of a ballet dancer."

Mickey, embarrassed and raging, suggests Columbo ask Bobby why Ding-Ding was blackmailing him. Bobby shrugs. He says he's been giving Ding-Ding small sums of money for years, but only out of pity. He simply couldn't stand the clown's begging phone calls.

That reminds Columbo that he has to make a call—to have headquarters send down a couple of officers to arrest Mickey. Not for murder, though; if Mickey had killed Ding-Ding, he would have used a baseball bat or a tire iron. Mickey is wanted in three states on various charges, all involving assault.

Columbo returns to William with an ice cream bar. The lad digs in, chocolate smearing across his face. They take a detour to a park, where boys about William's age are playing adult-supervised tag football. Columbo suggests they watch the game for a bit. William sees it as a distraction from their investigation. Columbo calls over one of the coaches, an old Army buddy, who says they could really use one more player. William, on the verge of tears, is onto them. He knows the whole trip's a setup so Columbo can ditch him.

Columbo takes William aside and kneels to be at his height. He knows the boy's smart enough to hear the truth: it's not that he wants to get rid of him; he's worried about his safety. That, Columbo says, is a responsibility of friendship, and he is William's friend.

The boy impulsively hugs Columbo. Columbo gives him a squeeze back, and promises to return shortly. William agrees to give football a chance.

Having learned that the loose hair came from a Kodiak bear, Columbo heads for a taxidermist shop. The taxidermist explains that people don't stuff Kodiak bears much anymore. The last one he stuffed was three years ago—for Gloria Van Nelson's late husband, who not long after was killed in a hunting accident.

Columbo then goes to the marina, where Andy the old propmaster lives on his yacht. Andy agrees to speak with Columbo if he joins him on his fishing trip. Repeating the schtick from Season 1's *Dead Weight*, Columbo gets progressively more seasick as the trip goes on. The cruise does give him an opportunity to ask Andy what happened to Elaine. Andy's surprised; he hadn't thought about that girl in forever, yet in the space of a few months two people have asked him about her—Columbo and Ding-Ding. Andy was the one who had introduced Sam to working with plastics and fiberglass. The night of Elaine's death, he and Sam had been working late in the prop room, then they left—without seeing anyone. Andy says he discovered the body the next morning. Columbo says it must have been tough on Sam when he heard about his girl.

"*His* girl?" Andy says. "She wasn't Sam's girl—anyhow, at least not his alone." Andy then shares his recollection in a third flashback sequence, in which Elaine is neither fairy princess nor tramp, but rather a pretty, young, hard-working ballerina. She was ambitious and in love… with Bobby. Bobby insisted she should tell Sam about their romance, but Elaine couldn't bear to hurt Sam, and this upset Bobby.

Columbo asks if Sam ever found out about Bobby and Elaine. Andy doesn't think so. He does remember that Sam had a nervous breakdown right there in the theater the day she was found dead.

Columbo returns to the park to pick up William. But the boy is having such a great time, he'd rather keep playing.

Come Sunday, the free puppet show on Sam's lawn is in full swing, in front of dozens of enthusiastic children. Columbo finds Bobby, Gloria and Andy gathered near the front door, watching the show. Columbo announces he's solved the case. He's convinced that Bobby was paying off Ding-Ding so the clown wouldn't tell Sam about his relationship with Elaine. Just then, Furry spots Columbo and calls him over to the puppet stage to "give an old pal a head rub." Columbo obliges, noting that his fur is really soft: "Kodiak bear, isn't it?"

"You bet!" Furry says, joyfully. "I'm a bear of a fellow!" The audience laughs.

Columbo asks if Furry knows a certain story, the one about the shy prince and the pretty dancing girl. Mr. Snip appears, the self-professed authority on fairy tales. Furry begins, "The shy prince was in love with the dancing girl…" Mr. Snip interjects: "But the dancing girl fell in love with a dancing boy." Furry confesses that the shy prince was real sad about that. He cried, and cried. Even the trees and grass cried. The prince was too shy to do anything about it. Fortunately, he had a lot of friends who loved him, especially Furry and Mr. Snip. The kids cheer. Then Furry and Mr. Snip discovered that the wicked dancing girl was really a wicked witch! The kids gasp.

Columbo asks what they did to help their friend.

Mr. Snip proudly declares, "They locked her in a dark box…"

"…where she faded away," Furry says. The kids cheer. Gloria breaks down and clings to Bobby.

Columbo asks if that's the end of the story. It most certainly is not! Later, a wicked Swan came to hurt the shy prince. "But Furry and Mr. Snip came to the rescue again!" Furry states. "They wrapped him up in a snowball and threw him away." The puppets laugh. The children cheer.

"And that's the end," Columbo says, sadly.

"You'll never learn how to tell fairy stories," Furry grouses. "They always end with 'and they lived happily ever after.'"

"Yeah… they lived happily ever after."

The curtains close. The kids applaud. Columbo slips behind the puppet theater, where Sam sits, stunned, a puppet in each hand. For the first time he realizes the killing of Ding-Ding wasn't a dream in which Furry and Mr. Snip were coming to Sam's rescue. "But it couldn't have been them," Sam laments. "It had to be me. It was me, Columbo… wasn't it?

"Yeah, Sam," Columbo frowns, "it was you."

Columbo's producers were confident enough in the script's viability that they assigned it a production number and placed it in holdover—where it would remain. With its unique kiddie-show setting, Columbo's touching relationship with the lonely boy, and memorable Insta-Foam murder, it's easy to see why they gave *Dead as a Duck* a hard look.

But since the script was penned by someone who'd never written for *Columbo* before, and was developed by a producer who also had never worked on the show, it lacked several necessary ingredients. Apart from the Kodiak bear fur, there weren't really any clues for Columbo to discover. There was no cat-and-mouse between Lieutenant and murderer, and no opportunity for the suspect to cover his tracks or make a fatal mistake that Columbo could pick up on.

Columbo was probably overdue for a tweaking. New wrinkles might freshen it up. But *Dead as a Duck* bent the formula too far. Columbo fingering a sympathetic-yet-absent-minded villain would have to wait. As well, a true whodunit would not surface until *Last Salute to the Commodore* (the final episode of Season 5).

While working on *Dead as a Duck*, Ted Flicker was simultaneously trying to find a buyer for his own detective show—a pilot called *My Husband the Detective*, about a middle-aged Jewish detective in the San Fernando Valley. His agent put him in touch with writer/producer Danny Arnold, who had been working on a similar idea. Flicker and Arnold merged their ideas into a pilot, *The Life and Times of Captain Barney Miller*, which Flicker directed. After the network passed, Arnold purchased the rights to the failed pilot, cut Flicker out, recast and reshot the original script, and the resultant series, *Barney Miller*, went on to run for eight seasons. Since Flicker co-wrote the script for the first pilot, the Writers Guild forced Arnold to bill Flicker as co-creator of the series. The series—which Flicker never worked on—became Flicker's most enduring credit.

As for *Dead as a Duck*, its prospects were not helped by the fact that another script arrived around the same time that also had an otherwise-sympathetic killer struggling with mental illness.

Sugar and Spice and Everything Nice/ The Dreamer

In mid-1973, Brad Radnitz submitted an even more unique story idea for *Columbo*. Radnitz had been a TV freelancer since the mid-1960s, writing spec scripts for one show after another—*Gilligan's Island, Mission: Impossible, Family Affair, The Brady Bunch*, and the like, both comedies and crime dramas. He was well familiar with *The NBC Mystery Movie*. In 1972, one of his old *Ironside* scripts was repurposed as a *McMillan & Wife*, and in mid-1973 he pitched story ideas for both a *Columbo* and a *Hec Ramsey*. He was given the green light to expand both into scripts. *Dead Heat*, his *Hec Ramsey*, went into production. His *Columbo* needed further polish.

The draft was passed to master script doctor David Rayfiel, who'd worked on dozens of high-profile movies (including *The Way We Were, Jeremiah Johnson*, and, with Peter Falk, *Castle Keep*—one of the few projects Rayfiel actually got credit for). While Rayfiel would admit story was not his strong suit, he was renowned for building highly dramatic scenes. Radnitz's scenes needed some pop.

Rayfiel had just finished expanding Stanley Ralph Ross' treatment for Season 3's *Swan Song* into a full script and went right into revising Radnitz's, completing his second draft on February 15, 1974, featuring the alternate titles *Sugar and Spice and Everything Nice* and *The Dreamer*.

Nighttime has fallen over the Willowbrook School. Across the wooded grounds are red brick buildings, overgrown with ivy but meticulously maintained, connected by worn footpaths, quaintly illuminated by old-fashioned gas lamps and the bright moonlight. The scene is absolutely tranquil—except for the faint sound of breathing. It grows louder and more labored.

In the distance, 15-year-old Janet Brownwell sprints away from the dormitory. She crosses the grounds and hurries down a grassy slope toward a bike rack. The exaggerated breathing persists. Janet leaps on a bicycle and takes off down a paved road, her legs pumping hard at the pedals. She arrives at the quiet, darkened Brownwell home. As Janet walks toward the house, the heavy breathing continues, but we now realize that it's not synchronized with Janet's breathing, which is only moderately strained from the bike ride. She unlocks the front door and steps into a large foyer, filled with fancy furniture. She moves down a dark hallway toward a door. Just as she reaches it, the door swings open and directly at the camera bursts a German shepherd. Janet grabs the dog's collar and hooks on its leash. The dog is excitable but not hostile. It barks—silently; we hear only the strange breathing and an occasional moan, as someone might elicit during a troubled sleep.

We now follow the dog straining forward, leash taut, down a dirt road and toward a large pond. As the dog nears the pond, Janet leads it to a weathered old rowboat, beached at the water's edge. With a pale smile, she ties the leash to a wooden oarlock. Though we hear only the sounds of the restless sleeper, we pull back to see the dog is whining and howling furiously.

Back at the Brownwell home, a half-packed valise sits open on a bed. Janet places a perfectly folded sweater inside—then immediately musses up the neatly arranged clothes so they appear to have been packed in haste. Janet enters the walk-in closet and gathers a parka, ski pants, and other winter gear. She freezes, as a woman's voice calls her: "Janet? Is that you?" Janet looks up at the bedroom door, forcing a smile as an attractive woman appears. It's Eileen Brownwell, Janet's 30-year-old stepmother. Eileen is puzzled yet pleasant. She asks Janet why she's home.

Janet says Daddy called her school. He wants the two of them to join him at their cabin in Lake Tahoe. He's flying in from Washington, D.C., and has arranged everything. Eileen figures she must have missed his call, while she was away at a class. She's pleased by the unexpected trip, but fearful of all the loose ends they'll need to tend to on short notice, like taking Frankie to the kennel.

Janet says that the dog escaped the yard, but not to worry. "I'm sure he's down at the pond, Mother. He likes to go after frogs." Eileen is stunned—and overjoyed. Janet had never called her "Mother" before.

The disturbed breathing suddenly stops, just long enough for us to zoom in on Eileen's left hand, where she wears a ring featuring a large, brilliant diamond in an elaborate antique setting.

A moment later, they're driving away in Eileen's sportscar, as passenger Janet regales her with animated conversation. Whatever she's saying greatly pleases Eileen. Eileen slips the ring off her finger and hands it to Janet. Subtly, Janet unclicks her own seatbelt, but keeps it in position, as if it were still fastened. Janet rolls down her window partway. The breathing and moaning become increasingly anguished, as if the sleeper were about to cry out.

As the sportscar travels the dirt path toward the moonlit pond, Eileen slows the car to negotiate the sharp curve around it. Suddenly, Janet slams her left foot over Eileen's right foot, flooring the accelerator. Confused, Eileen turns to Janet. Janet smiles an evil, determined smile. Eileen reaches for the ignition, but Janet blocks her. Terrified, Eileen swerves the car right and left. She's losing control. She misses the curve. The car flies off the embankment into the air and plunges into the pond. The tiny car quickly fills with water, as Janet fights off Eileen's panicky attempts to free herself from her seatbelt and the sinking vehicle. When all seems lost, Janet flings her own seatbelt aside, opens the passenger door, and slips out. Through the murky water, Eileen remains bewildered. She stops struggling and opens her mouth to scream. Janet swims away furiously, as if desperate to avoid the cry. She hurries out of the water, toward the rowboat. She frees the whining animal, which instantly moves into the shallow water, sniffing, whimpering, until it's called by Janet.

Janet breaks a branch off a nearby scrub pine. She walks to the embankment, using the branch to wipe away the car's tire tracks.

Back at the house, Janet crosses the carpeted foyer. She's taken off her sneakers, to avoid leaving a muddy trail. She opens the door to the yard, leads the dog through it, and closes it behind him. Janet smiles, satisfied. She puts her shoes back on and returns to the bike. She pedals quickly back toward the pond, as the pained breathing resumes even louder. She skids to a stop at the water's edge and looks out. The pond is absolutely still, but we begin to hear what we did not hear earlier: the sounds of the struggle that took place inside the sinking sportscar, growing louder as the gasps for breath now sync with the sounds of the disturbed sleeper.

In Janet's eyes, we see the final seconds of Eileen's life and her desperate watery scream. Janet lunges to one side—as if to grab someone—but she's tangled in something. She struggles, as if tentacles were pulling her underwater. Janet jolts forward and shrieks.

She's bolt upright in her own bed at the dorm, awakened by her own cry. Her nightgown is soaked with sweat, her hair wild and plastered to her face. She shakes her head, trying to rid the nightmare from her mind. Still gasping, she climbs out of bed, intent on staying busy to keep the horrible thoughts away.

As she crosses the bedroom, we notice that all her shelves are covered with eight-inch-tall dolls from around the world. Gifts from her diplomat father, each one is dressed in ornate national costume. Janet heads for the lavatory. She splashes water over her face and neck. A small bundle sits beneath the washbasin. Janet opens the bundle, revealing the blouse, skirt and sneakers she was wearing in her dream, all dripping wet. She recoils in horror—for an instant. The fear quickly drains from her face, replaced by a mildly puzzled look, then one of exasperation: obviously she's forgotten to hang dry her laundry. She begins twisting the water from her clothes and hanging them, humming to make the routine chore pass by more quickly.

The next morning, a black limousine rolls up the whitewashed gravel drive toward the Brownwell home. It momentarily swerves off the path to avoid a pedestrian—Columbo, who's parked his Peugeot near the gatehouse, out of respect.

The limo stops and out climbs a diplomatic courier, an attaché case chained to his wrist. A grieving, tired Craig Brownwell is waiting at the open front door to welcome the courier. Brownwell informs his courier friend there's still no word on his wife. As Brownwell reviews the contents of the attaché, his friend tries to console him, aware that men in their line of work are usually too busy to hold on to their spouses. "My wife says she's going to get a divorce on grounds of desertion, and name the State Department as co-respondent," the courier jokes.

But Brownwell fears the worst and has notified the local police's Homicide Department. The courier is shocked. Homicide? "Yes, they have someone… quite good," Brownwell says. "He'd just… see if any, if… He's first rate, I'm told, this chap—"

Meanwhile, Columbo is at the front door, trying to figure out how to work the complicated antique doorbell, which he accidentally rings multiple times. Brownwell answers the door and is dismayed to see who the chief has sent over to locate his wife. The courier drives off. Columbo marvels at how quiet the vehicle glides away. "What d'you figure they get to the gallon?" Columbo asks. "Got any idea?" Brownwell does not.

Columbo is next distracted by the attaché case and wants to examine the handcuff and chain. "I thought these were just props for spy movies!" He also compliments the lovely home, at which Brownwell admits he spends little time due to his constant travels for the government. His daughter's away at school, but he does bring back beautiful dolls for her. Columbo detects that Brownwell is implying his wife is unhappy. So why then did he call Homicide? Because the diplomat simply can't believe his wife left him. They'd only been married a year, but as soon as he could tell she was unhappy, he applied for a fixed assignment, which was approved. As soon as he completes his current project, he'll be transferred to Los Angeles, a short commute from home. He and his wife would be together for dinner every night.

Just the two of them?, Columbo asks. Yes, since his daughter lives at the Willowbrook School. Columbo's not too keen on private schools in general. He has a nephew who used to cause a lot of trouble and was expelled, then transferred to a public school and "overnight won the Good Citizenship Award!"

Brownwell says his daughter has never been a disciplinary problem, and she doesn't have a "wicked stepmother." He insists on returning to the facts—namely that his wife didn't tell anyone where she was going, which is unlike her. He encourages Columbo to search the house for clues. Columbo reluctantly agrees. As they climb the stairs, Columbo shares how, when he has a spat with his wife, Mrs. Columbo just gives him the silent treatment. Brownwell is exasperated. "Lieutenant, my God! This isn't about a spat! My wife has disappeared! Without a trace! I'm worried—and fearful—for her life!"

They pass Janet's bedroom, where the girl is playing with her international dolls and listening to classical music. The men enter the master bedroom. Brownwell says the only items missing are two small suitcases and a few pieces of winter clothing. That suggested to Brownwell that she may have been heading to their cabin near Lake Tahoe. But he checked with a neighbor up there who readies the place whenever they're planning to visit and he hadn't heard from her.

Columbo notices that all the summer clothes in his wife's closet are neat and organized, but the winter clothes are scattered—a jacket half off a hanger, another on the floor, empty hangers strewn about. Columbo wonders if she might have been angry or upset when she packed. "Or in a hurry," Brownwell adds.

Columbo stops at the nightstand and picks up an ornately framed photo depicting Eileen's parents. If she were leaving for good, surely she would have taken the picture, not to mention more of her clothes—no matter how much of a hurry she was in when she packed.

"Unless she didn't pack," Brownwell says, suggesting maybe someone packed for her. Columbo notes there are no servants. Brownwell meant someone with a gun. But it's been five days, and no one has contacted him about a ransom. They walk to the garage, and Columbo asks for a description of the car Eileen was driving—a red Alfa two-seater her husband gave her as a wedding present. Janet joins them in the garage. She's looking for a wrench to tighten the chain on her bicycle. She's in a far more chipper mood than the last time we saw her. Brownwell introduces her to Lt. Columbo, then she goes to work on her bike in the driveway. "Like the Little Red Hen," Columbo observes. "Does things for herself."

Brownwell notes how well Janet has been dealing with the drama. Willowbrook is nearby, so Janet's welcome to come home whenever she likes, but the school discourages students from going home too often.

Janet's "real mother" died about five years ago, when the girl was 10, almost 11. Janet remembers her but, according to Brownwell, "doesn't mention her, though. Hasn't in some time. Out of consideration for Eileen's feelings, I suppose."

Columbo asks if he can wander a bit before he leaves. He cuts across the lawn, passing Janet. They exchange waves, but he keeps walking. He hears a dog whining. It's in an enclosed yard, lunging against the fence. Columbo asks Janet if the animal is okay. She explains that her dog gets agitated when it sees her with her bike. It knows she's going away.

Columbo continues his walk across the grounds and down the dirt road toward the pond. The surface is absolutely still. He notes the sharp 90-degree turn in the road and continues along the water's edge to the rowboat. Something catches his eye, and he kneels to examine it. He rubs the mud between his fingers and smells it. In the distance, the dog's whining intensifies. Columbo heads back to the house, just as Janet is getting ready to bike back to school. Your pup really doesn't want you to go, Columbo notes. "His name's Frankie," Janet says, explaining that her parents were bobbysoxers and used to go see Frank Sinatra at a big theater in New York. Janet says Frankie likes to run through the woods and chase frogs into the pond. But Eileen didn't like him to go out there because she couldn't wash the oil out of his coat. Columbo had noticed the oil along the water's edge. She says she'd better head out before the dog really gets upset.

Back at police headquarters, the chief is getting an earful over the phone from Brownwell, as Columbo and a younger officer, Newmark, listen. The police chief agrees to put an additional man on the job. It's the third time today Brownwell has called. Columbo admits he still has nothing to go on. All he knows is that Eileen didn't tell anyone she was leaving—but an angry woman might not. And she didn't board the dog at a kennel, knowing the gardener would take care of it. The chief asks if Columbo would be okay with arriving home, opening the door, and not seeing Mrs. Columbo. Of course, Columbo replies. She'd be in the kitchen.

The chief says, no, she's not in the kitchen. It's been six days. Something must be seriously wrong.

Columbo resists: "There's no sign of forcible entry, no sign of a struggle, and you can't compare this to my wife! This is a lady with a wallet full of credit cards and a red Italian sportscar!" Columbo finds it funny that a man like Brownwell would rather believe his wife's been murdered or kidnapped than that she left him.

Columbo heads for his Peugeot, and Newmark joins him. Twelve hours earlier, Newmark was "in a black-and-white unit prowling downtown L.A. and now here I am assigned to you, Lt. Columbo! What a way to start a career in crime detection!" Columbo is not quite as enthusiastic. He starts up the engine; it races furiously. Newmark advises to cut back on the throttle. Columbo eases off the accelerator. The engine idles rough. Newmark hops out and checks under the hood. The oil mixture is too leaned out. Newmark pulls a dime from his pocket and uses it to adjust the carburetor. The engine purrs like a kitten.

They arrive at the Brownwell home. Newmark suddenly sniffs, eager to show his skills. "The gardener's been here this morning," Newmark says.

Columbo is impressed: "You know what he smells like?"

"New-mown grass! Very distinctive smell. Fleeting… it'll be gone in another hour."

Newmark is so proud of his observation, he trips over a rake left on the driveway. Columbo keeps walking, as the dog whines in the background. At the door, Columbo introduces Brownwell to Newmark, and says he was going to ask permission to visit the Willowbrook School to talk to Janet, since she saw Eileen most recently. Maybe she noticed some little thing that might indicate where she was going. But, hearing the dog, Columbo figures Janet's home.

Brownwell is perturbed. The dog has been carrying on like that for as long as Eileen's been gone. Janet may like to think that Frankie's her dog—they got him as a pup, right after Janet's mother died—but Eileen has been taking care of him. Eileen is the one Frankie's attached to.

Columbo sees the dog barking and lunging at the fence. He decides to free him. Frankie races down the dirt road. Columbo and Newmark follow. The dog reaches the pond and starts pacing back and forth, agitated. "Shall I get a crew out here, Lieutenant?" Newmark asks.

Columbo is forlorn. "Two divers'll be enough, and a recovery vehicle. And the medical examiner."

The recovery operation includes an army of police, two scuba divers, an ambulance, and a tank retriever vehicle that begins winching up the submerged sportscar. As the car breaks the surface, Columbo notes that the passenger-side window is a little more than halfway open. As the car clears the pond and the water drains out, Eileen's body is visible behind the wheel. He waits until most everyone's gone before taking a closer look at the open window. Was someone with her? Is there a big enough opening for someone to have swum out? Columbo checks the steering wheel, to make sure it's working properly, just as Janet comes cycling down the dirt path. The girl seems troubled by the sight of the car. "It's… it's not real," she whispers to herself. An instant later, her terrified expression vanishes. She's fine.

Meanwhile, Newmark has opened the trunk of the Alfa and discovered the suitcases. The clothes inside are well soaked, and all for winter. Columbo notes no dress-up clothes—she didn't plan on going out. "Eileen liked to go out," Janet offers. Columbo notes the girl did not call her "Mother." "She wasn't my mother," Janet explains.

Columbo suggests maybe, in time, that might have changed. Janet doesn't think so. Columbo has heard that she was a sweet woman. Janet agrees. Suddenly, Columbo's startled by a blast of classical music. Newmark has turned on the sportscar's radio. "KFAC," Newmark says. "She liked serious music." Janet adds that she does, too.

Columbo continues digging through the suitcase. No pills, no creams, no lotions. She obviously packed in a hurry. Two suitcases, both hers, so she was alone. But why would she take the dirt road toward the pond instead of city streets to the highway?

As he ponders, Columbo wanders over to the rowboat and sits inside. Janet joins him. They sit silently for a moment, until Columbo catches sight of the wooden oarlock. It's splintered. Someone must be a tremendous rower! But Janet says no one uses the boat anymore—it leaks and Eileen is terrified of the pond. Columbo spots teeth marks near the oarlock and pawprints in the mud. Janet reasons someone must have tied up a dog there, and it chewed on the wood to get free. Columbo figures it was Frankie. Janet says no; neither she nor Eileen would ever tie up Frankie that way. Columbo encourages Janet to go back to the house and cheer up her father, the same way she's made him feel better. He then rejoins Newmark, who's been going over the inside of the car. Newmark wonders why Mrs. Brownwell didn't try to unlock her seatbelt. Columbo wonders if she panicked. Janet, about to ride off, answers: "Eileen isn't the type to—she was a cool, composed person… she was almost perfect."

Newmark locks and releases the seatbelt a couple of times, demonstrating its quick, simple action. Columbo speculates that maybe when the car hit the water, Mrs. Brownwell struck her head and was knocked unconscious. The gas pedal and brake were still operable.

Columbo scans the shoreline for tire tracks. There are none. To fly right over the shore, the car must have been speeding, maybe even accelerating. When Columbo reaches the embankment, he discovers that there also are no tire tracks at the edge of the dirt road. Someone must have deliberately brushed them away. Either someone who saw the accident happen or who was in the car and escaped.

The officers pay Brownwell a visit, to ask if he knows anyone who might have been with his wife. Brownwell's furious. He knows his wife. She would never have gone off with another man.

Columbo and Newmark next go see the medical examiner, who confirms Eileen was alive—and probably conscious—when her car submerged. Columbo can't understand how someone, especially a woman who's afraid of the water, could be compelled to race her car over an embankment into a pond. Newmark wonders if maybe she was hypnotized. The medical examiner suggests suicide; he notes that suicides often divest themselves of anything valuable or sentimental, and the corpse wasn't wearing her wedding ring. The slight tissue atrophy and loss of pigmentation around her ring finger proved she usually wore one—a big, ornate one at that.

Back at the victim's house, Columbo has Brownwell look through all of his wife's belongings. He can't find the ring. He's flabbergasted. She loved that ring and rarely took it off. It's a family heirloom—a single diamond in a beautiful antique gold setting. Brownwell's mother purchased it long ago in a foreign country and gave it to his first wife when they married. After she died, Brownwell kept it, until giving it to Eileen.

Columbo comes across Eileen's long list of appointments and activities, all well organized. According to her schedule, she had attended a karate class on the evening she disappeared.

Columbo calls on Eileen's karate instructor, who's in the middle of teaching her class. She has a half-dozen housewives, dressed in karate whites, grunting, chopping and kicking in unison. The women break off in pairs so their instructor can talk to Columbo. She confirms that Eileen was capable enough to defend herself from an attacker. But did she have it in her? The teacher's not sure; it would depend on how scared she was or who was doing the attacking. She points out one student, who's going easy on her partner. "You see?" the instructor says. "They're friends. It gets in the way."

On his way out, Columbo sees the students stop at a desk to reclaim their valuables. The attendant is familiar with Mrs. Brownwell's ring. She checked it that night, as she always did.

Columbo meets Newmark at the chili parlor. The young officer has checked out Brownwell's alibi. His plane landed at 8 p.m. His wife's karate class was at 8:30. The autopsy estimated the time of death as about 9:30 or 10:00. The limo dropped Brownwell off at 11:00.

Columbo's next stop is a psychiatric social worker who consults for the police department. Meeting in a frosted glass cubicle, the worker shows Columbo a Rorschach card. The analyst thinks the Lieutenant seems troubled. Columbo admits he is. He understands that the social worker meets with all kinds of unusual criminals, young and old. The doctor interrupts: "You feel like smashing the glass partition, don't you?"

Columbo looks at him like he's nuts: "This glass here? No. What would I want to do that for?"

Columbo relates that his suspect is a 15-year-old girl, who's either innocent, a brilliant actress, or guilty without remembering. Has the doctor ever come across someone who had no recollection of a murder they'd committed? The social worker nods; a complete blackout is rare, but possible.

Soon after, Brownwell begins packing up Janet's things for an indefinite trip abroad, to get a change of scenery for the two of them. The house is a constant reminder of Eileen, and Janet has complained of recurring nightmares. Columbo is skeptical. He'd like to visit Janet at her school. Brownwell doesn't like the idea; Columbo's presence would needlessly upset the girl. But wasn't she upset already, by the nightmares?

Columbo shares a story about the youngest of his two kids who, when she was 5, used to have bad dreams. She called them "nightbears," because one of them was about a bear. So she thought every bad dream would be about bears. Once she understood that wasn't true, no more nightbears. Brownwell relents; just understand that he'll be picking her up in about an hour on their way to the airport.

As he exits Janet's bedroom, Columbo compliments the doll collection. He asks Brownwell if he was on an overseas assignment when Janet's birth mother died. Yes, he was in Iran when he received news from the State Department and rushed home.

Columbo arrives at Willowbrook looking especially troubled. Janet is in her room, playing with a doll. There's a knock on the door. The doll reacts sharply. Another knock. Janet whispers to the doll, then holds it close to her ear, as if the doll were whispering to her. They decide to allow the visitor to enter.

It's Columbo. Janet doesn't turn, but whispers audibly to the doll: "Who is he?" A moment later, she snaps back to normal. Janet asks the Lieutenant how he's doing and if he's heard about her trip. She anticipates an African safari. She should be packing, but there's nothing at school she feels she needs. "Just your dolls," Columbo offers.

No, Janet won't be taking them. They are for when Daddy's traveling. Now she'll be with him.

Columbo wonders if she'll be able to leave everything behind when she goes to Africa... including the bad dream. Janet doesn't seem to understand. Columbo suggests that, if she got rid of her nightmare before she left, she could travel and do anything else she'd like in the future. Just then, Janet sits upright, sure she's heard her father's car. She goes to the window.

Columbo says her father will be arriving after a bit, and then she can tell him she'd like to stay. Daddy could request that transfer to Los Angeles, so he'd be close by. Would she consider staying? Janet looks down at the doll and asks what it thinks. She then turns to Columbo. "Yes, it would probably be better that way, with Daddy not very far away," she says, adding quietly to herself, "I would like to be able to sleep through the whole night without waking up once."

Columbo asks what wakes her up. A bad dream? Possibly; she doesn't remember. She wakes up in the middle of the night, feeling as if she's lost something but can't find it no matter how hard she looks. "The ring?" Columbo asks.

"Yes!" Janet is stunned that he knows.

They now hear the limo pulling up the gravel driveway. Janet starts for the door, but Columbo stands in the way. Janet grows agitated; she doesn't want to be late. Columbo needs just one second: the day your mother died, your Daddy flew right home... from where? Iran, she says; now will he please move?

"And he brought you a doll, didn't he?"

"Yes!" she blurts out, desperate to get to her father.

Columbo asks where it is. Janet doesn't keep it with the others. It gets cold,

THIRD TIME'S the charm: Columbo finally got to face off against a sympathetic-yet-absent-minded villain in the Season 5 opener, *Forgotten Lady*, co-starring John Payne and a forgetful Janet Leigh. *[Credit: NBCUniversal]*

so she keeps it covered. Columbo walks to the bed, opening a path for Janet to get by. He pulls the bedspread aside, uncovering an Iranian doll wearing a fancy, glittering costume with the antique diamond ring pinned to it as if it were a belt.

Columbo somberly heads outside, where the headmistress is saying goodbye to Janet and her father as they begin to climb into the limo. Janet sees Columbo approaching, holding the doll. She freezes. The sight distresses Brownwell, which makes Janet concerned for him. She tells him she can't go with him, at least not now. Maybe someday. She knows she has to go with Columbo.

There's little doubt that *Sugar and Spice and Everything Nice* would have made an unforgettable *Columbo*. From its powerful dreamlike opening sequence to the audacity of having a seemingly sweet 15-year-old girl murder her even sweeter stepmother, it truly would have pushed the boundaries of a show that rarely strayed far from its formula.

The character of Newmark is quite reminiscent of the overeager Sgt. Wilson from Season 2's *The Greenhouse Jungle*—minus the laughs. In fact, the whole story hangs a little heavy. There's a smile or two during Columbo's visit to the social worker. But other opportunities for humor—particularly at the karate class—were sidestepped. Imagine how much fun Peter Falk could have had with the instructor shanghaiing Columbo into participating in the drills. I suspect the producers felt the story was so serious that anything overly comedic would have struck the wrong note. In the end, they were left with an overly serious story that was probably too much of a departure to ever be made.

Assigning the proper age to the girl proved similarly problematic. She had to be old enough to wrest the steering wheel away from her stepmother, but young enough to elicit sympathy. Consequently, the script featured a 15-year-old who, at times, acted like a 5-year-old.

The story also lacked the cat-and-mouse game and verbal sparring of past cases. There's no showdown with the villain. There's little intentional deception on the part of the killer—she can't even remember she's guilty. Columbo acts kindly and protective toward her at all times.

That said, the producers thought highly enough of the project to have new story editor Peter Fischer give it another full rewrite. Yet, ultimately, the story was never filmed. Some months later, however, writer Bill Driskill pitched a story about a sympathetic actress who, as she drifts into dementia, kills her husband and, soon after, loses all memory of doing so. It would become the Season 5 opener, *Forgotten Lady* starring Janet Leigh.

Original writer Brad Radnitz, meanwhile, had long since moved on to other projects—including the bullfighting mystery *A Matter of Honor*. It was produced as the fourth episode of *Columbo's* fifth season.

4
Season 5 (1975-1976)
Lethal Athletes

Entering the fifth season, producer Everett Chambers was finally on his own. Having worked under Hargrove and Kibbee for the bulk of the prior year, he was now free to dump most of the unproduced story ideas he had inherited, and start generating his own, through story editor Peter S. Fischer. Chambers intended to freshen up the series by setting stories in new locations and reviving characters that the audience enjoyed. His main opposition was Peter Falk.

Falk found the foreign settings gimmicky. As a result, over the show's first three years, Columbo had rarely been permitted to venture beyond Beverly Hills and Malibu—aside from his jaunt to London in Season 2's *Dagger of the Mind*. In Season 4 under Chambers, Columbo had traveled to a military academy (*By Dawn's Early Light*) and on a Mexican cruise (*Troubled Waters* by Bill Driskill). For Season 5, stories in development had Columbo journeying to an embassy in the Middle East and a hacienda in Mexico.

From the beginning of the series, Falk was against recurring characters. So much of the show's charm grew out of how he interacted with different personalities and, if he dealt with the same characters week in and week out, it might get repetitive. Falk did consent to share screen time with Dog at the start of Season 2, but up to that point even the mutt had appeared infrequently—just once more in Season 2, once in Season 3, and once in Season 4.

Yet another supporting player was nearly as memorable—Bob Dishy's

SGT. WILSON, Bob Dishy's overly officious character from Season 2's *The Greenhouse Jungle*, appeared just once more—in Season 5's *Now You See Him* (*above*)—despite the producers' continued efforts to bring him back more frequently. *[Credit: NBCUniversal]*

officious Sgt. Wilson from Season 2's *The Greenhouse Jungle*. The producers had been trying desperately to bring him back ever since. Falk and Dishy were actually close, longtime friends, who'd worked together on stage at Syracuse University. On *Columbo*, they played off each other brilliantly, with perfect timing and an adeptness for comedy. Their characters' relationship brought out an especially amusing dynamic—for a change, Columbo was the one who was constantly annoyed.

Executive producer Dean Hargrove could hardly wait to bring Dishy back. During Season 3, Hargrove and Roland Kibbee revised one draft of *Candidate for Crime* to feature Sgt. Wilson. Dishy's character was to serve as senatorial candidate Nelson Hayward's primary plainclothes bodyguard. He would take his job extremely seriously, impressed with the importance of his assignment, enthusiastically admiring, and ready to serve Hayward.

The next year, Hargrove and Kibbee considered giving Dishy his own detective show on the wheel—*McCoy*—about a conman with a heart of gold. But NBC wanted a bigger name, and opted for Tony Curtis. (Dishy did guest-star on the second episode of *McCoy*, playing the crook.)

Then, while prepping for *Columbo's* fifth season, story editor Peter Fischer received a spec script from freelancer Michael Sloan, in which Columbo battled a murderous magician—with "assistance" from Sgt. Wilson. Screenwriter Howard Berk took notice of Wilson's return and decided to incorporate the character into a script he was working on.

Roar of the Crowd/ A Lion in Season

Berk had made a name for himself writing four episodes of *Mission: Impossible*. He then settled nicely into detective-show writing, successfully pitching to *The Magician*, *The Rockford Files*, *McMillan & Wife*, and *Get Christie Love!* According to his son Peter, Berk was especially adept at humor, though his first *Columbo* script, Season 4's *By Dawn's Early Light*, had few laughs. Writing for Sgt. Wilson and placing the story in the unusual setting of a circus would give him more opportunities for humor.

Berk submitted his "circus story" in early June 1975, a few weeks after Peter Fischer had left the series to work on *Ellery Queen* with Levinson and Link. Chambers had decided on the first five episodes for *Columbo's* fifth season, and now had three options to choose from for the last: the circus tale, a "marina story" by Jackson Gillis, and "Orient Express in the Air" by Steven Bochco.

Chambers favored Berk's circus story, but story editor Bill Driskill disagreed. It lacked a strong finish, he argued. Also, network executives were nervous that it would be too expensive to produce, based on the projected budget for a proposed episode of *McCloud* set at a circus. So Chambers had all three story ideas expanded to full teleplays. Berk submitted his 97-page script, *Roar of the Crowd*, on December 8, 1975—four weeks before the sixth and final episode of the season was scheduled to begin production.

At dawn, a small circus begins coming to life, as workmen tidy up after last night's performance and get ready for tonight's. Out of the main tent exits Rick Banner, 30ish, a superb athlete—and he knows it. He's dressed in a gym outfit, and carries a small overnight bag. He heads for the nearby main gate, where a guard is posted to keep out non-circus personnel. The guard is surprised that, so early in the morning, Banner has already been practicing.

"That's why I'm perfect, Andy—I keep practicing," Banner smiles. "Have you seen Mr. Gurney this morning?"

The guard says the owner of the circus just left, presumably for the bank. Banner thanks the guard and moves on, past a fence adorned with dozens of circus posters—most of them bearing his likeness and the legend: "World's Greatest Aerialist—Rick Banner."

Banner approaches Ned Gurney's motorhome/office, parked just beyond the cluster of trailers for the circus' top performers. He looks about. Nobody's around. He takes out a key, quickly opens the motorhome door, and slips inside. Seconds later, a large truck-and-trailer parks between the motorhome and the big tent, preparing to unload supplies.

Inside Gurney's motorhome, Banner opens his bag and removes a gas cylinder and a small electronic receiver unit. It's metal, about the size of a matchbox, and has a wire protruding from it. He magnetically attaches the receiver to the valve area of the cylinder, then affixes the wire to a valve control. He sets the cylinder upright on the desk, then pulls from his bag another small, metal object—an electronic receiver with a switch. Banner flicks the switch, triggering a distinct click from the receiver. The valve starts to open. Banner immediately flicks the switch back. The valve starts to close. Banner smiles. He pockets the transmitter, opens a bottom drawer of the desk, places the cylinder inside, and slides the drawer shut. He slips out the door.

As evening approaches, masses of guests line up at the ticket booths near the main gate. Others pour into the tent; the stands begin to fill. A band entertains the preshow audience.

Just as the opening act begins, Columbo walks into the tent, a dripping ice cream cone in one hand, cotton candy in the other. He apologizes as he makes his way past crowds of people surging in both directions. Columbo arrives at his fourth-row bench to find three empty seats along the aisle. He looks on, bewildered, then turns to the large woman who occupies the next seat (and a half): "Excuse me, ma'am. I'm looking for my nephews. You know, those two young fellows who were sitting next to you—one's about 8, one's about 10. I wonder if they happened to tell you where they were going?"

She shakes her head no, without turning from the ring... until she looks down at her dress and notices a splotch of ice cream. She stares murderously at Columbo. He apologizes profusely and tries to shift the cone to the same hand as the cotton candy, so he can fish a handkerchief from his pocket—thereby dripping more ice cream on the lady's dress. The woman takes a Kleenex from her purse and tells Columbo to beat it.

Meanwhile, Banner pays a visit to his girlfriend, Alicia, Ned Gurney's pretty, 20-something daughter, who works as a show assistant. Her father had told her that Rick's been upset all week about the impending sale of the circus to Gabe Hausmann, a significantly larger operator. Banner shrugs. Of course, if it were up to him, he'd keep the circus just the way it is—small and independent; he'd just "tighten some belts." But he knows it's not up to him; Ned's the boss.

Alicia says she knows that initially it'll be difficult for Rick to have to share top billing with other acts. "But what difference does that make?" she asks. "You're still better than all of them... especially to me."

They embrace, until he glances at his watch and realizes that they'd better get ready for their act.

Banner next calls on Gurney, who's alone in his motorhome, working at his desk. The men eye each other warily. "Again?" Gurney sighs. Banner pleads one last time for Gurney to change his mind and not sell out to someone like Hausmann, who'll turn his circus into a factory. Exasperated, Gurney explains he has no choice. Either he merges or goes bankrupt.

"You're pussyfooting around the truth, Ned!" Banner argues. "All it would take is cutting out most of these second-rate acts you're too soft to get rid of! People like Otto Prinz with those flea-bitten animals he's too soft to get rid of!"

Gurney says he and Rick are just two different generations of circus people. Some of his acts have been with him 25, 30 years. By merging with Hausmann maybe he can give them a few more years. Agitated, Gurney fumbles in his desk for a bottle of pills. He throws a couple in his mouth and washes them down with a nervously poured glass of water.

But Banner wants to know, what about him? "I'm the guy who's marrying your daughter! What's going to happen to me?"

Gurney knows the only thing Rick is worried about is his ego. He'll survive. What the hell difference does it make if he has to split top billing?

"All the difference in the world," Banner intones solemnly. He leaves Gurney's motorhome, just as Otto the lion tamer exits his trailer. A huge man with a thick mustache, Otto is costumed in a safari outfit ready to go onstage. The men pause a fraction of a second to glare at each other, then move off in different directions.

Back in the main tent, Columbo is still looking for his lost nephews, their treats melted beyond recognition. He finally dumps the snacks in a nearby trashcan and asks a security guard near the tent's exit if he's seen the boys. The officer suggests checking with the information office.

Just then, Columbo is distracted by a great fanfare of music. A spotlight shines on the Ringmaster, backed by Alicia and fellow beauty Sue, as he introduces "Otto Prinz, master of the world's most dangerous animals!"

Otto enters a large cage and cracks his whip. Ferocious felines follow close behind and, with another snap of Otto's whip, they assume their positions atop various props, eliciting a rippling of applause from the audience.

Back in his motorhome, as Gurney works over his desk, he hears a dog whining outside the door. He smiles and welcomes in the amiable mongrel, tail wagging. Gurney pats the dog and sets out some leftovers on the floor. The dog happily attacks the food.

They're interrupted by a knock on the door. It's Wally the security guard, just checking in. Gurney has to cut their conversation short to take a call from Gabe Hausmann in New York.

At the information office, Columbo is describing his missing nephews when he hears a stir from the big tent. It's the Ringmaster introducing Rick Banner, perched atop the high-wire platform. Columbo heads back in, just as Banner begins his suspenseful walk across the wire. The audience gasps. Banner successfully traverses the high wire, to tremendous applause from Columbo and the rest of the crowd. Banner acknowledges the adulation, while subtly moving his foot along the edge of the platform, to which he earlier attached the magnetized mini transmitter. His foot finds the switch and delicately flips it, activating the transmitter and, in turn, the gas cylinder in Gurney's desk drawer. The valve begins to open, unknown to Gurney, who continues playing with the dog as he chats with Hausmann. Suddenly, there's a faint hiss as gas begins to escape. Gurney's speech slows. His eyes blink. His breath comes in shorter gasps.

Gurney hangs up the phone, slowly. He stares straight ahead, trying to catch his breath. He's confused. The dog lets out a single, peculiar whine. Gurney's head starts to droop. His eyes close. His head drops to the desk. The dog crawls to the door. It whines pitifully, scratching the door and pressing its nose underneath, searching for a sliver of fresh air.

By now, Banner has descended to the floor of the tent, where he is mobbed by adoring fans. He exchanges greetings and signs autographs. Columbo, too, is irresistibly drawn to the magnetic aerialist, until he remembers the lost boys. He returns to the officer near the exit. But before the guard can share an update, Alicia rushes into the main tent, hysterical. "Rick! Hurry!" She rushes into his arms. Something horrible has happened to Daddy.

Banner gestures to Sue to get a doctor and for the security officer to come follow Alicia. Columbo hurries after them, in need of the guard's news about his nephews.

The group rushes to the motorhome. Inside, Banner checks Gurney. He's dead. Alicia turns away and buries her face in her hands. Banner comforts her and instructs the officer to call an ambulance. The doctor arrives and confirms that Gurney's dead. Banner has Sue take Alicia away. The doctor wants to know if Gurney had a history of heart trouble. Banner nods; Ned had had several heart attacks. Columbo agrees: "Face that color—that's what it usually is…" The interruption enrages Banner. Who is this interloper? Columbo apologizes. He's from the police and just wanted to ask the guard about his nephews. The guard hands Columbo a note from the boys, who went looking for their uncle and, when they couldn't find him, decided to take the bus home.

Columbo thanks them both and begins to head out, when he notices a vase on the desk filled with a dozen carnations, their petals closed. "First time I ever saw them closed," he notes. Banner frowns at Columbo, displeased by the strange, indelicate remark.

As Columbo steps out of the trailer, he hears whining from under the motorhome. Columbo kneels, and the stray dog staggers closer, its movements akin to a drunken wobble. Twice its legs buckle. The dog continues to whine as Columbo pets it. He can't understand what could be troubling the erratic pooch. The Lieutenant pokes his head back inside the motorhome, just as Banner and the doctor are covering the corpse with a blanket. Columbo wonders if anyone's familiar with the sick dog outside. Banner, growing even more impatient, retorts, "I'm sure it's just a stray, Lieutenant. Mr. Gurney had a habit of picking them up wherever we went, feeding them, taking care of them. I suppose this was his latest."

Columbo decides to take the pooch in for the night. The dog nestles contentedly into the passenger seat of the Peugeot. But, as he's driving home, Columbo starts having second thoughts. "This may not be such a good idea," Columbo tells his canine passenger. "You know why? By tomorrow morning, we're going to be pretty sloppy about each other. I'm going to decide to keep you, and you're going to decide to stay. Then you know what's going to happen? My basset hound's going to raise the roof. There'll be a regular war."

Instead, Columbo changes course to a friend's home. "Bachelor… nice fellow… lives alone. Perfect. Now all we've got to do is find out if he likes dogs."

Back at the circus, the crowds have gone. It's dark. Banner sneaks back into the motorhome to retrieve the gas cylinder. He then heads to Alicia's quarters, to console her and make sure she knows that he'll be there to help her with everything, including postponing the Hausmann deal.

Columbo arrives at the apartment of one Detective Sgt. Wilson. Wilson opens the door, and Columbo thrusts the stray into his hands. Wilson is stunned. Despite Columbo's best arguments, Wilson does not want a dog, particularly a dog that can barely walk. But as the night goes on, the dog gets its legs back and playfully scampers about the apartment. Wilson now has a theory: what if the dog ate something that was tainted? But that doesn't explain the closed carnations. Columbo asks Wilson if he'd like to join him on a late-night ride to the circus. Wilson agrees to go—and to keep the dog on "a trial basis."

At the circus, they convince security guard Wally and Alicia to let them snoop around the motorhome. Suddenly, Banner barges in, furious at Columbo. "At this hour, Lieutenant? And isn't this just a little bit tasteless? Forcing her to come here?" Banner insists on taking Alicia back to her trailer.

Wally then shares how he visited Gurney shortly before his death. Ned was feeding the dog scraps and received a call from Hausmann. "Never saw a friskier dog in my life, Lieutenant. Peppy as all get-out."

That tells Wilson the dog was poisoned by something it ate. Columbo remains unconvinced. He suspects poisonous gas—the only thing that would account for a sick dog, a dead man, and closed flowers. "Carnations don't like noxious gases any more than we do," he explains. "When they're hit, they close right up. The reason I know that is: my wife once left a bunch of carnations next to the stove—which, as it turned out, had this gas leak. Next thing you know, every one of those carnations closed up tighter than a drum." (This, of course, contradicts Columbo's earlier statement that he'd never seen closed carnations before.)

Columbo and Wilson check the motorhome's vents and exhaust system. No leaks. And the stove is electric.

They call the doctor. He confirms that, while a gas leak would usually have a lesser impact on a large man than on a small dog, it would have a greater effect if the man had a bad heart.

Columbo's suspicions are confirmed the next morning when the autopsy report arrives: "Death by inhalation of noxious gas." A police lab technician's examination of the motorhome proves it couldn't have been an accident: there were no leaks, the motor hasn't been run for at least a week, and the air conditioner is electric. It looks like murder.

Banner enters, in disbelief that it wasn't an accident. He postulates that maybe Gurney inhaled gas outside the motorhome. Wilson is swayed, but Columbo proves there wasn't time, considering how soon after the Hausmann call ended that Alicia discovered the body.

If it really is murder, though, Banner has a perfect suspect: Otto. Only the day before, the hotheaded lion tamer got into a raging argument with Gurney.

Columbo and Wilson separate to look for Otto. The Lieutenant discovers that the tamer is not at his cage, but should return shortly. Columbo takes the opportunity to look a little closer. The cage is empty and the door ajar. The detective eases inside. He picks up the whip and acts out an old fantasy: Columbo the lion tamer. He cracks the whip.

At the same time, the lions and tigers are pacing about in a caged van that's connected to the main tent. Moxie, a short, middle-aged man partially dressed in a clown costume, walks up to the van, smoking a fat cigar. He blows a mouthful of smoke at the cats. A lion snarls. Pleased, Moxie blows more smoke toward the cage. As Moxie continues taunting the lion, Otto silently comes up behind him and kicks him in the rear. Moxie and his cigar go flying.

"If I ever find you near here again, I'll tear you apart," Otto bellows, in a thick German accent. "Now get out of here."

Terrified, Moxie scrambles to his feet and scurries off. Otto then walks to the main cage, as a helper opens the passageway that connects it to the vans.

Otto is furious to find Columbo in the cage, playacting with his whip. Columbo sheepishly apologizes, unaware that—behind him—the big cats have entered the cage and jumped onto their perches. Columbo questions Otto about his argument with Gurney, since Gurney's death has been ruled a murder. Otto demands to know if he's being accused of the killing, but Columbo has a bigger concern. He realizes he's surrounded. The Lieutenant freezes in terror, now only concerned with escaping from the cage in one piece. "You walk out," Otto advises. "Very slowly."

"I can't move," Columbo replies.

With tremendous concentration, Columbo does make his way out. Otto then elaborates on his earlier argument. Gurney wanted Otto to use different, more exciting animals in the act. "I refused," Otto declares. "They are old, but they are not ready for a zoo."

Columbo asks him where he was at 9:00 last night, since he was finished performing. Otto insists he was in his trailer, then snaps his fingers, signaling his cats to roar.

Columbo meets up with Wilson, who has discovered that no one likes old Otto. He's a loner who never talks to anyone—except over shortwave; he's a ham radio operator.

They are approached by Moxie, who confesses that he's been eavesdropping. He also overheard Otto's argument with Gurney—and it had nothing to

HOWARD BERK'S *Roar of the Crowd* was never produced for television, but years later it was novelized in Japanese.

do with his animals. It was over Otto's gambling. "Otto's up to his neck in gambling debts, Lieutenant. Only this time, Mr. Gurney put his foot down—no more advances, no more loans. Otto really blew his top; you could hear him half a mile away."

Columbo and Wilson then have Alicia and Banner let them back into the motorhome, where they discover a folder full of receipts for money Otto owed to Gurney. During their search, Hausmann calls to discuss the deal with Alicia. But Banner takes the phone and informs him that, with everything going on, they've decided to postpone the sale.

Later, Wilson posits that Otto probably ran an exhaust hose from his trailer to Gurney's. Columbo reminds him that Wally didn't hear Otto's engine running and had mentioned no hose.

They catch up with Banner, who's heading to practice. Columbo mentions that, while searching the motorhome, he came across a letter from Gurney to Hausmann, warning that Banner was insistent on retaining sole top billing after the merger, even though he understood that it would not be possible. Banner sloughs it off, saying a closer look at the files would show the one who really was against the merger—Otto, since Hausmann already has a first-class animal act and wouldn't need another.

As they talk, Wilson notices Otto leaving the grounds. He follows him. Otto takes a cab to a sleazy apartment building, where he spends the next 20 minutes. Wilson reports his findings to Columbo and shares his hunch: Otto must have been paying off an accomplice, who had acted as a lookout when Otto ran a hose from his trailer's exhaust to Gurney's motorhome. Wilson wants to confront Otto with the theory.

Otto admits he and Gurney didn't argue about the animals, but about his gambling, because he didn't want his debts made public. Then Wilson asks about the clandestine trip into town. Otto refuses to talk. "You don't have to bother, Prinz!" Wilson counters. "Let me tell you what you were doing: you were paying off your accomplice in murder!"

Otto explodes. He towers over Wilson and threatens that if he ever makes another accusation, he'd better be ready to arrest him—or he'll be fed to his cats. Columbo steps in to soothe the situation. He offhandedly asks Otto if he won or lost. "That is what you were doing in town, wasn't it, sir? Placing some bets?" Columbo asks. Grudgingly, Otto admits he lost, as usual.

Banner has been eavesdropping from the shadows and doesn't like what he's overheard. He sneaks into the tent and scales a ladder to the high-wire platform, unseen by the busy workmen below. Using tiny wire cutters, Banner snips partially through the high wire.

For that evening's performance, an enthusiastic audience fills the stands. The Ringmaster moves into the spotlight and signals for silence. "And now, ladies and gentlemen, the high point of our show! That greatest of all daredevils of the high wire… Rick Banner!"

Banner bounds from the wings with the confidence of a master bullfighter. He acknowledges the crowd, then glides up to the platform. In the stands, Wilson continues pleading his case against Otto to Columbo, who's fixated on Banner making his way across the wire. "Look at him," Columbo remarks.

"That's sensational timing." It gradually occurs to Wilson that Columbo actually suspects Banner.

On the wire, Banner goes into a trampoline effect, preparing to launch into a somersault. The wire snaps. Banner grabs one end. The spectators gasp, rising to their feet. Alicia looks on, wide-eyed. Banner, however, swings Tarzan-like on the severed wire, then pendulums back before releasing his grip above a pile of hay. He rolls over several times, then starts to pick himself up, slightly dazed. Alicia and other circus workers rush to his side. A security guard arrives and reaches for Banner's arm. Banner winces in pain. "Look out, you clumsy idiot!"

Banner pushes past Alicia and the others, and mounts a nearby prop. Frantically, he signals for a spotlight. Obviously in pain, his left arm hanging limp, Rick triumphantly waves to the crowd, receiving a tremendous ovation.

Columbo and Wilson follow Banner and his entourage out of the tent, as the band begins playing and another act hurries into the center ring. In Banner's trailer, the doctor bandages his shoulder and advises going to the hospital for X-rays. Banner doesn't like the idea, but the doctor insists. The doctor offers to pull his car around. Banner then turns to Columbo, demanding Otto be arrested before he kills again. Columbo doesn't understand why Otto would want to kill Banner. Banner explains that, earlier in the day, he had informed Otto that the merger was off and the lion tamer "was going to be out in the fall, the minute his contract was up."

Banner reluctantly heads for the doctor's car. Alicia advises him to take the next few days off.

Banner erupts: "Where the hell do you get off telling me what to do? Nobody tells me what to do! Nobody knocks Rick Banner off that high wire! Nobody! Ever! And if that's too straight for you, Alicia, let's break it off right now! And don't bother mothering me over to the hospital! I can handle it!"

The doctor drives off with Banner. Alicia watches, her eyes welling with tears.

Columbo and Wilson head back to the now-deserted tent. In disbelief, Wilson watches as Columbo hesitantly mounts the ladder up to the high-wire platform. Columbo looks up, then down, then hesitantly climbs. He agrees with Wilson that it's probably a mistake, but continues. Further up, he stops and looks up. The platform seems to sway dizzyingly. He looks down. Even worse. With only a few rungs left, Columbo's foot slips; for one second, he's hanging. Wilson closes his eyes, anticipating a body to come crashing down. Columbo slides his foot back onto the rung. Slowly now, he pulls himself onto the platform. He's made it.

On his knees, Columbo examines the jagged, short end of the wire. Finally, he starts inching back and, in doing so, his fingers close over a metal object along the side of the platform. Columbo pulls it free, and looks over the small, magnetized piece of metal. He shrugs and shoves his finding into his pocket.

The next morning, Columbo learns from Alicia that the doctor is refusing to allow Rick to perform, so her boyfriend is probably "off sulking somewhere." A circus worker has heard that Banner will be spending his unwanted day off at the Beachside Demolition Derby.

When Columbo and Wilson arrive at the stadium, a parking lot attendant directs the Peugeot to a side entrance. A guard raises a gate and they drive through, heading down a short, dark tunnel. They emerge into daylight, stunned.

According to Berk's script, "Somehow or other, our intrepid cops have stumbled onto the field of combat. Maniacally driven cars are racing around in every direction, trying to smash each other to pieces. As Columbo tries to turn around, a car bears down at 700 miles an hour. A terrified Columbo wrenches the wheel and shoots the car into an evasive arc. Another car bears down; again Columbo wrenches the wheel. The Peugeot zigzags downfield, weaving in and out between destruction-bent cars."

Wilson yelps and throws his arms around Columbo, which does not improve Columbo's driving. Columbo slams on the brakes to narrowly avoid being smashed to pieces. He spins the car around and races toward the tunnel.

As Columbo tries to navigate through a sea of surface missiles, Wilson grows optimistic: "Keep going! Keep going! You've almost got it!"

Then, they both react to a new threat: another speeding car heading straight for them; there's no escape. Columbo and Wilson brace for impact—just as another car shoots in front of them, knocking the oncoming vehicle off course. Relieved, Columbo brakes just short of the tunnel and exchanges a dazed look with Wilson. Just then, the savior car pulls up alongside. Behind the wheel is a helmeted Rick Banner. He agrees to meet them back at the motorhome in a few hours.

While they're waiting, Wilson turns on Gurney's television with the remote control. Columbo is lost deep in thought and idly begins jangling his keys. Without warning, the TV screen goes dark. Wilson turns the TV back on, but it goes out again as soon as Columbo resumes his jangling. "That's happened at my house a couple of times," Columbo offers. "The dog does it with his collar…" Suddenly, Columbo's attention is drawn to the keys in his hand: the magnetized slug of metal found on the platform has stuck to one of the keys. He wants to visit the police's electronics expert for an explanation.

Later that night, Banner has returned to his trailer and is exercising his injured shoulder, tugging at a wall pulley. It still hurts, but he's determined. There's a knock at the door. It's Wilson and Columbo, holding a package.

Banner's wearing his costume, having persuaded the doctor to let him perform. He's convinced that the demolition derby loosened his shoulder.

"You really took quite a chance, though, didn't you, sir?" Columbo wonders. "I mean, you could have damaged that shoulder permanently."

Rick smiles: "I'm in the risk business, Lieutenant. That's my game. It's the same with you guys, isn't it? You put your rear ends on the line every day of the week. And you know why we do it? Because we're different. Because we can't live without the danger."

Columbo disagrees: "Well, speaking strictly for myself, sir, I do just fine without the danger. I guess that's why I'm in Homicide. Nobody takes shots at you; the people you get involved with are dead."

Columbo has come to share the latest development in the case. He unwraps the package to reveal a small gas cylinder, similar to the murder weapon. Banner theorizes that Otto must have somehow slipped one into the motorhome. Columbo agrees, but says he can't figure out how, since Wally saw Otto in his trailer at about the time of the murder. Banner has an idea. He used to be an electrician's mate in the Navy, and remembers that a lot of valves and other equipment on shipboard are activated by electronic impulses. The cylinder could easily have been made to operate by remote control. All it would take would be a miniature receiver unit attached to the valve apparatus. "The killer could be 50 feet away, 500 feet away," explains Banner. "All he'd need is a transmitter tuned to the same frequency as the receiver, and he's in business!" All Otto would have had to do was hide the cylinder then later flick the switch from his trailer.

"What switch is *that*, sir?" Columbo asks. "The minute it's something technical, I get a little lost."

Banner demonstrates with the cylinder, speaking slowly as if to a child: "The switch on his transmitter, Lieutenant, so he could send an impulse to the receiver, which, in turn, would activate this valve and release the gas." Obviously Otto used his ham radio equipment to send the signal.

Columbo, though, knows Otto's equipment was out for repairs on the night of the murder. Banner suggests Otto instead used a mini transmitter. Columbo is skeptical. He wants to make sure it would really work. He has Banner place a mini receiver with the attached magnet slug against the cylinder, and connect the wire from the valve to the receiver. It works. They try to send the signal again from outside the trailer. Again, it works. But when they try it from Otto's trailer, it doesn't work. Something is blocking the signal. Columbo has made sure the large supply truck-and-trailer is parked outside, just as it was on the night of the murder. Columbo explains that Otto couldn't have killed Gurney. He didn't make an attempt on Banner's life, either. Banner staged that himself—to divert suspicion from the fact that he was the one who had killed Ned Gurney.

Unmoved, Banner reminds Columbo that, at the time, he was performing in front of 3,000 people. Columbo takes him back to the high wire, again shakily climbs up to the platform, and demonstrates that the signal could be sent from that distance—over the truck parked outside.

Banner confesses, but asks for one favor, which Columbo allows: to perform one last time to an appreciative audience.

There are so many great elements at play in *Roar of the Crowd*: the cute puppy, the always-lovable Wilson, and one fantastic set piece after another: the remote-controlled gassing, the lions, Columbo on the high wire, and the demolition derby. Unfortunately, the promising mystery is undone by an abrupt, unconvincing ending. Columbo presents no hard evidence linking Banner to the murder. There's not even any closure on Wilson or the puppy.

Chambers said he found the script "full of holes," and thought it would be too difficult to cast. He, supported by Falk, chose to go with the marina story (*Last Salute to the Commodore*) instead. They would continue working on *Roar of the Crowd* and, ideally, have it open Season 6, to be directed by Bernie Kowalski.

The following summer, they hired Les and Tina Pine (who originated Season 1's *Short Fuse*) to rewrite *Roar of the Crowd*. Unfortunately, the Pines' revision, now titled *A Lion in Season*, was demonstrably worse than Berk's original.

Chambers wasn't giving up. The Pines were given another crack, as Universal sent *Columbo* unit manager Bob Anderson to Atlanta to scout locations for the circus story. In the meantime, an even stronger script by Ken Kolb arrived that knocked the circus project permanently out of the running.

Some months later, producer Richard Alan Simmons did bring Berk back to transform an unproduced pilot script into the *Columbo* Season 7 finale, *The Conspirators*. And a year later, Simmons had Berk serve as executive story consultant on three episodes of *Mrs. Columbo*, two of which he received writing credit on. Berk would also contribute to *Columbo* in the early 1990s, penning the final draft of the never-produced *Double Vision*.

Murder in B Flat

Normally, a production studio pleads and prays for a TV network to renew its series for another year. Not so with *Columbo*. Primarily due to Falk's protracted work habits, production schedules and costs were blowing past budgets—in some cases doubling the amount of time and money allotted. Universal's newly promoted vice president in charge of controlling expenses, Richard Irving—the same man who, seven years earlier, had produced and directed *Columbo's* first pilot, *Prescription: Murder*, vowed his studio would not proceed with any show that could not stick to budgets and schedules, *Columbo* included. Yet, NBC needed *Columbo*—the foundation for its Sunday nights. So the TV network agreed to pay any costs that exceeded budget. In exchange, NBC would be afforded an on-site liaison to ensure any expenditures were absolutely necessary.

NBC's man on site needed to be someone with business sense and production knowledge, to make sure things were being done efficiently. He needed to be able to handle big personalities firmly yet fondly. And he needed a background in writing, since Falk's biggest issues were with the scripts.

NBC found its man in 60-year-old Bob Metzler, a longtime writer for film, radio and television, who since 1955 had served as business manager for the Academy Awards ceremony. Metzler broke into the movie business in 1939, after winning a national scriptwriting contest sponsored by MGM. His prize was a job. He contributed to the *Andy Hardy* film series, *The Philadelphia Story*, and more, before earning his first credits on Clark Gable's *Honky Tonk*, *Riders of the Purple Sage*, and B pictures for other studios. On the side, he wrote for such radio series as *The Adventures of Philip Marlowe* and *The Count of Monte Cristo*. After the war, he became a producer at Walt Disney Productions, overseeing numerous *True-Life Adventures*.

On *Columbo*, Metzler's primary responsibility was to keep costs controlled and production moving. Although Falk typically despised studio and network executives, the actor took a liking to Metzler. He viewed him as sincere and aboveboard. But, best of all, Falk liked that Metzler was an experienced writer and script doctor, who could help identify problems with existing scripts and recognize talented writers who could fix them.

Emboldened by the show's need for good scripts, within weeks of coming on board in the spring of 1975, Metzler pitched a story of his own, a murder-by-bow-and-arrow mystery, *Solo for the Bowstring*. He quickly developed a strong relationship with Peter S. Fischer, and asked *Columbo's* story editor to look over his treatment. But before the story could progress, Fischer was reassigned to Levinson and Link's new series, *Ellery Queen*. Metzler approached Fischer's successor on *Columbo*, Bill Driskill. Driskill, though, was partial to the other stories in development. He suggested Metzler change the setting to the 1940s and rewrite his idea for *Ellery Queen*. Metzler decided to go over Driskill's head. Later that afternoon, he pitched his idea to Falk. Falk said he liked the idea, but would not commit any further. And, quickly caught up in the whir of deadlines, Metzler reluctantly set his own story on the back burner.

Once Season 5 wrapped, Falk's contract was up and he intimated that he was finished with *Columbo*. Yet Metzler knew that Patrick McGoohan, who had just directed the season finale, *Last Salute to the Commodore*, had Falk's ear—and McGoohan had Falk's backing to write a *Columbo* script of his own, revolving around the kidnapping of Columbo's wife. So Metzler arranged to meet McGoohan for lunch (a lunch that included "several drinks" for McGoohan) to gauge the prospects for future *Columbos*. Metzler proposed selling Falk on—rather than a full sixth season—having a package of two two-hour specials, one McGoohan's story, the other Metzler's. McGoohan seemed receptive.

Two days later, Metzler went to Falk with the two-story proposal. Falk said it was possible, subject to him reading and liking the scripts, but that he would give "first consideration" to McGoohan's story. Metzler immediately returned to work on *Solo for the Bowstring*. He retitled it *Murder in B Flat*, then called the local police department to investigate whether his murder and clues were forensically sound. Might a fatal arrow wound be mistaken for a gunshot wound, after the arrow was removed? (It might.) Could fine wood scrapings or varnish from the shaft of the arrow be deposited on the killer's finger ring when he pulled the arrow out of the body? (Possibly.) The police expert thought the whole setup rather ingenious.

A few weeks later, Metzler met with McGoohan to update him on *Murder in B Flat*. McGoohan agreed to pass Metzler's script on to Falk, along with his endorsement. Although nothing official had yet been signed, McGoohan said that Falk had confided in him that "there will be more *Columbos* made."

Universal suspected as much, and placed Bill Driskill in charge of coming up with six scripts for a possible Season 6. Weeks later, Falk signed on for four more episodes, again under producer Everett Chambers. Chambers quickly called Metzler to say that he liked *Murder in B Flat*, but he wanted Driskill to read the latest version before he decided whether or not to purchase it.

The following week, Metzler met with Driskill, who said he had three other scripts he preferred. He suggested several changes for Metzler. In particular, Driskill thought the story needed another clue, and found the bloodthirsty bowman to be too weak a character. He should be "less of an obvious pigeon" for his accomplice. Metzler also took the script to Universal executive Dick Irving, who "hoped that it would be made."

After two more weeks of meetings, rewrites and negotiating, Metzler was given $1,000 for a one-year option. If Universal ended up buying the script he'd get another $4,000, an additional $5,000 once filming started, and up to $1,500 more, based on how many other writers received screen credit, for a possible total of $11,500.

Soon after, director Bernie Kowalski (who was on the lot prepping to direct *Fade In to Murder*) told Metzler that he, too, had read the script and liked it very much—which surprised Metzler, who thought Kowalski was lined up to direct *Roar of the Crowd*. Chambers and Falk also praised Metzler's latest revision, dated June 22, 1976. Prospects were high that *Murder in B Flat* would be filmed as either the third or fourth show of Season 6.

— 📖 —

We open in a small-yet-elegant bachelor pad that looks out on a golf course; the home is comfortably furnished and color-coordinated to the tastes of a sportsman. Golf photos and trophies abound. The lights and music are low, as pro golfer Stan Allen and archery champion Margaret Butler finish an intimate candlelit dinner. Stan is 38, Margaret says she's the same (though her ID would say 45). They're both good looking and finely clothed over their athletic bodies.

They also both have big-money sponsorship deals with sporting goods tycoon Gregory Baird "G.B." Butler, Margaret's husband, with whom she also shares a prenuptial agreement. If she files for divorce or is found cheating, she'll get nothing. The only way she gets anything is if G.B. dies and she inherits it.

Margaret picks up a candlestick and sashays toward Stan's large sliding glass door and onto his patio. She sets the candlestick down on a wrought iron table and turns up the sexy: "Shall we have dessert out here?" Stan confesses he doesn't have any dessert. Margaret reminds him they have each other. Unable to resist, Stan hurries onto the patio to embrace her. What he doesn't see is, in the darkness behind a hedge, a shadowy figure is watching the love scene through the lens of a Minox infrared spy camera. The peeping tom near-silently snaps a few shots, then pockets the Minox and takes out a larger 35mm camera. He clicks a series of slightly louder shots, as Stan and Margaret writhe ever more passionately. Suddenly, Stan freezes and opens his eyes. He listens. Stan pulls away from Margaret and charges toward the hedge. Nothing. So he dashes onto the golf course, where he spots the fleeing photographer.

The next morning, Margaret approaches an office door marked "Cooper's Confidential Investigations: Pictures Don't Lie." Behind a cluttered desk sits Don Cooper, private eye, sporting a fresh black eye and a swollen lip. Margaret chuckles at his condition. "This is going to cost you extra," Cooper says.

Margaret pulls a wad of cash from her purse and drops it on his desk: the $300 balance she owes him for the job, $50 for the beating he incurred, another $400 for the beating Stan gave his camera, plus an extra $100 to keep quiet. In return, she wants the film. Cooper shrugs: "It's in the sand trap where your boyfriend caught me. He ripped it right out of the camera before he smashed it… and me."

Margaret's savvier than that. Stan heard the camera she wanted him to hear. Margaret heard both cameras. She makes Cooper hand over the infrared film from the Minox.

The Butlers live in the penthouse of a posh 15-story tower in West Los Angeles. Their maid, Bessie, is tending to the rooftop garden when the phone rings. It's G.B., calling to inform his wife that he'll be home from New York that evening. Bessie brings the phone to Margaret, who's in her bedroom, sitting at an antique desk in a French-windowed alcove. She's been clipping words from newspapers and magazines, and placing them on a blank piece of paper. G.B. is 58, old-fashioned, and harsh. His bags are packed, and he wears a conservative topcoat, hat and steel-rimmed glasses. He's tired and in a foul mood. Margaret offers to make him feel better by meeting him at their beach house after he lands. He has no interest in carousing with her coterie of "hard-drinking sponges."

But Margaret has other plans: "Alone, darling. You and I, alone. Just the two of us."

G.B. hadn't joined her at the beach house in seven or eight months, but Margaret convinces him she'll make it worth his while. He consents.

Margaret tells Bessie she can take the weekend off, since she'll be at the beach with G.B. She then resumes rearranging her news clippings to spell out: "Negatives of prints - $10,000. No bills over $100. Call you Saturday. No police." Margaret admires her handiwork for a moment, then removes the "$10,000" and replaces it with "$50,000." The blackmail note complete, she picks up the phone and dials.

The headquarters of G.B. Butler Sporting Goods boasts beautifully

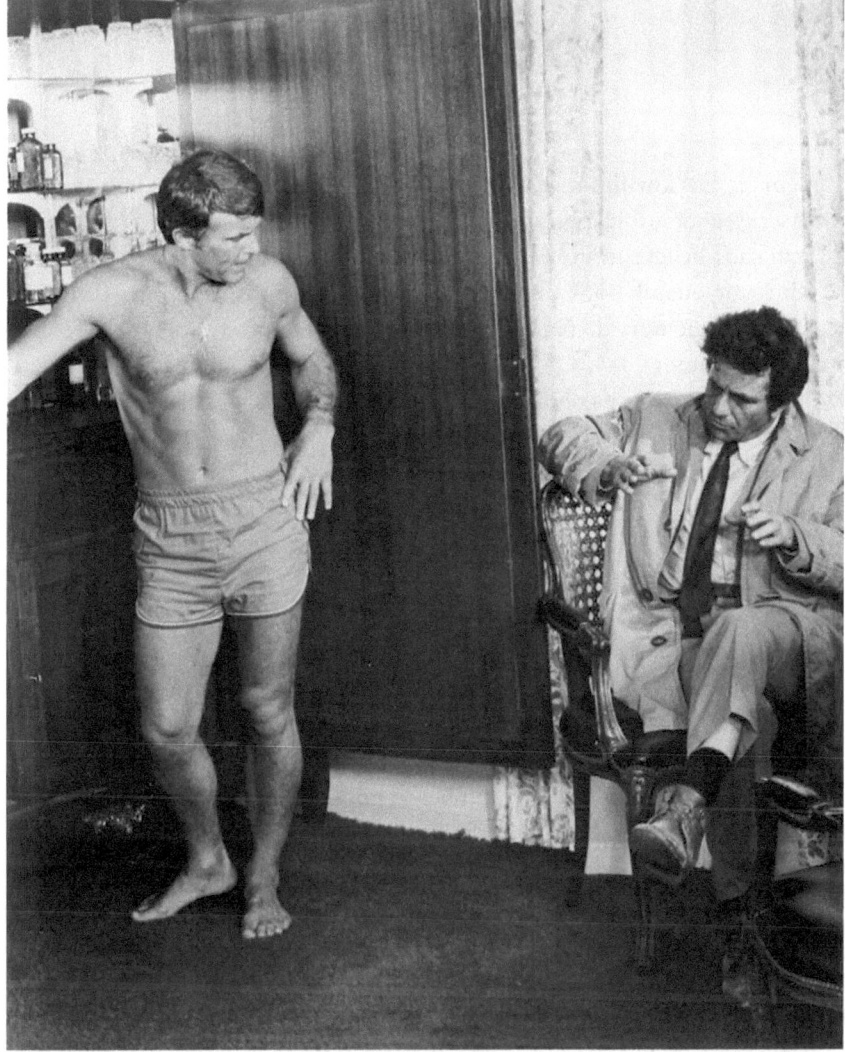

PETER FALK played off Robert Conrad's Milo Janus so well in Season 4's *An Exercise in Fatality*, producers tried to pit Columbo against similarly vain professional athletes during Season 5. *[Credit: NBCUniversal]*

manicured lawns, expansive parking, and a modern, luxurious factory. Inside the president's office sits G.B.'s secretary, Miss Blanchard. Her severe hairstyle, suit and rimmed glasses are near-duplicates of G.B.'s. The walls are adorned with sepia-toned photographs of their licensed sports stars, including golfer Stan and archer Margaret. Miss Blanchard sets aside her crossword puzzle when the phone rings. It's Margaret on the line, informing her that she'll be in at 3:00 to meet with Stan.

At 3:00, Margaret arrives carrying an 8x10 envelope. Stan is waiting in her office. She bursts in. Stan's pacing. He knows something's amiss. He closes the door. "We're in trouble," she says. From the envelope she removes her homemade blackmail note and several 8x10 prints of the lovers on the patio "in a series of amorous positions."

Stan can't believe it. He yanked the film right out of the snoop's camera.

"But not out of both cameras," Margaret responds. She next turns his attention to the note demanding $50,000. There's no way she can raise that amount by tomorrow.

"It wouldn't do any good anyway," Stan adds. "This louse'll never give you the negatives. He'll just keep bleeding you."

She doesn't know what to do, certain that G.B. will have copies within a day.

"I should have killed him when I had him in my hands," Stan snarls, throttling an imaginary neck.

"Too late for that," Margaret says. "But you should kill somebody."

"Yeah. Myself."

That's not who Margaret says she was thinking of—since she'd hate to lose her lover.

Stan slowly catches on… and smiles. Margaret shares that, right at that moment, G.B. is on his way to their beach house. They are supposed to spend the weekend there together. But she loves Stan. So, in short order, she'll end up a poor divorcee… or a tremendously wealthy widow.

Stan paces as he ponders. All right, he's game. Margaret hands him the key to the gun cabinet. Stan says a gun is too noisy. He suggests a knife. That's a no go for Margaret; she wants G.B. to die, but not suffer. Then Stan thinks of the perfect weapon: a bow and arrow—silent, untraceable, deadly.

Margaret, though, reminds Stan that she's an archer. But that's why his plan is perfect—the authorities will never pin an archery murder on her, assuming she forges an airtight alibi with ultra-proficient secretary Blanchard.

Stan heads for the factory's display room, which is filled with large cut-out figures of the champions who endorse Butler Sporting Goods. The golf display depicts the collection of signature Stan Allen golf clubs arranged in a sunburst pattern on each side of a smiling, life-sized cutout of Stan. A similar archery display has a cutout of shapely Margaret Daley Butler, dressed in a provocative blouse and shorts, an arrow nocked on her bowstring, drawn back to the head. Custom-made bows of various strengths for men, women and children sit in individual slots at either side. Tennis, skiing, baseball and fishing are displayed in a similar manner, although the guns for the skeet shooting champ's cutout are locked in a glass-doored cabinet.

Stan heads directly for the archery display, and pulls out a short, powerful, man's fiberglass hunting bow. Then he takes two target arrows from a box of

12, and slips them into his golf bag. He disassembles the bow and slides the pieces into his bag. He covers his tracks by resealing the box of arrows, and placing a stock bow in the empty slot in the sunburst pattern. Stan slings his golf bag over his shoulder and exits.

Meanwhile, Margaret has been occupying Miss Blanchard in conversation, expressing her concern over how hard her husband has been working. They chat long enough to establish a foolproof alibi for the murder-to-come.

Stan races up Pacific Coast Highway to north Malibu. He parks at a vacant lot that slopes down to the beach. He slips out of his car, golf bag in tow. He quickly reassembles the bow, just as another vehicle approaches. It's G.B., who parks at the closest beachfront cottage and climbs out with one piece of luggage. Stan takes the two arrows from his bag. G.B. walks up to the front door and, as he fishes into his pocket for his key, notices a broken window. Inside, he sees a dead seagull that flew through the glass. Grimacing, G.B. enters the house. The living room is nicely furnished, but caked in dust. G.B. runs a finger across the top of a table, leaving a streak in the dust. Suddenly, he's startled by Stan's voice behind him: "Surprise!" G.B. whirls around to see Stan in the open doorway.

G.B. demands to know what in the hell Stan is doing there. He's in no mood for surprises. Stan says it's more of a joke—one that will kill him. Stan picks up the bow and arrows, and moves closer. As he nocks an arrow onto the bowstring, Stan explains that he and Margaret love each other—as well as all of G.B.'s beautiful money. G.B. keeps backing up, until he's cornered near a baby grand piano. Stan cocks the bowstring, trembling from the pull of the mighty weapon. He shoots. The bowstring twangs. G.B. falls, dead.

Just then, the telephone rings, startling Stan. He instinctively reaches for the phone, then notices the finger streak across the dusty table. He pulls his hand away and lets the phone keep ringing. Stan yanks the arrow from G.B.'s chest. He hurries out, as the phone continues to ring.

The next morning, stanchions and ropes cordon off the beach house. Several police officers are stationed out front but, rather than standing guard, they're "in leisurely postures, sunning themselves. A photographer even uses a flash bulb reflector to direct the sun's rays under his chin."

Up walks Columbo, but no one notices, since most of the policemen have their eyes closed and their faces tilted up to the sun. Columbo is incredulous, wondering if he's got the wrong address. No, this is actually the murder scene. Columbo is directed inside, where he's greeted by the far-more-officious Sgt. Ann Jenkins. The attractive, smartly attired officer gently kicks a roll of paper across the carpeting, to create a path for Columbo to walk over without disrupting any evidence. But first she needs to check Columbo's credentials. He's surprised… to encounter a female sergeant.

She fills him in on their findings so far. On the floor, under a sheet, lies Gregory Baird Butler. Cause of death? She *thinks* he was shot.

Thinks he was shot? Columbo asks if the wound is "through-and-through." The coroner isn't entirely certain, because the victim's fists are clenched over his heart. Columbo gingerly raises G.B.'s fists, so the coroner can check the size and positioning of the wound. It's tiny and through-and-through, confirming G.B. was not shot, but more likely stabbed. Sgt. Ann doesn't understand, so Columbo explains bullets are highly deflectable. They usually come out higher or lower than the point of entry, particularly if they hit bone. Also, bullets tend to flatten out as they go through the body, making the exit wound larger than the entry wound. "I'd say the murder weapon was a long, sharp something-or-other," Columbo surmises, based on the position of the hands. "Victims have a tendency to grab anything that punctures them."

Columbo has now noticed some sort of scrapings stuck to G.B.'s ring. He flicks some of the flakes into an envelope, and hands it to an officer for analysis.

Continuing his investigation, Columbo makes his way along the paper pathway until he reaches the piano. He peers under the keyboard. A lead weight holds down the piano's three pedals. Ann points out that that's what people do if they're not going to use a piano for a long time. She demonstrates how the weight lifts the dampers off the strings to prevent grooves from being cut into the felts. Columbo sticks his head under the raised top of the piano for a closer look. He notices that all the strings are uniformly covered with dust—except one group of three, which glisten. He speculates that much of the dust entered via the broken window. But what about the shiny strings?

Enter Stan, a "friend of the family" who says he was called by the distraught Mrs. Butler. Columbo tells him not to touch anything, as Ann photographs footprints in the carpeting near the body. While Columbo asks how Mrs. Butler is taking the news, and who he thinks might be responsible, Ann begins comparing one of Stan's fresh footprints to those next to the body. Stan's are considerably smaller. He's relieved, thinking this exonerates him. But Ann explains that the older prints were made with rubber-soled shoes, which leave larger marks than leather-soled ones.

While the investigators finish up, Columbo asks Stan if he can wait outside for a moment. Stan is happy to wait on the beach, practicing his golf swing. Columbo heads for the piano to count the piano strings from right to left. He then joins Stan on the beach, who's using a sand wedge to loft one ball after another straight into a circle he's drawn in the sand 30 feet away.

"Boy, I wish I could hit 'em that way out of a trap," Columbo smiles. Stan shares his secret and has Columbo give it a try with his wedge. He even offers to let Columbo keep the club. Columbo declines ("That'd break up your set!"), then does a double take at the club head. He's *the* Stan Allen, PGA champion! Columbo even bought his book, though it hasn't helped his game. Maybe one day, once the case is resolved, he might take him up on the offer.

Later that day, Stan and Margaret celebrate at her penthouse. He mentions how the officers investigating G.B.'s murder are singularly stupid. They even compared two sets of footprints—both of which he created, but which they'll never be able to prove. As a precaution, Margaret instructs him to dispose of the shoes and return the bow and arrows to the factory. No archery equipment should go missing from inventory—and it must be spotlessly clean.

Their revelry is interrupted by the arrival of Columbo. The Lieutenant extends his condolences. He admits he can't tell if Mr. Butler was shot or stabbed, by what, or by whom. As Columbo begins to question Margaret, Stan leaves. Margaret reveals that she was supposed to meet G.B. at the beach house an hour after his plane arrived, but she was to first wait for his call. She tried calling him from the office—as Miss Blanchard can testify—but when he didn't pick up, she figured he must have caught a later flight, so she headed home.

In the meantime, Sgt. Ann has been sitting in her car outside the Butlers' apartment. She sees Stan exit and decides to tail him. He pulls up to the Butler Sporting Goods complex, removes his golf bag from the trunk of his car, and takes it inside the factory. Ann watches from a distance, jotting down notes. Inside, Stan goes to a small high-powered forge. He pulls a pair of rubber-soled shoes from his bag, places them in the forge, and sets them on fire. He then turns on the powerful suction fan in the hood over the forge.

Outside, Ann looks up to see a puff of smoke, then heatwaves emanating from a vent in the factory's roof. She glances at her watch and marks the time in her notebook.

At the same time Stan is watching the shoes burn, Margaret is setting fire to her blackmail notes, 8x10 photos, and roll of infrared film, in her rooftop barbecue.

With the shoes incinerated, Stan turns off the forge and fan, and goes to the display room. He pulls two arrows from his bag and replaces them in the appropriate box. He reassembles the fiberglass bow from his bag and replaces it in the sunburst. He tosses the generic replacement bow onto the pile where he originally found it. He starts to move away, then stops. He unclips the small towel from his golf bag and carefully wipes down the two bows.

That evening, Columbo visits a piano store. As he begins counting the strings inside a baby grand, up walks a snooty salesman (picture Vito Scotti). "It's a lovely instrument, sir. Are you interested in buying?" the clerk asks. The interruption causes the detective to lose count. Columbo says he's listening for a certain note; he doesn't know what note that is, only that if each note has three strings, it would be 39 notes down from the right. The salesman runs down the chromatic scale from right to left until he reaches the B flat above middle C. Columbo hits the key, then asks if he can record the sound. The clerk wonders if this is his normal criterion for selecting a piano.

At the police lab, Columbo plays the recording for the technician, and says, "Now, that's the sound that would be made by the only clean strings in the piano in the beach house. All the other strings are dirty. Everything's dirty in that house."

The technician posits that it's highly unlikely the strings were wiped clean. More likely they were "vibrated clean." If something near the piano elicited the same B flat tone, it would send out a frequency that could cause the B flat strings in the piano to resonate.

"It's called sympathetic vibration," the tech explains. "The original sound would be louder than the secondary sound—from the piano strings—so you probably wouldn't hear it. But the strings would be vibrating and sounding, nonetheless… and, of course, the dust would be vibrated off of them."

The weapon must have been made of something similar to piano wire. Columbo deduces he's "looking for some type of a lethal harp or guitar."

But what about the scrapings? The technician identifies them as varnish and Port Orford cedar.

The next morning, Columbo meets Sgt. Ann at the factory, where she's discovered a suspicious blob in the cinders of the forge. They continue on to the president's office, where about 10 somber employees have gathered. Margaret announces that she will be taking her husband's place, with assistance from Mr. Allen and Miss Blanchard. Columbo pulls the secretary aside, so she can confirm the times Stan and Margaret left on the afternoon of the murder.

Columbo then goes to Stan, who is giving pointers to Ann on a putting green in the display room. Columbo has Ann, with notebook, recount Stan's suspicious movements on the day after the murder. Margaret acts dumbfounded. Stan says he was just picking up a half-dozen golf balls on his way to the course. Picking them up or burning them? Stan says he didn't burn anything—or, no, he did. A bundle of old checks.

"They must have been rubber," Columbo muses, "because this is what Sgt. Jenkins found in the forge this morning." He pulls from his pocket a glob of rubber, then bounces it on the floor like a ball and catches it. Stan argues that could have been in the forge for months. Columbo thinks it looks and acts like rubber—recently melted rubber. And why would he carry checks around in his golf bag? Stan grows increasingly defensive. Once the police leave, Margaret tells Stan to go home and keep quiet.

Outside the factory, Columbo and Ann discuss the sympathetic vibration theory. All they've got to do is come up with a stringed weapon. "Like my violin?" Ann asks, pretending to strum an imaginary one. Her invisible bow makes Columbo think of an archery bow. He smiles. "Shoot it near a piano, and you got a dead man and three clean piano strings."

"If it twangs like the B flat above middle C," she adds.

Just then, Stan pulls out of his parking space and stops, waiting for Ann to follow him. She hurries to her car and obliges.

Columbo returns to Margaret's penthouse, where she's practicing her archery in her rooftop garden. She wears a white blouse, a black skirt, and an armguard covering the inside of her left forearm. As Columbo approaches, Margaret lets off a shot, striking the dead center of a target on the other side of the garden. Her second shot is identical.

"Two bullseyes," Columbo notes. "Score 18."

Margaret is impressed by Columbo's knowledge of archery. He's been doing a little research, he explains. He's convinced that G.B. was killed by an arrow shot from a bow, using equipment just like hers. She's shocked. Columbo then asks her to pluck the string of her bow. Though confused, she plucks her string. It makes a tone that Columbo hums. He pulls out his tape recorder and plays the B flat. Margaret's tone is much lower than the recording. He asks her to pluck again, but the two tones are clearly different.

"It's not that bow," Columbo concludes. "Each tone has a wavelength… a frequency all its own. The tone of your bowstring is not the one I'm looking for."

Columbo then asks if Margaret's arrows are made of wood. No, she uses fiberglass arrows and, before that, she used aluminum. She hasn't used wooden arrows in about 15 years.

But does she have wooden arrows at the factory? Yes. And what species of wood are they made of? Port Orford cedar, she responds, because of its nice straight grain. The company buys the wood in Northern California and Oregon, because those are the only areas where it grows. But anyone who manufactures wooden arrows likely uses Port Orford cedar.

Are these arrows varnished? Yes, she says, with spar varnish, right before the flight feathers are glued on.

Margaret despairs at the thought that she's now a prime suspect. Columbo tries to set her at ease. He can't logically rule out the national women's archery champion, yet he knows she didn't kill her husband. The lab showed that it took at least 90 pounds to drive that arrow "and there isn't a woman alive who can pull a 90-pound bow back far enough."

Margaret agrees; she's never used over 32 pounds. Columbo says he's looking for a husky man who's a good archer.

"Husky, yes," Margaret says. "But he doesn't have to be any kind of an archer at close range."

"Is that right?"

"The bow, of course, would almost have to be a man's fiberglass hunting bow… a short one."

Columbo asks if they have any such bows.

She says they have a few, in the factory.

That night, Columbo takes two officers to the G.B. Butler Display Room to find the murder weapon. He plays the B flat recording from his tape recorder. "I'm going to leave this with you guys. So get busy with the bows. Stick to short, tough ones. String them up and twang them to see if they sound like…" He replays the sound.

"What about fingerprints, Lieutenant?"

Columbo says to forget about prints. The weapon definitely would have been wiped clean. But the question does give him an idea. He peers closely at several bows in the sunburst display of the cutout. "Get me a sample of this dust. After you find the bow, look for the arrow. It'll be scratched. The varnish'll be scraped off… right down to bare wood."

Columbo leaves to meet Sgt. Ann, who's staking out Stan's house. The suspect is inside, peeking from behind the curtains. The Lieutenant, holding a paper bag, sends Ann off, instructing her to be at the beach house at 1:30. Columbo rings the doorbell and immediately a furious Stan swings open the door. Upon hearing his nemesis doesn't have a warrant, Stan slams the door in his face. Columbo smiles and rings the bell again. Stan yanks open the door, but before he can close it again, Columbo pulls from his paper bag a plaster cast of the murderer's footprint. He says he doesn't think it will match any footwear Stan has in the house and, if true, then he can call off the stakeout. Stan sighs and lets Columbo enter. Stan retrieves his one pair of rubber-soled shoes from the bedroom. The shoe is the same size as the cast, but its rippled sole doesn't match the pebbly pattern in the plaster. Columbo admits he was wrong.

"I've known that all along," Stan snarls. "But what about the glob of rubber in the forge?"

"Inadmissible evidence," Columbo replies. "A defense attorney would crucify me if I tried to present it in court."

Columbo hands the shoe back to Stan, along with the glob of rubber from his pocket. Stan is free to come and go, but Columbo asks him for one final favor—to join him after lunch at the Butler beach house. He has some news to share, because he's discovered that G.B. was killed by a bow and arrow.

Stan's astounded. "No! Then it was she… Oh, poor Margaret. Are you sure she did it?"

Columbo says she's one of a couple of suspects. And also, if he could bring his clubs with him.

"You like that wedge," Stan laughs.

"It's a beaut."

Stan, in fact, arrives at the beach house before Columbo. He steps onto the porch, carrying his golf bag, when he spots Margaret walking on the sand near the water's edge. He leaves his bag and hurries to her. She thinks Columbo's gotten too close. He thinks Columbo's off the scent, but he is concerned that his relationship with Margaret is cooling. She says it's because he's "blowing it." Stan, motioning toward the officers at the house, wonders if she's trying to throw him to the wolves, to save her own hide.

Margaret shakes her head pathetically and smiles sweetly at Stan. "Stanley, darling, like Little Red Riding Hood, it's your frightful stupidity that makes you so vulnerable to those wolves."

Margaret and Stan snip back and forth, convinced that it's not them but their partner whom Columbo has in his crosshairs. Just then, up walk Columbo and Ann. Columbo sees Stan's bag and pulls out the prized wedge. He takes a few practice swings, then returns it to the bag. "Work before pleasure," he frowns. As they head for the house, Stan reminds Columbo that the club's all his if he'll take it. But Columbo reiterates that he can't accept a gift from a suspect.

Stan is taken aback: "A suspect? But I thought that was all cleared up… you know, the footprints, the shoes."

Columbo agrees. The shoes are out. He says he thinks Stan burned a pair in the factory, but he can't prove it.

"I burned checks," Stan repeats. "Now, what's to prevent you from accepting a promotional golf club?"

Columbo holds the golf club closer and rubs its head. Then he shoves it back into the bag. "The fact that you killed Gregory Baird Butler… with a bow and arrow."

Suppressing his shock, Stan calls the contention ridiculous. He's no archer, he says, trying to deflect the attention to Margaret. But Columbo knows the murder didn't require a skilled archer, just a strong man. Margaret laps it up.

Ann brings in the officers from the display room. One carries a package. He tears off the paper to reveal an arrow and the hunting bow in two pieces. Columbo takes the bow and fits the two parts together. He declares that these are the bow and the arrow that were used to kill G.B.

"You can tell from the rifling marks, of course," Stan sneers.

No, Columbo corrects him, but from the scrapings under Mr. Butler's ring. Columbo turns the arrow to reveal scratches from the tip to about three inches down the shaft. G.B. must have been clutching the arrow when he died, so varnish and wood were caught under his ring when the arrow was pulled from his chest.

Stan wants to know where the arrow was found. In a box of arrows in the factory. Couldn't it have been scratched in the factory? Columbo shares that microscopic traces of blood—the same type as G.B.'s—were found along the rim of the metal point. To demonstrate the sound the now-strung bow makes, Columbo plucks the bowstring just as Ann holds down the B flat above middle C on the piano. The tones are identical.

"Sympathetic vibration," Columbo smiles. "There's only one chance in nine million that two bow strings would have the same tone."

Acting as if he's wrapped the case, Columbo dismisses the other officers, except for Ann. Stan remains unconvinced.

So Columbo recounts the entire story of what happened on the day of the murder, and how Stan transported the murder weapon in his golf bag. Stan asks if his fingerprints were on the bow and arrow. No, they were wiped clean—by the towel on Stan's golf bag, which has traces of the same red varnish. Stan reasons that when the substance is applied in the factory, "it flies all over the place." But Ann points out that the streak is in a straight line along the towel, like a wipe mark.

Margaret increasingly enjoys Stan's predicament.

Columbo now wants to reenact the murder. He takes off his raincoat and tosses it aside. He positions Ann where G.B. was standing when he was shot. Columbo picks up the bow and moves toward the piano. He raises it and starts to pull back the string with an imaginary arrow, while having Margaret check his technique. He's having trouble, though, getting a good pull. He removes his suit coat and the gun from his shoulder holster, and drops them onto the sofa. "That's better," he says.

Columbo again picks up the bow and takes his stance with fingers properly curved on the bowstring. He looks to Margaret for approval. She gives him an "OK" sign. Columbo pulls the string back, and back, and back. His arm begins to shake. He lets go. Pow.

Immediately, Columbo grabs his forearm. He unbuttons his shirt cuff and pulls up his sleeve, revealing a red area on the tender inside skin of his arm. Margaret explains it's a common archery injury—that's why seasoned archers wear an armguard.

Suddenly, Columbo grabs Stan's forearm. Stan winces in pain.

"Did you have an armguard, Mr. Allen?" Columbo asks. He pulls up the sleeve of Stan's sweater to uncover a similar injury on his forearm. Stan, however, laughs. He says he got that mark at the factory, "not with your musical bow that killed G.B."

But Columbo has one last card to play. He shows Stan that the feather on the killer arrow is broken and a fragment is missing. He went over every inch of the murder scene, and the sand outside, and found no sign of the missing feather. Columbo suspects there's only one place it can be—inside whatever was used to transport the bow from the beach house to the factory. Columbo points to Stan's golf bag. Stan scoffs. He warns Columbo not to touch his bag without a search warrant. Columbo, though, says he's entitled to look because he currently has the bag in his possession and it was at the scene of the crime. Columbo begins pulling the clubs out of the bag. Stan panics. He grabs Columbo's gun off the couch and aims it at the detective. "That's enough," Stan barks. "Okay! All right! I did it for us—Margaret and me."

"You did NOT," Margaret corrects him.

Columbo and Ann, however, are unperturbed about being held at bay by a nervous murderer. Columbo continues fishing through the golf bag, as Ann removes a gun from her purse. She calmly points it at Stan.

"Her gun is loaded, Mr. Allen," Columbo says.

Figuring he has nothing to lose, Stan pulls the trigger. All he gets is a "click." He had no idea that Columbo never carries a loaded gun. "Too bulky… too confining."

Columbo did bring along a pair of handcuffs, just for Stan, while Ann has a matching pair for Margaret. Columbo explains, "You were the only one who knew Mr. Butler would be here. You sent Mr. Allen to kill your husband."

Ann calls the uniformed officers back so they can take the couple away. Columbo, meanwhile, turns the now-empty golf bag upside down, and bangs it on the bottom. The broken piece of feather falls out.

"Well, what do you know?" Columbo says. "It really was there."

Metzler's script was solid and packed with ingenious clues, but it did have a few imperfections. The story is rather straightforward, with no twists and a couple of headscratchers. A murderer might feel compelled to return the unique hunting bow to the factory, but why the arrow? The feather clue—a late addition to the script—is reminiscent of the wayward pearl in the umbrella from Season 2's *Dagger of the Mind*.

The real problematic character is Margaret. She sets up her boyfriend to kill her husband, then does nothing to protect him. Does she love him or is she just using him to get G.B.'s money? And why would she go along with having Stan kill her husband with her trademark, a bow and arrow? And, finally, while Columbo compiles a mountain of evidence against the golfer, the only thing he's got on Margaret is that she was the one who must have told Stan that G.B. was at the beach house. That doesn't mean she plotted with Stan to kill G.B.

The shortcomings were correctable. Unfortunately, after the second show of Season 6, Falk forced Universal to fire producer Chambers and the entire series was put on hold. After a month of no movement, Metzler approached Falk and asked him about his intentions toward *Murder in B Flat*. Falk said he still liked the story. Metzler thought he could repurpose the story elsewhere. Falk reiterated that he wanted to keep it for *Columbo*.

It took another two months before a new producer was hired—Richard Alan Simmons. Simmons was given the scripts under consideration to review, but after one meeting Metzler could tell that Simmons wanted to generate his own story ideas.

Metzler tried pitching *Murder in B Flat* to NBC and Universal as a movie of the week or as a pilot for a series in which the lead detective and the sergeant are married. Both passed, although NBC did ask Metzler to write a *Little House on the Prairie*–perhaps out of gratitude for his work on *Columbo*. Universal's Dick Irving suggested *B Flat* might work better for *Quincy, M.E.* than *Columbo*. So Metzler went to writer/producer Bob Blees, who explained that star Jack Klugman had to approve all stories on *Quincy*—and that Klugman would not read teleplays. If Metzler wanted *Murder in B Flat* to be considered for *Quincy*, he'd first have to convert his script into a treatment.

At that point, Metzler had had enough. He no longer wished to place his fate in the hands of another over-empowered actor, and dropped the project cold. He'd stick to managing the Academy Awards.

5
Season 6 (1976-1977)
Old-Fashioned Murders

Peter S. Fischer had been among the most prolific writers to ever work on *Columbo*. After reading Fischer's one-shot script for Season 3's *Publish or Perish*, Falk demanded he be assigned to his show full-time. Contractually, Fischer had to wait until his current series, *Griff*, was canceled. He then scrambled to script *Columbo's* final show of the third season (*A Friend in Deed*) before being appointed executive story consultant for Season 4.

That year, in addition to revising everyone's drafts, Fischer also wrote three of the six scripts himself (*An Exercise in Fatality*, *Negative Reaction*, and *A Deadly State of Mind*). Pressured by Falk into endless revisions, Fischer was exhausted. Early in Season 5, he could tell he was in for more of the same. Two shows in, Fischer was able to get reassigned to Levinson and Link's forthcoming *Ellery Queen* as a producer and writer. As a favor to Falk, Fischer agreed to stay on the *Columbo* payroll as co-story editor, though it wasn't much more than a credit.

Fischer's departure from *Columbo* hurt the show—and enraged Falk. The actor told Fischer he was happy for him. But, in truth, he was incensed that Universal would move his star writer from one of its highest-rated shows to a pilot seemingly done as a favor to Levinson and Link.

Ellery Queen ran for just 22 weeks. As the final installment aired in April of 1976, NBC announced that, due to poor ratings, it would not be renewing the show.

In Deadly Hate

With Fischer suddenly free, he was asked to write another *Columbo*. Fischer had a few weeks before he was to start his next regular gig, so he wrote a spec script inspired by Shakespeare's *Richard III*, the tale of a king's jealous, hunchbacked brother who manipulates, deceives and arranges the murders of his other brother, his nephew, and anyone else standing between him and the throne.

"I had a vision of some old king of England who was wandering around this big museum," Fischer recalled. "I could just see a little guy, a Burgess Meredith or somebody like that, running the place, everything but the hunchback."

Fischer completed his 86-page script, *In Deadly Hate*, on May 10, 1976.

A schoolteacher leads a small group of children through the English wing of the Costaine Museum. It's a sumptuously decorated edifice housing one of the world's foremost collections of European artifacts, concentrating on the Middle Ages and the Renaissance. Shields and armaments hang from the tall marble walls. Suits of armor line the corridors. As she leads, the teacher shares the history of the exhibits. The kids stare back at her with blank looks.

Off to the side stands the museum's curator, Richard Costaine. He's a smallish man in his early 50s, described as "courtly, with a well-practiced smile, whose eyes take in everything and reveal nothing. A true lover of the arts and a patron of gentility, he is in reality a Renaissance man transplanted to the 20th century, a man as at home with technology and progress as the mongoose with the cobra."

Costaine stares up at a large painting of Richard III being defeated at Bosworth Field, and nods to himself. Under his breath he quotes Shakespeare's *Richard III*: "Go, gentlemen, every man unto his charge. Let not our babbling dreams affright our souls."

Enter James Costaine, the younger of Richard's two nephews—tall, handsome, engaging. He approaches his uncle apprehensively, unsure why he's been summoned. Richard asks why James is still at the museum on a Friday afternoon. It's past 2:30.

But, James points out, it's also the last day of the month and his brother, Edward, is balancing the books. Richard says Edward wouldn't need *James'* help for that. Edward, though, made clear he wanted James' help. Richard

BURGESS MEREDITH, who had recently completed the horror film *Burnt Offerings* (1976) and was best known as the Penguin from the 1960s TV show *Batman*, was the original choice to play *In Deadly Hate's* malevolent museum manager, Richard Costaine.

smiles and instructs James to run along; he'll deal with Edward.

James is elated. As he hurries off, Richard looks back up at the painting and softly intones another *Richard III* quote: "Plots have I laid, inductions dangerous, by drunken prophecies, libels and dreams to set my brother, Clarence, and the king in deadly hate the one against the other."

Several hours later, Edward, up to his ears in paperwork, is incensed to learn that James has gone. Richard confesses that he gave James permission to leave. By whose authority, Edward demands to know. Richard's no longer in charge of the museum. *He* is. Richard had no right to let James leave. It's the 30th of April and the books must be closed out. Edward will be stuck taking inventory past 10:00 at night.

Ah, Richard mock-sympathizes, the burdens of responsibility. At least, Edward points out, the museum is finally showing a profit for the first time in 20 years. Richard isn't impressed, since he doesn't view turning a profit as the goal of such a "magnificent structure." It had better be profitable, Edward threatens, or he'll get rid of it.

"With your mother's blessing, of course," Richard interjects.

No, Edward says, he's calling the shots now. Edward also wants to know if Lewis Schafer, the private detective whom Richard hired, has discovered who's been pilfering the inventory. Because if the P.I. doesn't make headway soon, he'll be canned.

Schafer, meanwhile, has run off to the Costaines' weekend cabin, located in a remote area of the San Gabriel Mountains, about two hours from Downtown L.A. He lugs a carton from the trunk of his old Pinto to the front door. Schafer pulls a key from his pocket, unlocks the door, and enters. He sets the carton on a chair and from it removes a gold, jewel-encrusted goblet, wrapped in tissue. The phone rings. Schafer checks his electric-powered calendar watch. It's 4:30. He picks up the receiver. It's Richard, checking to make sure Schafer found the cabin and planted the evidence. Schafer says he's working on it, but he thinks the whole plan is screwy. Richard explodes. He will not be questioned! James left at 2:30. Edward will be working late. Schafer will proceed, as instructed. Schafer agrees.

Schafer hangs up the phone and removes a pistol from his jacket. He takes a bullet out, puts it in his pocket, and places a blank cartridge in the gun. Schafer then phones his wife, Nell, who's busy preparing dinner. He asks for a favor, with a sense of urgency. He needs his 35mm camera with the closeup lens right away. As he begins describing the camera, his voice breaks off. Someone's coming. "Hey—please!" he shouts. "No! Don't—"

A gunshot rings out over the phone line. Nell gasps. She calls for her husband, but there's no answer.

On the other end of the line, Schafer sets the receiver on the cradle. He removes the spent blank from his pistol and replaces the bullet.

Columbo responds to Nell's call to the police. She's upset and confused. She heard a gunshot and is certain her husband's dead. She doesn't know where he was calling from, but after the shot someone did hang up the phone. Since she didn't hear any coins being dropped in a slot, Columbo figures he wasn't calling from a phonebooth. He asks what case her husband was working on.

She says he had three active cases: investigating an accident for an insurance company, tracking down a Mr. Ciccarelli's 17-year-old daughter who's run away from home, and looking into some recent thefts at the Costaine Museum. She brings Columbo the files.

That night at the Costaine home, family matriarch Phyliss Costaine is entertaining friends. She's a feisty, gray-haired woman of great beauty and enthusiasm. Richard joins them, explaining that he had been on the phone purchasing a first-edition Chaucer from a rare-book collector in Tokyo. Phyliss wants to know if the purchase was approved by Edward. Richard gets testy. Phyliss promptly shuts Richard down, humiliating him. The other guests ask where Edward is. Phyliss says he's staying late at the museum—putting business first, just like his uncle. Richard pleasantly corrects her; he doesn't think they're at all alike.

Outside the museum, a shadowy figure approaches—Lewis Schafer. He pulls a stocking mask over his head. He uses a special tool to pry open a window. He silently climbs through. He crosses the corridor and heads for the stairway. Reaching the second floor, he stops outside an office where, inside, Edward is seated at his desk, working at a calculator and jotting down notes. Quietly, Schafer reaches through the half-open doorway and flips off the light switch. Edward looks up and demands to know who's there. Dead silence. Edward rises and walks toward the doorway. In the darkness, Schafer slides a hunting knife from his belt and raises it. Edward opens the door and steps into the hallway. From behind, Schafer grabs Edward around the neck and plunges the knife into his back. Edward gasps, then drops to the floor.

Schafer hurries down the stairs and crosses to a case containing antique jewels. With a glasscutter, he scribes a circle on top of the glass. Just then, he hears footsteps approaching. Schafer ducks back into the shadows. It's a security guard, who notices the scratches on the glass case. A shadow falls over it. Startled, the guard turns, to see a masked intruder, holding a gun by the barrel. Schafer strikes the guard on the head with the butt of the gun. The guard falls. Schafer returns to the display case.

The next morning, vehicles are parked all around the front of the museum, including several police cars, an ambulance, and a pristine beautiful Jaguar XJ6 sedan. Columbo's Peugeot rolls into the slot to the right of the Jag. Looking sleepy, Columbo opens his car door, inadvertently banging it into the side of the Jaguar. He bends down to see if he's nicked it. Meticulously, Columbo wipes at the spot with his finger, then polishes it with his coat sleeve. Satisfied that everything's fine, he starts off toward the museum entrance.

A cop inside brings Columbo up to speed—somebody broke in last night. Slugged the guard. Grabbed some jewels. Killed the guy who runs the place.

Lt. Donnelly has given orders to his men to check the grounds for footprints and tire tracks. He's now questioning the guard. When Donnelly hears Columbo is from Homicide he directs him to the dead guy upstairs. Columbo just has one question—who's the dead guy? Told it's Edward Costaine, who runs the museum, Columbo says he's working on a different case. Just then, two paramedics bring a stretcher down the stairs, carrying the sheet-covered body of Edward. They are followed by Richard and a "beefy cop" named Lt. Mal Jacobs. Columbo asks what happened. Richard says that a burglar stabbed his nephew. Lt. Jacobs adds that the killer used a bone-handled hunting knife, and it looks like an inside job. The perpetrator knew how to evade the alarm system and where to find the loot. But what's Columbo doing here?

He says he's looking for a private detective named Lewis Schafer. Columbo had heard Richard hired him about a month ago. Richard explains he brought in Schafer to investigate a series of thefts at the museum. Columbo reveals that yesterday, while Schafer was talking to his wife on the phone, there was a shot and the line went dead. Jacobs wonders if there's a connection between the two cases.

"I wouldn't know," Columbo replies. "I mean, maybe the guy's dead, maybe he's alive. Right now, I'm just trying to find him."

Columbo asks if Richard spoke to Schafer yesterday. Richard says no, it's been several days.

Actually, Richard plans to meet Schafer later that day at the cabin. Schafer is washing up. He starts to slip his calendar watch onto his wrist, then hesitates. He checks the kitchen wall clock and sets his watch to the proper date. As he finishes, he hears Richard drive up. The phone rings, but Schafer ignores it. He looks through the window as Richard exits the Jag and heads to the cabin door carrying a black valise. Schafer opens the door to let Richard in—and to let him know he's late.

"It would have been unseemly to hasten from the corpse too quickly," Richard says. He compliments Schafer on not answering the phone and assures him that the authorities are totally perplexed with the killing. But, not to worry, Richard will happily "help them unravel their tangled web—much to the consternation—and, I hope—the everlasting confinement of my nephew, James." Richard presumes that, in short order, James will be convicted of murdering his brother, by which time Schafer will be enjoying the good life on some remote island.

Schafer grins, thinking the scheme just might work. Of course, it would have been just as easy to kill them both.

"Easier, perhaps, but infinitely less satisfying, my dear Tyrell," Richard smiles, again referring to *Richard III*.

"Who's Tyrell?" Schafer asks, as he starts to open the valise.

"A man like yourself, Mr. Schafer. A hired assassin."

Schafer shrugs: "After today, I'm long gone."

"Aptly put, sir. Very aptly put," says Richard, as pulls out a .38 pistol and shoots Schafer dead. Richard wipes his prints off the pistol and puts it back in his pocket. He buries the body in a shallow grave outside the cabin, then rolls Schafer's car over an embankment into the thick underbrush below.

Columbo has gone to visit Schafer's client Antonio Ciccarelli. He finds the barber half-asleep in his barber chair, a copy of *Playboy* open in his lap. Columbo's arrival startles Ciccarelli from his nap. The barber takes one look at Columbo's long, uncombed hair and figures he has quite a challenge ahead of him. But Columbo's not there for a haircut; he wants to know if Schafer was working for him yesterday.

The name depresses Ciccarelli. He hired Schafer to find his daughter, then promptly *un*hired him. He hasn't seen him in a while. Schafer was happy to take his money and run up travel expenses traveling to Seattle, but never seriously looked for her. Turns out she's in Jersey City, married and pregnant. Well, at least pregnant.

At the Costaine home, Phyliss is distraught. Richard arrives to console her. She's not sure where James is. She assumes that, like usual, he went to the cabin to write. But when she called, no one picked up the phone.

Just then, the phone rings. It's James, calling from a payphone in a hotel lobby, with gorgeous gal-pal Julie standing silently, off to the side. He just heard about his brother on the radio. Lying, James says he's at a little roadside diner, not far from the cabin. He must have been down at the lake when she called. He hangs up and turns to Julie. He's got to go back. Julie feels badly for his brother and mother, despite how poorly they treated her. She asks if she'll see him again next weekend. James will try, but with his brother gone, he fears things are about to change. Thank goodness his Uncle Richard is around to run the museum again.

Columbo's Peugeot pulls into the Costaines' driveway and parks behind the Jaguar. As he starts toward the house, he notices dirt and mud on the fenders of Richard's car. Richard watches from an upstairs window. He's in James' boyhood bedroom, to hide the gun and the stolen jewelry. He quickly stashes them under the mattress and bolts downstairs.

Columbo apologizes to Phyliss. He doesn't want to bother her—he's come to talk to her brother. His kid-gloves treatment angers Phyliss. She doesn't want to be treated like "some doddering invalid." She'd be most happy to answer any questions about Edward's death.

But Columbo's not working on that case—he's looking for a Mr. Schafer. Richard reminds his sister that Schafer is the detective he'd engaged to look into the thefts at the museum. Columbo explains that Schafer had been fired from his last few cases. The robberies were the only one he was currently working on. He wonders if his disappearance is related to the museum break-in. Richard suggests that, since the police think the break-in was an inside job, the intruder might be the same person who committed the previous thefts… perhaps someone Edward recently dismissed. Costaine advises Columbo to check everyone's alibi for last night. The museum investigation is not under Columbo's authority, but he could probably look into it.

That night, Richard makes an anonymous call to Julie. Cryptically, he says that her friends in Kansas City miss her. Julie becomes alarmed. Who is it? Richard says it's someone concerned about her welfare. By tomorrow morning, the local authorities will know all about her sudden departure from Missouri 16 months ago. Click. Unnerved, Julie hurries to her bedroom to pack.

The next morning, gray skies hang over the cemetery for Edward's burial. Columbo watches from a bench, trying to light his cigar with a damp pack of matches. As the mourners file out, Columbo offers his condolences. This time, Columbo has questions for James; he's the only one without an alibi for the time of the murder. James insists he was at the cabin, alone.

Once back home, Phyliss announces she must call her lawyer, to formalize who will become the new head of the museum. The news perks up Richard—until he discovers that she wants James to be in charge. Richard is mortified. James knows nothing about running the museum. He'll learn, Phyliss assures him. After all, he is her son and, according to her late father's will, the decision is hers. And, besides, Richard nearly succeeded in destroying the place. James can hardly do worse.

"*If* he gets the chance," Richard murmurs. Pouring himself a brandy, Richard confesses that there's something Phyliss should know before she phones her attorney. Richard says that as soon as he heard about the break-in and Edward's murder, he drove to the cabin to inform James. Phyliss is afraid to hear what he discovered.

Columbo drives up to the cabin, where the sheriff has already uncovered mounds of museum artifacts inside, the Pinto buried in the bushes, and Schafer buried in the backyard. Columbo takes a closer look at the body. One shot—straight through the heart. Loaded gun, still in the holster. And his calendar watch, buried for four days and still running, with the precise time and date, May 5. In the Pinto's glovebox, a deputy turns up Schafer's passport—but it carries the name "George Thurmond."

Late in the night, long after operating hours have ended, Columbo arrives at the museum, where he finds Richard hunched over a table, magnifying glass in hand, reading a huge volume of Chaucer. With reverence, Costaine savors each cracked, yellowing page, "delight danc(ing) in his eyes as he nods to himself, his lips moving reflexively as he follows the lines."

Columbo looks over his shoulder. "What is that? Greek?"

"English," Richard replies, condescendingly.

But the first word, in fancy script, is unrecognizable: "What is that—'Fabbath'?"

"Sabbath," Richard corrects him with a weary sigh, lamenting the literary shortcomings of the current age.

Columbo didn't come to discuss literature. He reports that the items stolen from the museum have been recovered, but he wanted to tell Richard before informing his sister, because they were found at James' cabin... along with Schafer's corpse. Richard turns away, as if deeply shaken. He can't believe his nephew capable of such an act.

Searching the Costaine house, the police locate the gun and stolen jewelry under the mattress. James is indignant; he hasn't been in his old bedroom for years. Lt. Jacobs is triumphant and begins making his arrest. Columbo is doubtful; he can't believe James would be dumb enough to leave both stolen property and the murder weapon under his bed.

Jacobs is convinced. "Columbo, believe me, the guy's a bad apple," the officer says. "A few months ago, he was seeing a lot of some Vegas showgirl. His mother found out and threatened to cut him off. Kid like that—million-dollar appetite on a two-dollar meal allowance—trust me. You got your guy, too."

As Jacobs hauls off James, Columbo asks for just one favor. When Ballistics examines the gun, can they perform an additional test?

The next day, Columbo goes to Schafer's house to retrieve some receipts from the Costaine file, as well as the Thurmond file—Lionel and Betty Thurmond, a divorce case from a few years prior.

At police headquarters, Columbo calls all the airlines to find out if a George Thurmond was booked to fly out on May 1 or May 2. He's not having any luck. Until his phone rings. It's Julie, calling from a phonebooth, about to leave town on a bus. She won't divulge her name but wants to assure Columbo that James couldn't have killed his brother, because he was with her all night. Columbo presses her to come in with her evidence. She hangs up.

Columbo summons James to the interrogation room. James enters and crosses to a long wooden table in the center of the room. On top of it are an odd-looking metallic "ashtray" and a paper bag. Columbo asks James if he'd like some coffee. He digs into the paper bag and pulls out some sugar, creamers, a pack of cigarettes, and some matches. He tosses them onto the table. As James fixes his coffee, he asks why he hasn't also been charged with Schafer's murder.

"Maybe because I haven't heard your story yet," Columbo says.

James lights up a cigarette and insists he was mistaken about being at the cabin that day. No, Columbo corrects him, you lied. He tells James he knows he went to see Julie. He started seeing her six months ago. His mother found out. She threatened to disinherit him. "But you didn't stop seeing her," Columbo says. "You saw her a month ago, two weeks ago, last weekend…"

James insists Julie's a terrific girl, just maybe a little mixed up, which got her into trouble.

Like in Kansas City?

James, who's been flicking his ashes into the "ashtray," is amazed that Columbo seems to know everything. He confesses. He left the city about 3:00, got to Julie's place around 7:30, and let himself in. She got home from the casino around 10:00. Then three days ago, the Las Vegas police receive an anonymous tip regarding "her problem in Kansas City." By the time they arrived at her apartment, she was gone.

James squashes his cigarette in the ashtray. Columbo reaches over, picks up the tray, and dumps the contents into a trash bin. He then takes out a ratty old handkerchief, wipes off the ashtray, and sticks it in his raincoat pocket. Columbo assures James that he believes his story. James thinks he's being patronized. What about the jewelry and the gun? Ballistics checked out the weapon. They confirmed it was the one used to kill Schafer. But Columbo also had them check the butt of the gun. There were no traces of blood. Whoever broke into the museum hit the security guard over the head with the butt of their pistol. It was a hard blow. He bled a lot. If James were the thief, there should have been traces of the guard's blood on the gun butt.

At the museum, Richard has moved into Edward's office. He's just taken a call from the family doctor, who's concerned about his sister's fast-declining health. Richard says he'd like her to remain at home, where he "can take care of her." He then continues dictating a letter to his secretary, negotiating another big-money purchase for the museum. Columbo drops in. He heard about Phyliss' condition. Richard is sure she'll be fine, after she's had a chance to process the shock of Edward's death, followed by James' arrest.

Then Columbo may have good news for her. He just spoke with James, and is certain he didn't steal anything or kill anyone. He was in Nevada, seeing a woman—a Julie.

Ah, Richard, nods. The casino girl. But he and Phyliss assumed he'd stopped seeing her months ago.

Columbo is surprised. He thought Richard was aware they were still seeing each other every weekend. Didn't Mr. Schafer tell him?

Richard insists Schafer was investigating the burglaries, not his nephew's affair. Troubled, Columbo reaches into his pockets for a handful of receipts. Gas stations, motels, all in the Las Vegas area—for the past three weekends—as if Schafer were keeping track of someone's activities.

Richard says that's news to him. But is there any proof that James was in Las Vegas last weekend? No, Columbo says, but James said he got to the girl's house around 7:30, so there's no way he could have gotten to the cabin in time to kill Schafer or to the museum in time to plug Edward.

Richard then is confident the girl will corroborate James' story. Actually, Columbo says, the girl has run off. But he does have one piece of proof. He pulls the "ashtray" from his pocket and sets it on the desk.

Richard is mortified. "Good Lord, Lieutenant," he cries. "You don't carry this around like a peanut butter sandwich!"

Columbo swears he's been very careful with the object. Richard explains that it's five centuries old.

"Yes, sir," Columbo says. "You know that and I know that—but James didn't... He used it for an ashtray."

Richard is disgusted. But Columbo presses on. James doesn't care about any of the stuff in the museum. And he knows little about it. Columbo is convinced that he was framed.

Columbo visits a travel agency, where a clerk produces a thick envelope intended for George Thurmond. Reservations for seven sunny days on Waikiki, plus three days on the Big Island, with free golf and waterskiing. Thurmond was supposed to pick it up last Saturday afternoon. The clerk even stayed late at the office, but he never showed. A real shame, since the package was prepaid in full and nonrefundable. She asks Columbo to tell Mr. Thurmond how sorry she is that he missed out on his trip. Columbo promises to give him the message.

Columbo shoves the envelope into his pocket and heads for the Peugeot. He slips behind the wheel and turns the key. Click. Nothing. Click. Click. Click. Columbo droops in his seat, frustrated.

Columbo has the car towed to a mechanic, who seems to have met his match. But the repairman has a friend with a knack for finding spare parts for "priceless antiques." He thinks he'll be able to get a secondhand starter by 5:00. As Columbo begins to walk off, Richard's Jaguar pulls up next to him and rolls down his window. Richard asks if he's had lunch. Not yet, Columbo says, he was just going to grab a cheeseburger. Richard invites him to join him at St. George's.

The restaurant is a posh one, with an Old English motif. The Costaine family lawyer sits in a corner booth, waiting for them. The maître d' asks Columbo if he can take his coat. Columbo says he'll just wear it; his suit's a little wrinkled and he doesn't want to look out of place. Richard tells Columbo he asked him to lunch because he knows he's been checking up on his activities. Richard presumes Columbo was able to verify his alibi for the night of the museum break-in, when he was at his sister's dinner party, but not for the following morning. Columbo reveals that Richard's neighbors had confirmed he was out. Columbo suspects that he'd been up at the cabin. The night before, the Jaguar was sparkling clean, like it'd just been washed. But the next afternoon it was dirty, as if he'd been driving on dirt roads.

The lawyer contends Columbo is mistaken. Richard, however, says he's correct. Schafer had already told him he suspected James of the thefts. So as soon as Richard heard Schafer had been shot, he feared the worst. He sped to the cabin to see for himself. He found no sign of James, but there was Schafer on the floor, dead for 12 to 14 hours. Richard says he understands that he should have immediately called the sheriff; however, he feared his sister wouldn't be able to bear the news. So, he buried the body and hid the car.

The lawyer begs for leniency, asking Columbo to "consider Mr. Costaine's motives in judging him."

"Oh, yes, sir. You have my word on that."

After lunch, Columbo leaves to hail a cab. Before he can stop one, a driver waves him over. It's Julie. At police headquarters, she testifies that James was at her house Friday night and didn't leave until the next morning, after they heard the news on the radio. During the interrogation, Columbo calls Richard, to see if Julie can recognize his voice as the man who called to threaten her. She can't. Just then, James is led in. He and Julie embrace.

When Columbo goes to pick up his car from the mechanic, he notices the wrong date has been written on his bill. It doesn't match the date on the page-a-day calendar on the wall. The mechanic insists the date on the bill is correct—and to prove it, tears off the top page from the wall calendar. "Now it's right, see?" the mechanic explains. "Half the time I forget to change that thing."

A lightbulb goes off in Columbo's head.

At home, Phyliss sits in the living room with a blanket over her legs, looking very pale. She stares blankly ahead, the fight gone out of her. Richard arrives, pleased to see her finally out of her bedroom, getting some air. He bends over and kisses her on the cheek. He pours her a cup of coffee and urges her to drink. Meekly, she thanks her brother for trying to protect James. She's talked to the lawyer and, if things should go poorly for James, she's leaving the museum to Richard, along with money to keep it going.

They are interrupted by the arrival of the police, with Columbo escorting James—uncuffed. Richard is shocked. Columbo apologizes for bothering them, but thought they'd be pleased at the news. All charges against James have been dropped. His girlfriend stepped forward and verified his story under oath. Richard asks if Columbo thinks the girl might be lying to protect James.

He does not. So who, Richard asks, does Columbo think killed his nephew?

Mr. Schafer. That's strange, Richard says. He thought his nephew killed Mr. Schafer.

"No, sir. You did."

Richard scoffs. He was seen at the museum Friday afternoon. Was it his "spirit-like alter ego" who was off at the cabin shooting Schafer, who must have come back to life that evening to kill Edward?

Columbo says it's not difficult to square, once you realize that Schafer was actually killed Saturday morning. Columbo retrieves a shopping bag, sets it on top of the piano, and pulls out a birth certificate. It's for George Thurmond, who would be 40 years old—except that he died when he was 2. This certificate was mailed to Schafer's address. From the bag, Columbo removes additional objects which Schafer obtained with his phony birth certificate: a passport, a Social Security card, airline tickets to Hawaii, and confirmed reservations for a beach hotel—for May 1. Lewis Schafer had become George Thurmond. He intended to leave his wife to start a new life. The shot his wife heard on the phone was an act, to make her think he was dead.

Richard finds the speculations preposterous. So Columbo reaches in the bag, pulls out a gun, and points it at Richard. Richard asks if he's intending to shoot him or just trying to scare him into confessing. Columbo flips the pistol over, so he's holding the barrel and showing the butt. The gun is Schafer's, the one found in his holster. The lab detected minute traces of blood on the barrel that match the security guard's blood type. Schafer had sneaked into the museum, using information Richard had provided to avoid tripping the alarms. He killed Edward, hit the guard, stole the jewels, and returned to the cabin. When he woke up the next morning, he had no idea that May 1 was going to be the last day of his life.

IN DEALY HATE was completely reimagined as Season 6's *Old Fashioned Murder*, starring Joyce Van Patten. *[Credit: NBCUniversal]*

Columbo has one more goodie in his shopping bag—a man's gold watch. He looks at it. He checks the time against Richard's pocket watch. He has Richard confirm that the date on the watch is also correct—May 7. Had Schafer been dead on April 30, his watch would have automatically changed to the nonexistent date April 31 at midnight. But the date was correct, because Schafer was alive to manually change it to May 1.

Phyliss is stunned. What has her brother done? Richard turns at her wildly. He insists it's a trick. Phyliss pauses a moment, then reaches back and slaps Richard across the face. He recoils with a gasp. She stares hard at him, then turns away. Richard shouts at her not to turn her back on him. But she crosses over to James, and her son puts his arms around her.

Richard realizes the museum will never be his; his defeat is complete. "You took everything away," he says. "You gave it to them. My treasures. To them."

In Deadly Hate feels like a serviceable *Columbo*—in part because it's fairly derivative of earlier episodes. The victim staging a phone call to his spouse from a mountain cabin? *Murder by the Book*. The manager of a family business who obsesses over the past, invests in overpriced antiques, dismisses profits over quality, and kills a relative who threatens to sell the unprofitable venture? *Any Old Port in a Storm*. Copying the basic plot from a Shakespeare classic and having the murderer frequently quote the Bard? *Dagger of the Mind*.

Fischer's story was also short on clever clues, a big gotcha, and light-hearted character moments. Yet when *Roar of the Crowd* fell out, Chambers gave the green light to *In Deadly Hate*.

Falk appreciated receiving anything from Fischer, but he didn't want to do a conventional *Columbo*. He wanted a rewrite—but Fischer was now tied up with a mini-series. So Falk called in a favor from his friend, screenwriter Elaine May, who—with fellow script doctor Peter Fiebleman—changed most of the characters and completely revised the story… and continued revising even after the cameras had started rolling.

The production, now called *Old Fashioned Murder*, was scheduled to take 10 days to film. It took six weeks—with NBC and Universal finally shutting down filming on day 30. They'd have to cobble together something to air from the hundreds of thousands of feet of film that had already been shot. Fischer was so disgusted at what had been done to *In Deadly Hate*, he had his name pulled off the credits and replaced by a pseudonym, "Lawrence Vail"—the playwright character in George S. Kaufman and Moss Hart's *Once in a Lifetime*, who is driven insane by the ineptitude of a Hollywood studio. Indeed, *Old Fashioned Murder* so extremely diverged from Fischer's original story that, in a sense, one could consider *In Deadly Hate* to never have been made, fake credit or not.

Fischer certainly had plenty with which to keep himself busy. He immediately began writing for the mini-series *Once an Eagle*, created a few series of his own (*The Eddie Capra Mysteries, The Law & Harry McGraw*) and several with Levinson and Link (*Blacke's Magic, Murder, She Wrote*, which would run for 264 episodes and four TV movies over 13 years), and—as a favor to Falk, would return to *Columbo* in the 1990s to write three more (*Rest in Peace, Mrs. Columbo; Butterfly in Shades of Grey;* and *Strange Bedfellows*).

The Lesser of Two Evils

In July 1976, three weeks before filming began on *Old Fashioned Murder*, producer Everett Chambers was uneasy about his options for the last two shows of Season 6. He lacked confidence in *Murder in B Flat* and *Roar of the Crowd*, and was racing the clock to identify another option… until a spec script arrived from longtime TV freelancer Ken Kolb.

Kolb had started his 20-plus-year career in television in the mid-1950s, becoming a regular contributor to *Have Gun – Will Travel* and *Dragnet*. On the side, he provided a treatment for Ray Harryhausen's *The 7th Voyage of Sinbad*. In the 1960s, Kolb wrote for series like *The Rifleman* and *The Wild Wild West*, but what he really wanted was to be a novelist. His first book, *Getting Straight* (1967), was made into a movie with Elliott Gould three years later. Kolb followed with the novels *The Couch Trip* (1970) and *Night Crossing* (1974). All the while, he continued cranking out TV scripts to fund his novelist habit.

Like *The Couch Trip*, his *Columbo* spec script centered on a rogue psychiatrist, though this one with murderous motives. It similarly provided the opportunity for a fair bit of offbeat humor, by including the inimitable Sgt. Wilson. Kolb finished his 85-page script, *The Lesser of Two Evils*, on July 23, 1976.

The psychiatry office is opulent and imposing—with Dr. Michael Medford the centerpiece, tall, slender, with long silvery hair, a hand-tailored Italian suit, and a cool, penetrating voice. He meets with attorney Roger Simon. Rumpled and overweight, Simon cultivates a disorderly appearance to disguise his rapacious legal mind. Medford notes that, in his professional opinion, the crime was committed while the defendant was in a state of "diminished mental capacity."

Simon is incredulous. How can his client—a millionaire who runs a company with over 1,000 employees—plead diminished capacity? Medford theorizes that the tremendous growth of the man's business has placed him under such a strain that he can no longer make rational judgments in his personal life.

Simon shrugs: "Well, you're the doctor. And I've seen you make juries believe stranger things than that." Simon agrees to build his entire defense around Medford's testimony.

Medford shows him out of the office and returns to his desk, just as his next appointment arrives: muscular, menacing Charles Kingsley. Medford says he is surprised—but delighted—to see Kingsley. He asks what his former patient could possibly need, now that he has been legally certified as "cured." Just one little thing. Kingsley wants his $200,000 back. Medford, however, is not in the habit of returning "professional fees."

Kingsley says what he paid wasn't a fee; it was a bribe. Medford corrects him: it was a fee for his diagnosis, testimony in court, and subsequent treatment, which led to Kingsley's recovery.

Kingsley is tired of semantics. He leans forward and announces grimly: "It was a bribe, solicited by you. To lie under oath that I was crazy. To teach me to feign insanity, then later to feign sanity again."

Well, Medford surmises, maybe he's not cured after all, since this now sounds like the ravings of a madman. Maybe Kingsley should be recommitted.

Kingsley laughs smugly: "Not before I could ruin you forever. I have your original report on me, dated and signed by you."

Medford thought he had shredded proof of his initial diagnosis, in which he declared Kingsley sane and responsible for his actions. In truth, all he'd destroyed was a photocopy.

Kingsley says he's spent four years in the psych ward, while the doctor has been getting richer and richer through his schemes. He wants his share. He hands Medford a card with his address and tells him to meet him there that night, at 11 p.m., with a sizable payoff. Medford claims he can't raise more than $10,000 on such short notice. "That's a start," Kingsley taunts. "I'll be patient, as long as you keep paying… and paying… and paying…"

Desperate, Medford first drives to meet down-on-his-luck ex-con Harry Sloan, who's looking to leave town and start anew. Medford offers to fund his escape, for a favor. They drive to Kane's Coin Shop, where Medford is a regular visitor. The proprietor, Kane, asks if the doctor has come back for another look at a prized set of ancient Roman denarii. Medford says he's returned to see if he'd consider a more rational price. Kane laughs, as he opens a display case, removes three silver Roman coins, sets them onto the counter, and hands Medford a magnifying glass. Sloan walks in and asks to look at old British coins. As the clerk turns to help him, Medford reaches across the glass countertop and into the case, pressing his fingers against a glass shelf inside. A moment later, Kane rejoins Medford, who's interested in one of the coins, but not at Kane's price.

Back in the car, Sloan tells Medford he'd have little trouble with the shop's alarm system or the locks on the cases. Medford reiterates that he wants just the three coins he was looking at, nothing else. Sloan is confused. The doctor's loaded; why doesn't he just buy them? Medford says it's a matter of principle; the dealer burned him with a fake coin that he refuses to refund. If Sloan does just what he asks, there's $5,000 in it for him and a ticket to Mexico City the next morning.

At 11 p.m., Medford arrives at Kingsley's apartment, where the host is practicing putting golf balls on the carpet. Kingsley sets aside his putter and opens a bottle of wine. They discuss terms until an antique clock on the mantel chimes 11:30. Medford walks to the hearth to take a closer look at the timepiece. He "accidentally" knocks it to the floor. Kingsley erupts. As the hothead bends over to assess the damage, Medford grabs the golf club and whacks Kingsley's skull.

Medford proceeds with surgical calm. He checks for a pulse, but finds none. He slips on leather driving gloves, takes out a handkerchief, and carefully wipes his prints off the clock, putter and wine bottle. He leaves the bottle and Kingsley's glass on the table, then rinses out his own glass, dries it, and puts it back on the shelf. Medford then begins searching for the medical report, finally locating it folded inside Kingsley's wallet. He pockets it, along with the money from the victim's wallet, which he tosses onto the rug. He then yanks off Kingsley's watch, leaving deep scratches on his hand. To simulate a struggle, Medford tips over chairs, knocks over a lamp, and rips the drapes, before opening a window that leads to the fire escape. Finally, he takes out a glass hypodermic syringe, drops it to the floor near the body, and smashes it underfoot.

Later that night, Medford returns to his office to meet Sloan. The ex-con hands over the three coins, the garage door opener for Medford's office, and the keys to Medford's car and office. Medford pays him, as Sloan recounts how everything went according to plan: he picked up Medford's car, drove to the coin shop, cased it out, parked in the back, quickly bridged the alarm, cut a hole in the back window, jumped the alarm, and snatched the coins. Then, just before leaving, at precisely 11:30, he triggered the alarm. Medford explains that that final touch was intended to ruin the coin dealer's night of sleep, since he always goes to bed at 11:00.

A few hours later, a yawning Columbo arrives at Kingsley's apartment. He's intercepted at the door by young, overeager Officer Blake, who offers his thoughts on what took place.

"This your first homicide?" Columbo asks.

"Yes, sir," the rookie responds, surprised. "How did you know?"

Blake points to the wallet, which has been emptied of money. He shows Columbo the open window, through which the burglar must have entered. The killer was probably lying in wait for the victim to return, then jumped him, upsetting the furnishings. An anonymous caller to the police station—probably a neighbor—reported a fight. The intruder likely clubbed Kingsley with a putter, stole his money and watch, and fled, but not before dropping his syringe. Must have been a junkie.

Based on the temperature of the body, the medical examiner confirms the time of death as 11:30—the same time as is displayed on the broken clock.

Meanwhile, Detective Sgt. Wilson is investigating the burglary at Kane's Coin Shop. He determines that only three denarii were taken. He also spies the fingerprints inside the glass case and a distinctive tire track out back. Since many more expensive coins were left behind, Wilson postulates that the theft must be the work of a collector. He instructs Kane to make a list of everyone he has recently shown the missing coins to.

The next day, Columbo visits the courthouse to watch Medford on the witness stand. The doctor calmly, forcefully persuades a jury that attorney Simon's client "has been—and still is—in a condition of diminished mental capacity, which makes it impossible for him to make rational judgments in some situations."

After the testimony, Columbo catches up with Medford in the hallway. The Lieutenant congratulates him on his "performance." The doctor is flattered, though he doesn't consider giving legal testimony an act.

Columbo introduces himself. He's investigating the murder of a former patient, Charles Kingsley. Medford is sorry to hear that he was killed, but hardly surprised. He speculates Kingsley had a few drinks, got into an argument with a stranger, assaulted the man, and got himself killed.

Columbo confirms that's pretty much how the murder was set up to look. But the apartment belonged to Kingsley's brother-in-law. Why would he get himself killed defending it?

"Because that's the personality defect that made him kill his wife," Medford explains. "He had a history of flying into violent rages whenever he felt threatened."

Perhaps, Columbo admits. But why would a burglar enter a window with the occupant seated at the table, drinking? Medford speculates that Kingsley may have gone out for a while, and surprised the murderer when he returned.

But, Columbo wonders, why would he leave without putting the wine bottle back in the cooler? And the bottle was nearly finished, yet there was only one glass of wine in Kingsley's stomach. Columbo ponders: "Did he give the burglar two glasses of wine before he flew into a rage and killed him?"

Medford suggests that he'd opened the bottle previously. But, when Columbo asks, the doctor won't speculate on who might have wanted to kill Kingsley. He'll only say that the people who hated him most were those who really loved his wife whom he murdered.

Following Medford to his car, Columbo asks if the doctor had seen Kingsley after he was released. Medford says no. Columbo comments on Medford's car, noting it's beautiful but not too practical in bad weather. He must have a second car. Medford agrees, and drives off.

Columbo heads for a country club, where he tracks down Kingsley's brother-in-law, Warren Gray, on the golf course. Gray admits he recently had a run-in with Kingsley, who was upset over not inheriting anything from his dead wife. Gray is pleased to hear of Kingsley's demise. "He was a leech," Gray says, impatiently wanting to get on with his game. "He married my sister for her money, then killed her when he couldn't get at it."

And then, Gray fumes, the lowlife used a fraudulent defense to escape justice.

Columbo wonders if Kingsley was prone to violent rages. Never, Gray says. "He had ice water in his veins."

Gray promptly misses a three-foot putt and slams his putter to the ground. He notes that "some fiend" stole his lucky putter last week—the same type, it turns out, that Kingsley was struck with.

Wilson returns to the coin shop to update Kane on his progress: the police have issued a bulletin to all the local coin dealers and checked with the known fences—but there's still no sign of his missing coins. Kane isn't surprised. He knew it wasn't a professional job. Wilson says he's started going over the list Kane provided of customers interested in the denarii, but so far all have confirmed alibis. Kane notes Wilson still hasn't crossed out Medford—probably the likeliest of the remaining names. "He's a sorehead," Kane says. "Got all the money in the world, but he wants the best of every deal. He gives me a hard time, yeah."

That evening, Columbo calls on Medford at his imposing mansion. Inside, Medford is enjoying a drink—and some smooching—with a beautiful woman, Natalie. They hear the doorbell, but ignore it. As the ringing turns into urgent rapping, Medford promises to quickly get rid of their visitor. He reluctantly allows Columbo in, and has Natalie check the dinner while they talk.

Columbo asks if Medford thought Kingsley used Demerol; traces of the opioid were found on the broken syringe in his apartment, but it's not a common drug for junkies. Or did he prescribe Kingsley any when he last called on him—on the morning before he was killed? Columbo had confirmed Kingsley's visit with the security guard at Medford's office building. Medford reminds the Lieutenant that a doctor/patient relationship is confidential. "Whatever name you gave me, I would say I had not seen them," he declares. "That is not only my right, it's my duty."

Columbo takes his answer as confirmation that Kingsley visited him, as a patient. Medford says Kingsley's problems were more financial than mental. He'd asked for a loan and the doctor declined.

Columbo thanks him and is about to leave when he thinks of just one more thing: what was Medford doing Tuesday night, at the time of the murder? Medford says he was in his office, dictating into a recorder.

Their conversation is interrupted by footsteps at the door. It's Sgt. Wilson. He and Columbo exchange surprised looks. More police? Medford is beyond frustrated. Wilson presents a warrant to search the home. Inside Medford's wall safe, he discovers the stolen coins. It's enough evidence that Wilson will have to take Medford down to headquarters for questioning.

As they leave, Natalie reappears from the kitchen. Columbo explains Medford is suspected of burglary. "Burglary?" she says. "I don't believe it."

"I'll tell you something, ma'am… neither do I."

At police headquarters, Columbo and Wilson argue in the hallway outside the interrogation room. Wilson doesn't understand why Columbo is interfering in his investigation. Columbo says he can't believe Medford was committing burglary at the exact moment Kingsley was murdered. But Wilson is certain of precisely when the alarm was triggered, and that the fingerprints inside the case and the tire tracks outside the shop both belonged to Medford.

Just then, the doctor exits the interrogation room. He hands Wilson his signed statement and expects to be booked. But Wilson says Columbo wants him released, pending further investigation. Columbo points out that a man of Medford's stature, with a big court case coming up, would not skip town. He's sure that, in time, Sgt. Wilson will discover there's been a mistake. Wilson assumes that the mistake is Columbo's.

Columbo offers to drive Medford home. Medford looks at the Peugeot with disdain. "This is your car?"

"Yeah. They don't make 'em like this anymore."

As they drive off, Medford asks why the Lieutenant believes he's innocent since, in his experience, policemen are always inclined to believe the worst.

Columbo explains that burglary seems out of character for someone like him. And that all of the evidence is circumstantial. His fingerprints could have been left during an earlier visit. The tracks could match thousands of cars. "It's just a matter of you being able to prove where you bought the coins."

Medford says that might be difficult to prove. He paid cash—to a dealer who's since moved.

Columbo's not worried. He promises to do everything he can to clear

Medford. And, maybe in exchange, Medford can give him some help on the Kingsley case.

In the police lab, Wilson has lab tech Spinelli compare mud taken from outside the coin shop to mud from Medford's front tire. They're a perfect match. The testing is interrupted by a phone call from Kane, who had forgotten to mention earlier that he always places a drop of clear liquid on the backs of his rarest coins. It dries invisible, but glows under blacklight. He's been doing this ever since he had a customer return some fakes. Sure enough, under an ultraviolet lamp, a glowing dot appears on each of the three denarii.

"I can hardly wait to see the look on Lt. Columbo's face," Wilson chuckles.

The Lieutenant goes to interview Abel Foxworth, chief administrator of the institution that Kingsley was recently released from. Foxworth is disheartened to hear about Kingsley, whom he considers "one of our best examples of total rehabilitation." He shares how Kingsley's sanity rapidly improved following each visit by Medford, who had ultimately recommended his release.

Columbo then summons Medford and Gray to Kingsley's apartment. Neither is happy to be there. Columbo tries playing them against one another. He hands Gray the murder weapon and asks him if it belongs to him. Gray says no, but it's very much like his putter that was stolen. Columbo is confused, since the pro at the country club identified it as Gray's from repairs he had made to the grip.

Asked where he was at the time of the murder, Gray says he was at home with his wife. Columbo says Gray's wife disagrees: "She seems to feel that you're having an affair… or maybe several. Anyhow, she won't confirm your alibi."

Increasingly nervous, Gray explains he certainly was with someone *like* his wife. Medford now thinks Columbo invited him to help make a case against Gray. The doctor recalls that Gray threatened Kingsley during the trial. And Kingsley naturally would have been angry with Gray for keeping him from inheriting his wife's estate. Medford concedes Kingsley may have held a grudge against Gray: "Of course, I believed his hostility was fully under control, or I'd never have—"

Columbo interrupts: "Never have recommended his release?"

Suddenly, it dawns on Medford that Columbo has shifted the focus of his attack. Columbo wants to know why he continued seeing Kingsley after he was committed. And why, if Kingsley was brawling because he was subject to violent rage, did Medford think the man was cured.

Out of the blue, Sgt. Wilson appears in the doorway. Columbo is irked, but Wilson says he has an airtight case against the doctor and has come to arrest him for burglary. Medford goes along happily, momentarily pausing to tell Columbo, "I realize you were firing off a lot of wild shots in the hope of scaring up something, Lieutenant. I hope you'll see how ridiculous your suspicions have been."

As Wilson takes Medford away, Gray is now even more worried and uncertain about him being the target of the murder investigation. But Columbo has no use for him: "Go on home to your wife… or somebody who looks like her."

Later, at the courthouse, Columbo locates Roger Simon, just as the attorney is posting Medford's bail. A preliminary hearing on the burglary charge is set for 10 a.m. the day after next. Columbo offers to help prove his client's innocence—if the lawyer will help prove where he was that night, if he wasn't in the coin shop.

At the police lab, a triumphant Wilson displays his proof to an increasingly puzzled Columbo. They then visit the coin shop, where Columbo makes several deductions. First, Medford could have left his fingerprints inside the glass case while the clerk was distracted. Second, on the night the coins were stolen, the case's lock must have been picked. Finally, Medford would have had to drive out of his way to park in the mud. Columbo also wonders, if the alarm had been tripped when the burglar broke in, how the crook would have had time to then steal the coins and escape, since the police were on the scene within four minutes.

They head for the police impound garage for a closer look at Medford's car. Columbo is suspicious since Medford still had mud on his car several days after the burglary, yet there were no prints—except Medford's—anywhere inside the vehicle. Wilson is beside himself. He's got Medford's car at the scene. Medford at the scene. Medford with a motive for stealing the coins. And the coins in Medford's safe. What more does Columbo want?

"I want him an hour away at the time of the burglary," Columbo explains.

On their way out, Columbo asks Wilson about something he'd overheard: Wilson warning Kane not to file false insurance claims in the event he suddenly discovers additional items "missing." This suggestion gives Columbo an idea.

At the next morning's hearing, Columbo is stunned to see Medford, in light of the evidence, plead no contest. The doctor offers to pay full restitution to Kane, plus any damages the court may assess. The court consents, and instructs the defendant and his counsel to return at 10 a.m. Monday for sentencing. Wilson exchanges congratulations with the assistant district attorney, Mark Collier, before going over to Columbo to gloat.

Later, Columbo heads to Medford's house, humbled and apologetic.

Having officially established his murder alibi, Medford no longer has anything to fear from Columbo. A gracious winner, he cheerfully welcomes his beaten adversary and has him join him in the living room, where he's polishing part of his coin collection. Columbo apologizes for his suspicions, but simply must know: why would a man in his position go to so much trouble and take such a risk?

Medford can see Columbo knows nothing about rare coin collecting. He holds up a gold aureus from ancient Rome. So beautiful, Columbo enthuses. Yes, Medford agrees, but fake. It's the reason he decided to burglarize Kane's shop. He felt compelled to even the score. But why didn't he hire a professional to steal it? Medford says he didn't know anyone: "What could I do—advertise?" Considering he was such an amateur thief, it's no wonder he was quickly found out.

That's something else that's been bothering Columbo. Medford had left a trail of clues that led right to him… almost as if he'd wanted to be caught. Medford chalks it up to perhaps subconsciously wanting to be discovered, to ease his feelings of guilt. Is that why he left the coins where they could easily be found?

"The true collector must have his collection where he can see it, feel it, enjoy it," Medford says. "To steal the coins and bury them somewhere would have been truly irrational."

As Columbo rises to depart, he thinks of just one more thing: Medford's collection appears to be entirely Roman coins, correct? Yes, all serious collectors specialize in a particular period or country. Otherwise, it's just an accumulation, not a collection.

"In that case, sir," Columbo asks, "why did you steal the English gold sovereign of 1489? I believe it's called the Henry VII sovereign."

Medford looks shocked, but it dawns on him that Sloan must have snatched the sovereign for himself. He has to cover. Medford explains that it's such a unique, beautiful coin that it needs no collection around it. He felt he was owed it, and promises to reimburse Kane for its value.

After Columbo has left, Medford heads for a small, upscale travel agency, to purchase airfare to Mexico City under an assumed name. A short while later, Columbo visits the travel agent to learn where "Mr. Smith" is going—and that Smith earlier paid cash for a one-way ticket to Mexico City for the day after the burglary.

Columbo's next stop is the police impound garage, for another look at Medford's car. He sits in the driver's seat, places his feet on the pedals, and grasps the steering wheel. Suddenly, he breaks into a big smile.

Come Monday, Columbo arrives a few minutes before the start of sentencing. He takes assistant DA Collier aside to request that he be allowed to speak his piece before any deal is finalized. The judge enters and confirms that an agreement has been reached. Simon vows his client is prepared to make full restitution. Collier agrees, but asks that Lt. Columbo be heard before they proceed.

Columbo rises from his seat in the gallery and announces that Dr. Medford did not commit the burglary and that he's prepared to prove it. Both sides murmur until the judge raps his gavel for order. The judge is perplexed. He thought Columbo would be speaking for the prosecution.

Columbo says he is. That all of the evidence previously presented by Sgt. Wilson was planted by Dr. Medford "for a misleading purpose." He explains how Medford set everything up so that he could be an hour across town murdering Kingsley. And how, once released from the hospital, Kingsley—now dead broke—came after Medford for money and must have threatened to expose his racket of falsifying his diagnoses. Columbo had first suspected him when he saw that Kingsley was killed by a blow to the base of the skull—an unlikely spot to get hit during a fight, but—as a doctor would know—the most vulnerable place for a fatal strike. Also, the planted syringe had traces of Demerol—uncommon for druggies but not for doctors.

Columbo asks that Dr. Medford stand, to illustrate just how tall he is. Columbo notes the doctor is much taller than someone like himself of "average height." Yet his car seat was positioned just right for the detective to reach the pedals. So he checked the adjustment lever under the seat and came up with a perfect print of Harry Sloan, a convicted burglar. Columbo has already contacted Mexican police to locate and detain Sloan. The Lieutenant shows the receipts for Sloan's and Medford's airline tickets. Columbo admits he "had to tell a little white lie" about another expensive coin being stolen so Medford would think Sloan took it for himself, and would follow him to Mexico to get it back before Sloan tried to sell it.

The judge instructs Wilson to take Medford away. His Honor congratulates Columbo, and tells him he would have doubted his entire story, except for one thing: he couldn't imagine someone with Medford's standing giving up without a fight. That's exactly why it made such a good alibi, Columbo explains. Nobody would have thought he'd have pinned it on himself. But, the judge says, even a suspended sentence would have been a disgrace.

"Maybe so, sir," Columbo surmises. "But he could still practice… and compared with a murder conviction, it was sure the lesser of two evils."

SCREENWRITER Kenneth Kolb's *The Lesser of Two Evils* was so well received, he was assigned to script a *Columbo* set in Japan. Neither were produced.

The plot was an ingenious one, if a touch far-fetched. The doctor repeatedly issuing then retracting insanity diagnoses should have played itself out in short fashion, once the DA had noticed that everyone the doctor deems crazy he later declares to be perfectly fine. Juries would stop believing Medford, as, too, would parole boards.

Although Falk resisted recurring characters, thinking they would grow repetitive, Kolb brought a fresh dynamic to Columbo and Wilson's relationship by, instead of having them work together, having them work against each other. In fact, the character who acts most like Wilson usually does isn't Wilson at all, but Officer Blake.

One definite change would have to have been the name of the assistant

DA, Mark Collier—since that was name of the murderous psychiatrist played by George Hamilton in Season 4's *A Deadly State of Mind*.

Chambers liked Kolb's script so much, he pegged it as the third show of the sixth season and tasked Kolb with writing the fourth show—to be set in Japan. Chambers even had Kolb accompany him to Japan to check out locations and get inspiration for his writing.

At Falk's insistence, Chambers passed *The Lesser of Two Evils* on to Peter Fiebleman to do a rewrite—one that was never submitted because, before Fiebleman could finish, Chambers was fired. The series was placed on pause until Universal could find a new producer, and Universal paid off Fiebleman to be rid of him, once and for all. In early 1977, Richard Alan Simmons took over as executive producer and promptly discarded all preexisting scripts. He wanted to generate all the story ideas himself.

Over the next year, Kolb wrote a few more teleplays for other short-lived series, then he was done. Still, about a decade later, his old novel *The Couch Trip* would be turned into a movie starring Dan Aykroyd and Walter Matthau.

6
Season 8 (1989)
The Return of the Raincoat

After executive producer Richard Alan Simmons completed Season 7, NBC did not renew *Columbo*. Instead, the network had Levinson, Link and Fischer develop a new show they thought would appeal to *Columbo's* large fanbase, but would be hipper and less expensive to produce: *Mrs. Columbo*. They envisioned a frumpy middle-aged Italian woman in the lead. After submitting the script for a pilot, they learned the series would instead star 23-year-old Kate Mulgrew. All three writers walked out.

Simmons stepped in to take over. Just as he did with *Columbo*, he tossed out any earlier writing and developed his own. The audience was not fooled. The series was retooled time and again, to remove more and more vestiges of *Columbo*. The ratings worsened, until NBC finally pulled the plug.

Over the next 10 years, various forces tried to revive *Columbo*. Falk remained interested in making an occasional special, perhaps one a year, but his movie career had taken off and he didn't have the time for a full season. Yet a series seemed to be the only thing a network was interested in. It took a full decade before Falk's schedule sufficiently loosened and a new network, ABC, was amenable to a short-run program, again as part of a rotating wheel. The network had lined up Burt Reynolds (in *B.L. Stryker*) and Lou Gossett Jr. (in *Gideon Oliver*), but it needed a known commodity as a headliner. It needed *Columbo*, and Falk—ever indecisive—was on the fence. He wanted to look over about a half-dozen scripts in advance, to make sure that the writing would be up to the standard of the best shows from the NBC years.

ABC turned to Bill Link; Link was offered the job of executive producing the entire wheel, if he could convince Falk to return to the raincoat. He knew Falk was only interested in a sure thing. He'd want familiar yet fresh. So, Link called on prior *Columbo* writers, like Jackson Gillis and Robert Van Scoyk, to help dream up scenarios to pitch to Falk.

Untitled Courtroom Story

The 59-year-old Van Scoyk had written for dozens of TV shows, including Peter Falk's earlier series, *The Trials of O'Brien*, and *Columbo's Murder Under Glass*. He had also served as story editor on Levinson and Link's *Ellery Queen* and *Banacek*, and was finishing up the fourth of his five seasons as executive story editor for *Murder, She Wrote*.

On January 8, 1988, Van Scoyk submitted a six-page, untitled scenario.

This year's "in" car pulls up in front of a Bel Air mansion. Out climbs a man in a tailored suit; we'll call him R.J. R.J. walks to the door and rings the bell, to be greeted warmly by his Best Friend, who assures him that they're alone in the house. His buddy's wife is away rehearsing for a charity show.

We jump to the Best Friend's wife in rehearsal; let's call her Jill. She's 30, and beautiful in spandex. She's also very conscious of the time; she has something urgent to discuss with her husband before he goes to bed. He's much older, tires easily, and sleeps in his own bedroom. Jill is young, vital and tireless.

Back at the mansion, the Best Friend has summoned R.J. because he's just learned that he is dying. R.J. is not surprised; he knew his friend had an appointment with a specialist, and surmised that that's why he had been invited to the empty house. Best Friend has come to grips with the doctor's news, but he needs to take care of one last thing before he passes. He knows his wife and R.J. had formerly been lovers, until she left R.J.'s charm and good looks in pursuit of his own money and power. Best Friend knows R.J. is still in love with his wife, and he gives him his blessing to take care of her and make her happy after he's gone. "She'll have all the money she can ever hope to spend, but needs someone to love her," Van Scoyk wrote in his treatment. "The visitor promises he will honor his Best Friend's request, and has even developed a plan for bringing it about."

R.J. bids his buddy goodbye, then flashes a small automatic weapon. He fires. Best Friend collapses to the floor. He's still alive, barely. R.J. didn't want to him to die immediately, but over several minutes, by internal bleeding. Fatally wounded, the friend staggers to his feet, egged on by R.J., who says his only chance to survive the night is to throw open the window and cry for help. "A single small caliber gunshot would pass unnoticed—but a human cry, even in this isolated corner of Bel Air, might attract someone's attention." In desperation, the wounded man complies. He slowly pulls open the window, but the effort drains him. He's too weak to cry out. His legs buckle. His eyesight fails.

R.J. wipes his own fingerprints from the gun, and places the weapon into his friend's hand. He now tells his friend to shoot him… if he can. "The weakened man places his finger on the trigger, trying to aim at the shadowy fading figure of his killer, but there is nothing left." The victim falls to the floor, lifeless.

R.J. carefully retrieves the gun, so as not to leave any prints. He leans out of the window, and tosses the gun up onto the roof. He listens as the firearm slides down the shingles before coming to rest in the rain gutter. "Satisfied, he says goodbye to his old friend, his best friend, assuring him that his last request will be granted."

Jill, meanwhile, has finished rehearsal. As she leaves, she tells a friend she hates the task that awaits her at home, but it must be done. She must tell her husband that she's leaving him.

Jill arrives home. Her husband's car sits in the garage. She goes upstairs and knocks on his bedroom door. No answer. She checks her watch. It's late. She'll talk to him in the morning. She goes to her bedroom, undresses and showers.

In the morning, Jill is awakened by rapping on her bedroom door. It's a police officer who requests she come downstairs. "Lt. Columbo would like to see you in the den," the officer announces.

Jill grabs a robe and heads for the den, where Columbo is bending over her dead husband. She screams in horror. She's so rattled, the medical examiner leaves the body to make sure she's okay.

Columbo quickly moves on to the open wall safe. It's empty. When Jill is finally able to speak, she reveals that her husband always kept wads of cash in the safe— $350,000 at last count.

Columbo locates the cash in Jill's safety deposit box, along with love letters her dead husband allegedly wrote to an unknown woman, announcing that he'd decided to leave his wife for her.

The case against Jill is mounting—there's the money, the letters, no alibi, her asleep in the house, and an admission that she no longer loved her husband. But what happened to the murder weapon? The police turn the house upside down, but can't find it.

And why was the window open? Columbo searches the ground outside, but there's no gun, footprints or fingerprints—just the victim's prints on the *inside* of the window.

With no gun, he obviously could not have killed himself. He was dead by the time the maid had arrived that morning. "The wife's name goes to the top of the shortlist. It *is* the shortlist."

The district attorney is positive he can get an indictment. Columbo advises Jill to get a real good lawyer. So she turns to her dead husband's lawyer—R.J.! Of course, R.J. will defend her. He knows she's innocent and someone is framing her. That's not so obvious to Columbo, but he's open to being convinced.

R.J. visits the scene of the murder with Columbo, running through what he thinks might have happened. It's a plausible scenario, but nothing like what really happened. Columbo is enthralled. He's never before met a lawyer who's able to get inside a victim's head like R.J. can. It's uncanny… almost like he was there when the murder took place.

The media loves the murder. Reporters play up the drama, punching holes in Jill's story and elaborating on her motives. They're trying the case before it even goes to court. "Viewers of *The Eleven O'Clock News* become well acquainted with the tragic-but-beautiful young woman and her attorney. All the while, the widow clings to her attorney, her protector, depending on him, believing in him, renewing old feelings, wondering why she ever left him for the husband who is already growing dim in her memory. She is falling in love with him all over again. As planned."

Jill is put on trial for murder. Her loving lawyer introduces the coroner's report, which reveals that her husband was dying of an incurable disease. Initially, the revelation appears irrelevant to the case, but it's only an opening move for R.J. Now he just needs Columbo to find the murder weapon.

Alone at the scene of the crime, Columbo eyes the den window. He slides it open and leans out. He looks down… then to the right… then to the left, and, disappointed, pulls his head back into the room. He paces, talking to himself… until it hits him. Columbo hurries back to the window, sticks his head out, and this time looks up at the roof.

Columbo fetches a ladder from the garage and struggles to set it up outside the window. The gardener begs him to mind the flowerbeds. Columbo assures him that he'd never harm a flower. Columbo asks the gardener to steady the ladder as he begins climbing. Just then, the DA shows up and wants to know what the heck Columbo is doing.

"I'm testing a law," Columbo explains. A law? "The law of gravity. Whatever goes up has gotta come down someplace." Columbo reaches up and, sure enough, there's the automatic in the rain gutter. The question is, why?

Back in court, R.J. calls Columbo back to the stand. He wants to introduce the newly discovered gun as evidence. The gun is tagged. The attorney asks if the gun was tested for prints.

"Yes."

"And whose prints were found on the gun?"

"Nobody's," Columbo replies.

The attorney is flabbergasted. "Was every part of the weapon tested?"

Columbo asks to see the gun for a moment. Pointing to each part of the weapon, Columbo testifies that he had Ballistics check the grip, the barrel, the trigger, the chamber…

R.J. looks closer at the gun Columbo's holding—it's a *pistol*! "Lieutenant, are you positive this is the gun you found in the rain gutter?"

Columbo pauses, suddenly having second thoughts. He's *pretty* sure it is. You know, a lot of guns look alike, especially if they're about the same size. He drones on about the subject of identification to the point of exasperation. Finally, the judge asks the defense attorney to interrupt his witness and get to the point. R.J. says he is convinced that there has been a miscarriage of justice. He believes that this is not the same gun Lt. Columbo found. Turning to his witness, R.J. declares, "This is a *pistol*. Wasn't the gun you found an *automatic*?"

The DA objects: "Leading the witness!" But Columbo smacks his forehead. He thinks the attorney is right! He brought two guns with him, he explains, so he could compare the weapons during his Ballistics testimony and demonstrate the differences to the jury. The sergeant must have handed him the wrong gun. The officer apologizes, and hands over the pistol, which Columbo positively identifies, all the while apologizing for his confusion. Oh, yeah, he remembers now—there *were* prints on the gun he found in the rain gutter. The *other* gun didn't have any prints on it, but that was from another case. "It's all straightened out now—this is the murder gun that had fingerprints on the barrel, the grip, the trigger," Columbo smiles.

The defense attorney dramatically asks, "And *whose* prints were on the gun?"

"The *victim's* prints."

"The victim's *wife's* prints?"

"No, sir. Only the victim's. *That* I'm sure of."

"Lieutenant, can you draw any conclusion from this fact regarding the weapon?"

"Yes, sir. The victim must've shot himself, then tossed the gun up on the roof to get rid of it."

"And why, in the Lieutenant's professional opinion, would the victim want to get rid of the *suicide* weapon?"

"Well, maybe to keep people from finding out it was a suicide."

Amid a shower of objections from the DA, the defense attorney turns to the jury and suggests, "Or maybe he wanted to frame his innocent wife for murder!" This way, R.J. argues, instead of waiting to succumb to the painful disease, he could extract revenge on his unfaithful wife from beyond the grave.

Jill is shocked by the suggestion. But it does make a crazy kind of sense: *somebody* framed her.

The judge gavels the courtroom back to some semblance of order and cautions both sides to refrain from further outbursts. Columbo then asks if he can question the defense attorney about something that's not clear to him. "Why not," sighs the long-suffering judge.

Columbo begins, "No, I can see what you're driving at about the victim being sore at his wife, and maybe being so far over the edge that he'd even kill himself in order to make it look like she did him in." The DA begs him to stop: "Lieutenant! You're the prosecution witness!" The judge instructs Columbo to stick to his question.

What Columbo wants to know is, how did the attorney know he was handling the wrong gun? "In order to know that, you'd have had to see the right gun before it was tossed on the roof. And to do that, you must've been in the room when the murder took place. I'm sorry, I must not be thinking straight, because all this time I figured there were only two people in that room: the victim and the killer."

Shaken, R.J. is about to reply when Columbo reminds him that he has the right to remain silent… and the right to an attorney.

In Van Scoyk's earlier *Murder Under Glass,* a famous chef injects blowfish poison into a bottle of wine using a syringe through the cork. It was a promising scenario severely weakened by gaping plot holes, and by characters—especially Columbo—acting in counterintuitive ways. This new story suffered from the same problems, only magnitudes worse.

The absurdities begin right out of the gate. Most ridiculously, why would R.J. kill his closest friend upon hearing that the old guy only had months to live and wanted his wife to get back together with R.J.? The night of the murder, why would R.J. have even thought to bring a gun with him?

R.J. is willing to torture his friend by keeping him alive just long enough for him to call for help and fire his gun. This would have increased R.J.'s chance of either being caught or being shot himself. And, once mortally wounded and in possession of the gun, why would the friend need to shoot at the now-unarmed R.J.?

If witnesses had heard the victim's scream, why did the police wait until the next morning to visit his house? And if no one had heard the scream, why did the police show up at all? Then, once they arrived, how come they didn't wake the wife before entering? What kind of murderer would Jill be if she killed her husband and then went straight to bed, leaving his corpse on the floor?

Hardest of all to believe is the stunt Columbo pulls on R.J. in court, as he misrepresents evidence and lies under oath. Columbo often bends the law to trick killers into showing their hand, but this time he flat-out breaks it—while on the witness stand. What makes him suspect R.J. so strongly that he'd risk his reputation if not his badge remains a mystery. And, worst of all, the point of the stunt—meant to be a surprising gotcha—is easy to anticipate.

Still, Falk liked Van Scoyk's writing and eventually agreed to revive the series. Yet once Richard Alan Simmons was brought back to serve as executive producer, he characteristically discarded all previous stories in favor of generating his own.

In time, Falk would take over as executive producer and bring back Van Scoyk in 1991 to polish *Death Hits the Jackpot* and to adapt the Ed McBain novel *So Long as You Both Shall Live* into *No Time to Die*.

Last of the Redcoats

As newly reinstated executive producer, Richard Alan Simmons had a list of requirements for an acceptable *Columbo* script. First, the script needed a powerful, fascinating villain with a backstory. The murderer should be modeled after a newsworthy celebrity (think Steven Spielberg as the inspiration for the hotshot young director in Season 8's *Murder, Smoke and Shadows*, or Dr. Ruth Westheimer for the sex therapist in *Sex and the Married Detective*).

Ideally, the crime or motive should also be torn from recent headlines (such as the accidental, movie-set death in *Murder, Smoke and Shadows*, which evoked the tragedy filming *Twilight Zone: The Movie*, or the psychic Uri Geller/Amazing Randi feud, which served as the basis for *Columbo Goes to the Guillotine*).

Sometimes freelancers would pitch ideas to Simmons, but more often Simmons would come up with the basic plot himself and hand it off to a grizzled pro, someone like Millard Kaufman. Kaufman was a highly decorated screenwriter—in the 1950s and 1960s, after a stint working in cartoons. Most famously, Kaufman had co-created the character of Mr. Magoo. He'd then quickly made a name for himself in features, earning Academy Award nominations for *Take the High Ground!* and *Bad Day at Black Rock*. By the mid-1970s, the feature offers had started to dry up, so producer Stanley Kallis lured the screenwriter into television, having him doctor a script for *Police Story*, and then having him write one of his own. Kaufman would co-write two made-for-TV movies—*The Nativity*, directed by *Columbo* regular Bernie Kowalski, and *Enola Gay*, produced by Kallis. But soon he found himself unable to sell anything—even to television. A decade later, Kallis called again—with an offer to write for *Columbo*. Kaufman was 72.

For Simmons, his age was a plus. He, too, had suffered the hardships of age discrimination in Hollywood. Simmons wanted to work with older, seasoned professionals, preferably those with whom he had worked before. He instructed Kaufman on the exact type of villain and setup he was looking for—a Barbara Walters-type celebrity interviewer willing to do anything to get a one-on-one with a reclusive, now-middle-aged rock star. Simmons greenlit Kaufman's six-page treatment to expand into a 121-page screenplay, *Last of the Redcoats*, which was completed on April 10, 1989.

A young and vibrant 40, celebrity interviewer Linda Hale is dining in the penthouse apartment of rock legend Andrew Braden. He's the last living member of the Redcoats, the legendary English trio that revolutionized the pop music of our times. Hale first interviewed him 18 years earlier, "a little ol' shirttail girl fresh out of Texas," and that led to their spending the weekend together. She questions why, 15 years ago, Braden walked away from music and turned off his "talent like a tap."

He shrugs, explaining he was good at his work, but bad at living. She likes the quote and reaches into her purse for a small pad and pen. He stops her, angrily. Those words were for her—not "for those cretins out there in TV land." She is to make no notes or recordings without his permission. And no explosive questions.

Hale acquiesces but, in depositing her pen and paper, she surreptitiously starts up a portable tape recorder she'd hidden inside her purse. Braden admits that, over the years, he's often thought of her—and their weekend together. "You were absolutely, irrepressibly... primitive," he says. "It was like... like wrestling a velvet alligator."

She thinks it's about time for a repeat performance.

The next morning, after they say their goodbyes, Braden phones to have the elevator sent up for her. Just arriving is his aide, Ian Macdavey. Braden has a few chores for him. Braden opens a massive walk-in refrigerator to see what food he'll need picked up. He also wants a particular book, as well as a few thousand dollars from the bank.

Hale is off to work at the TV network. Her assistant, Annie Stewart, and her boss, Victor, the vice president of specials, are waiting, anxious to hear if she's gotten a commitment from Braden. It's been a while since she's had a big scoop and her contract is up for renewal.

"I have stormed his fortress," Hale says. "I have penetrated his inner sanctum." Braden, she says, is interested, but has a few reservations.

During her meeting with Victor, Braden calls to say he's consented to her request. She should stop by his apartment at 7:00 to discuss. She's surprised. Victor is ecstatic and hugs her. She's to return to his office at 9:00 with the details.

That night, while sipping wine by the fire, Braden shares with Linda why he lives like a hermit: "The whole world's a prison. My cell has two advantages: it supplies my rather simple needs, and it keeps people out."

She notes that his "simple needs" appear to require a refrigerator as big as the Ritz. Braden says he can live without music or books, but not fine dining.

As Hale walks to the fireplace to jab a log with a poker, Braden glances inside her purse. He sees the tape recorder, and explodes. She apologizes profusely, explaining how badly she needs him on her show.

Braden confesses he never had any intention of appearing. He was only leading her on to see how far she would crawl. He continues belittling her, as her frustration boils. She can't stop herself any longer and whacks him with the poker. He collapses. She's mortified. She quickly drapes a towel around his head, drags his body into the refrigerator, and turns down the temperature dial. She places Scotch tape over the striker on the back door, so it won't lock when closed. She then phones for the elevator, and plays her recording from last night of Braden saying, "My guest is leaving."

Visibly exhausted, Hale arrives at her meeting with Victor. She assures him that Braden is all-in. She then heads back to the apartment building, and enters through a fire door inside the parking garage. She gets inside Braden's penthouse via the taped-up back door. She opens the refrigerator door, but there's no body—only a bloody towel and a mess of jars and tins, presumably knocked over by Braden.

Hale discovers the lifeless body on the floor of the study. She washes the poker, cleans up the mess inside the fridge, and returns the dial to the proper temperature. She grabs a book from a shelf, sits at Braden's desk, puts on her tortoiseshell glasses, and types a passage from the book into the computer. To momentarily catch her breath, she removes her glasses, sets them beside the computer, and rubs her eyes. Reinvigorated, Hale drags the corpse to the balcony and hoists it on top of the railing—just as the phone rings. The voice belongs to Ian Macdavey; he's heading up with the book Braden requested. Hale tosses the body down 14 stories, hurries back to the study, and grabs her purse, just as Ian walks in. She ducks behind a Chinese screen.

Ian notices a light on in the study but, before he can investigate, he hears screams from the street below. He strides to the balcony and sees Braden's crumpled body. Quickly, Ian heads to the bedroom, giving Hale an opportunity to slip out the back door. Ian, meanwhile, places the money he withdrew from the bank into a pillowcase. He retrieves additional stacks of bills from the nightstand and a humidor, and adds that cash to his stash. He then hides the pillowcase in a bin inside the refrigerator.

Later that night, Hale returns yet again to the apartment, now a busy police scene. Columbo is investigating. He recognizes her immediately. She spies the poem typed up on the computer:

*"The time has come to say goodbye
To friends and lovers, earth and sky.
We press toward nothingness soon or late,
There's no such thing as an opiate.
Why wait?"*

Columbo remembers the song. He and Mrs. Columbo really enjoyed Mr. Braden's music. Hale says Andrew wrote the lyrics shortly after the first of the Redcoats died.

Columbo walks out onto the balcony. He detects a small gem, from Braden's vest, on the floor. He places his hands on the railing, but notices they get grimy from the filthy rail. Yet Braden's hands were clean. He must never have touched the rail—but then how would he have managed to climb over it?

The next morning, Hale is having breakfast with her agent at the Polo Lounge at the Beverly Hills Hotel. He informs her that, since Braden is dead, she has no show and the network is not going to renew her contract. They are soon joined by Columbo. Hale's assistant had told him she'd be there. Breakfast sounds good—until he sees the menu. Eggs and sausage, $21.50. Informed the price is not a typo, Columbo decides to stick with coffee. He delicately tries to ask if she and Braden were more than friends. Hale is dismayed by his indirect interviewing style. "Let me give you a few invaluable hints," she advises. "Hit hard. Dig deep. Sympathize with a silvery smile, with an air of spontaneity and nonchalance. Be direct, sincere, but not belligerent. Don't flounder, don't lose your cool, and never, never sweat."

Columbo fesses up. He had checked the apartment logbook. She was Braden's only visitor over the past two weeks. And twice she had signed in at 7 p.m. and hadn't signed out until 9:00 the following morning.

Hale neither confirms nor denies they were sleeping together, but confesses she questioned him a lot—and wonders if forcing him to reflect on all his wasted years may have contributed to his suicide.

She then meets with Victor, to announce she wants to do a memorial special, featuring tapes of Braden's voice she'd recorded in his final days. She'll need three days to interview his agent and music publisher, and put it all together.

Columbo has tracked down Ian at the Corps of Bagpipers. He asks about a doctor's appointment noted in Braden's desk diary. Ian doesn't know anything about it. He also can't answer why there was nothing in the diary about appearing on Hale's show.

Hale returns to the penthouse to retrieve her glasses. While she's in the study, Ian shows up to retrieve the pillowcase. Just then, Columbo arrives and surprises both of them. Hale explains that she was scoping out the apartment for use in her TV memorial. Ian says he was removing a bag of vegetables that had gone bad. Columbo shares that he found scratches on Braden's belt buckle, suggesting he was likely pushed over the railing. He also found a sliver of Scotch tape on the back door, and the entry wasn't bolted. Hale asks Columbo if he'd appear on her special. He agrees.

Once home, Hale is visited by Annie Stewart, who wonders where she was last night. She'd banged on her apartment door for a half-hour but no one answered. She's onto her. Once Annie leaves, Hale goes to the kitchen, places her tortoiseshell glasses on the counter, and smashes them to pieces with a meat mallet. She sweeps the rubble into the garbage disposal.

That afternoon, Hale conducts a mock interview with Columbo at the studio. He talks about his curiosity. "The question I've always asked myself is, why am I always asking questions?" he says. "I figure, you ask to learn." He explains that asking questions is like rolling a snowball downhill. "It can start an avalanche before it gets to the bottom."

Soon after, Ian returns to the penthouse. He opens the refrigerator to find Columbo inside. Ian says he's checking for spoilage. Columbo hands him the pillowcase: "This one's out of place." Ian assures him that everything is present and accounted for. "Oh, yes, sir," replies Columbo. "All except the money."

That night, Columbo and Hale fine-dine together. He shares that he discovered icicles on the caviar in Braden's refrigerator. Someone must have turned the thermostat way down, which would also explain why so many vegetables went bad—and how the murderer could have made the body appear to have died later.

The next day, the TV crew begins filming at the penthouse. With cameras rolling, Columbo reconstructs the case, even mixing in a few new discoveries. He's now sure the murder weapon is the poker, since it's the only fireplace tool not covered in soot and ashes. Braden's vest had long ketchup stains, suggesting his bloodied body was dragged out of the refrigerator. He swings open the fridge. Ian's inside, holding a bulgy pillowcase. "Look what I found!" he proclaims, explaining that Braden must have hidden his money there. Columbo wonders how Ian knows it's money. Ian reaches inside and pulls out clumps of paper. Columbo has set him up.

Finally, Columbo asks Hale to read a notation in Braden's diary. Hale says she can't; she doesn't have her reading glasses. Columbo lends her a pair. She reads that on the morning Braden was supposed to be filming her show, he had a dentist appointment to have two teeth pulled. He would have been in no condition to do a TV show. Oh, and Columbo also checked with Hale's optometrist. She had an unusual prescription—that matched both the glasses he just leant her, as well as a pair of tortoiseshell glasses he'd noticed at the crime scene.

Although Kaufman's clues and main characters (the caustic rocker and the ambitious newscaster) are interesting, his story never progresses anywhere—except in circles. There are so many scenes that take place at the penthouse, with characters rushing from one room to the next, hiding, and repeatedly being found in the refrigerator, it seems more like a setup for a British farce.

The non-premeditated murder recalls the rage-fueled attacks in *Death Lends a Hand* 18 years earlier and *Columbo Likes the Nightlife* 13 years in the future. The choice of a poker as weapon is straight from *A Deadly State of Mind*. The ambitious TV star feels exactly like the ambitious network executive in *Make Me a Perfect Murder*, produced by Simmons for Season 7. And the assistant who figures out the boss' deed was a Columbo chestnut by this time (see *Requiem for a Falling Star, Lovely But Lethal, Any Old Port in a Storm*, and Simmons' own *Try and Catch Me*, among others).

Simmons sent notes to Kaufman on the changes he wanted to see, hoping that the episode could make the cut for Season 9. Ultimately, according to producer Stanley Kallis, "Richard (Simmons) saw no hope for it, even though the basic story was (his own). Richard was out of patience with Peter who wanted to do his own story about Columbo in love. Yick."

As a final nail in the coffin, shortly after Kaufman submitted his revised draft, Simmons was relieved of his duties. Post-production on Season 9's first episode—*Murder, a Self Portrait*—was completed without Simmons. *Last of the Redcoats* was permanently shelved.

Undeterred, Kaufman kept writing. Unable to sell any more scripts, he finally turned to writing novels. He sold his first one—*Bowl of Cherries*—in 2007 at the age of 90. It was so successful, his publisher asked for a follow-up, *Misadventure*, which was published three years later, posthumously.

7
Season 9 (1989-1990)
The Last of Link

Before Richard Alan Simmons was named executive producer for *Columbo's* second go-round, Bill Link held out hope of dusting off a story he and Dick Levinson had conceived 10 years earlier… to serve as the pilot for *Mrs. Columbo*. They had first passed their treatment to Peter Fischer, who'd expanded it into a full screenplay. *The Lady's Set for Death* concerned Columbo's wife bringing to justice the murderous host of a *Let's Make a Deal*-type game show called *Set for Life*. Back in 1979, NBC was so certain they would film Fischer's script that they submitted it to a Japanese publisher to be novelized, under the title *The Murder Network*. The *Mrs. Columbo* book came out, but the story was never shot.

The Bride of Frankenstein

Nearly a decade later, Link thought Fischer's unused *Mrs. Columbo* could be rewritten for *Columbo*. In the summer of 1988, Link hired mystery author Joe Gores. Best known for his 1975 novel *Hammett*, which was made into a movie in 1982, Gores had published over 100 short stories, most frequently in *Ellery Queen Mystery Magazine* and featuring Dan Kearney and Associates. To supplement his prose writing, Gores agreed to the occasional *Kojak, Remington Steele, Magnum, P.I., T.J. Hooker*, even a *Mrs. Columbo*.

But as soon as Simmons rejoined *Columbo*, *The Lady's Set for Death* was again shelved. The minute Simmons was let go, Link had Gores complete

BEFORE IT WAS scrapped, Peter Fischer's 1978 script for the *Mrs. Columbo* pilot inspired a Japanese novelization... and years later an unmade episode of *Columbo*.

his rewrite. Gores submitted his revised first draft, now titled *The Bride of Frankenstein,* on June 28, 1989.

A Skid Row drunk finishes off his whiskey, discards the bottle in a trash bin, then staggers off into the night. A moment later, a gloved hand retrieves the bottle covered with the derelict's fingerprints.

The next day, a limo heads for the television studio. Inside the vehicle, game-show host Joshua Blair is dictating a memo into a cassette recorder, instructing all staff members to gather that evening on Stage 3 for a surprise birthday party for his wife. He then records a memo to his producer, Carleton Lange: "We are *not* talking about 25% profit participation and a seven-year deal. We *are* talking half ownership—two years max—and if Weinberg and his network programming geniuses don't like it, I'll take my overripe tomatoes, greedy gorillas, dancing washboards—and 35 share—to a network that will."

As the limo passes through the studio gates, an assortment of oddly costumed audience members clamor for a glimpse of their idol. Uncle Sam, the Mad Hatter, Batman, a tomato, a radish, a mousetrap, a thermometer, a deck of cards, a chicken, and a rooster are waiting in line for the 11 a.m. taping of *Set for Life.*

Blair smiles and waves at the faces pressed against the outside of his window, then dictates: "As of tomorrow, I want this human zoo kept away from my limousine. I don't care if you have to douse 'em with gasoline and light 'em—just keep 'em away from me."

The limo pulls up to a small one-story bungalow, situated at the remote end of the lot. A sign out front reads "Joshua Blair Productions." Muscular chauffeur/bodyguard Tommy Pearl opens the door for Blair. The boss demands to know why Tommy didn't get the car a tune-up as he'd requested. The driver says he did. Blair says the engine still doesn't sound right and instructs Tommy to take care of it. He'll ride home with his wife after the surprise party.

The bungalow consists of a two-room office fronted by a main reception area. Blair is greeted by his lovely, young secretary, Linda McCready. He has two orders: give me the overnight ratings, then quickly transcribe and send out my memos. That is until Blair sees that the second office, now used as a storeroom, is still piled up with boxes and old furnishings. He had told her he wanted the room cleaned out and the floor shellacked first thing in the morning. Maintenance had better show up in the next 20 minutes, or else.

Blair enters his office, which has a sash window on the left and a door to the second office on the right. He pulls a yellow phone from his desk and calls his wife, Caroline. She sits at the vanity of their master bedroom—"a huge room, thick carpet, round sybaritic bed with a maroon velvet canopy, tasteless in the way that only a man who hosts a game show with vegetables for contestants can be tasteless."

Caroline cuts short a call on the other line, instructing her caller that they had their moment, it was nice, but it's time to move on. She's sending back his letters, and he shouldn't call her again—but he should hold while she picks up the other line.

Switching to the other line, Caroline asks her husband if he's calling about divorce court. Blair apologizes profusely; he knows he's been an utter bastard, but he wants to make it up to her, with a birthday surprise. As he smooth-talks her, he unpacks his briefcase—a portable electric razor, a plastic grocery bag with two rocks inside, the half-pint whiskey bottle, an old .38-caliber revolver, and a pair of black leather gloves, which he puts on. Blair tells Caroline he's made an offer on the rustic property she's been eying, and is meeting the realtor there at 1:15. Caroline wants to see for herself.

Blair heads for the soundstage to tape his program. On the way, he runs into the director, Dave Raskin. He's hypertense, and tired of Blair ducking him and refusing to listen to his idea for a new show. Once again, Blair blows him off.

Blair passes six famous wrestlers, rehearsing for a commercial. They're trying—unsuccessfully—to pull apart blocks of wood joined by the show's sponsor, Bond-All Glue, under the watchful eye of beautiful-but-harried production assistant Mavis Cox. Blair sidles up to her, and says he tried to call her last night. She says she was out. Blair wants to know where. Mavis responds that he'd got her into bed by saying he was leaving his wife; now she hears he's throwing her a surprise birthday party. Just keeping up appearances, he responds. Mavis doesn't buy it. He snaps at her to have the commercial filmed and assembled by 1:00 p.m.

Minutes later, Blair's cold visage instantly transforms to a charming one, as he takes the stage to record his *Let's Make a Deal*-type game show. The audience goes crazy—particularly the females.

After the taping, Blair returns to his bungalow, where Linda is busy typing away and the floor of the secondary office glistens from a fresh coat of wet shellac. He instructs her to hold his calls and make sure no one disturbs him until 2:00, so he can have a quick shave and a nap. That means no one—not even Mavis when she brings over the commercial. He locks his office door

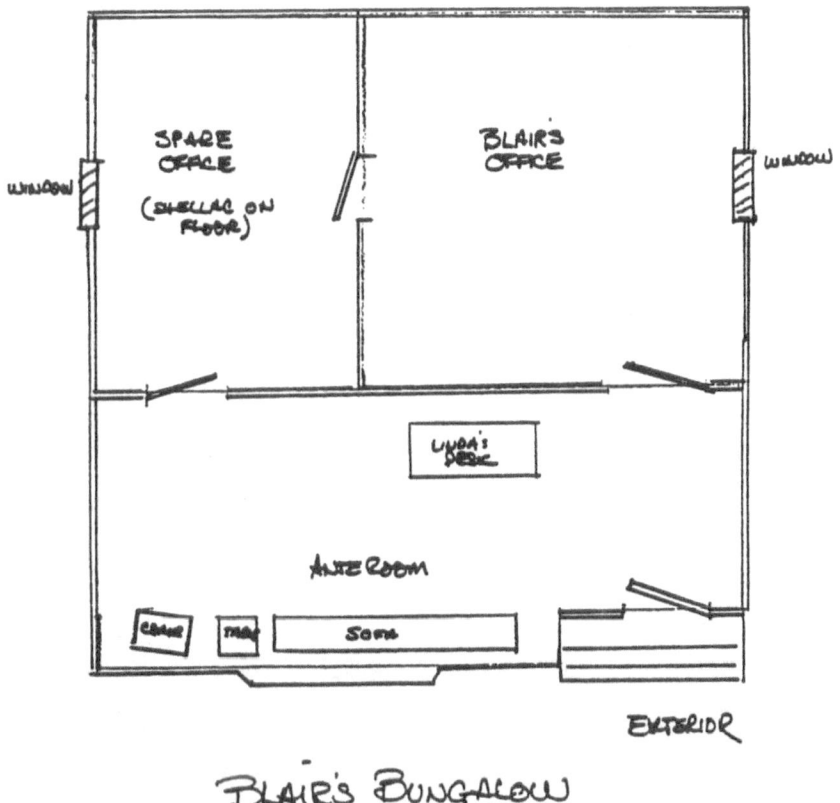

THIS HANDY FLOORPLAN would help the production team properly design the murderer's seemingly inescapable bungalow.

behind him and clicks on the tape player on his desk, although it emits only silence. He then unlocks a desk drawer and removes a green rubber mask, monstrous rubber gloves, oversized boots, and an undersized black jacket.

Minutes later, the Frankenstein monster emerges from the shrubs outside and lumbers to an old gray sedan parked nearby. The figure climbs in and drives off through a seldom-used rear studio gate.

A while later, back in the office, Mavis stops by to drop off her commercial, just in time for her and Linda to hear the sound of an electric razor emanating from Blair's cassette recorder.

Caroline gets to the wooded cabin first, parking her new Cadillac Seville outside the chained fence. Minutes later, here comes the gray sedan, driven by Frankenstein. The monster gets out and approaches.

"Josh?" she asks, laughing. "Did you decide to become a contestant on your own show? Why are you driving our old car? Where's the real estate woman?"

She's not coming, Blair answers. Then why are we here? Blair blames California community property laws. He's spent 20 years building a $50-million-a-year business while she's spent five years as his wife serving on committees, going to beauty salons, hiring and firing French chefs, and sleeping around. He removes a gun from his jacket pocket.

She doesn't understand. She says she hasn't even seen an attorney. "Good," Blair says. "Dead women don't need lawyers."

She runs. Blair calmly raises his pistol and fires. She drops. He walks over, kneels, removes a glove, and checks her pulse. Finding none, he wishes her a "happy death day." He takes a roadside hose and waters the ground around the Cadillac. Blair rubs his boots in the mud, then climbs into the Cadillac's passenger seat to leave muddy footprints on the floor. He takes the cash and credit cards from Caroline's purse and places them in the grocery bag with the rocks, which will be tossed into the reservoir during his drive back to the studio. Blair throws the purse to the ground. He slips the whiskey bottle between the seats. Then he hoses the mud off his boots.

Producer Lange has been reviewing the Bond-All Glue commercial with director Raskin, who wonders why Blair isn't present. Lange says he's taking a nap and Linda left strict orders that he not be disturbed. Raskin's eyes narrow. He strides into Blair's bungalow and tells Linda he must see Blair immediately. Linda tells him her boss is sleeping, for another three minutes. "With a little bimbo, maybe?" Raskin inquires.

He goes to the door, but it's locked. So he grabs the keys off the desk and jerks open the door. Blair is inside, rewinding his cassette recorder. Raskin turns red-faced. Linda is mortified. Blair just smiles, then starts dictating a memo to Maintenance into his recorder: his walls still need painting and his office window was warped by the rain and hasn't opened in months. While dictating, Blair glimpses a photo of Caroline on his desk. He pushes the frame over, cracking the glass.

That night, the *Set for Life* crew gathers inside the darkened studio, waiting to surprise Caroline. The door slowly opens. A shadowy figure enters. Blair gives the cue, the lights come up, 40 people scream "surprise," and a six-piece band starts playing "Sweet Caroline." The figure, they now realize, is a short, scruffy stranger in a ratty raincoat, holding an unlit cigar.

Later that night, Columbo enters Blair's bungalow through the side door into the storeroom. He walks halfway across the freshly varnished floor before he finds his shoes stuck, a trail of footprints behind him. Blair appears in the doorway to his office, frowning. As Columbo slips out of his shoes and steps, stocking feet, onto a rug, he explains he was looking for the men's room. Yes, in the dark.

Wiping off his shoes, Columbo shares that the police suspect a hitchhiker killed Blair's wife. Some joggers found the body about 3:00 in the afternoon. The medical examiner estimated she had been dead for about two or three hours. Blair snarls, "If I could get my hands on—"

But Columbo cautions him that it was a very large man, judging by the size of the muddy prints in her car. The man also left behind a bottle with fingerprints on it. Columbo theorizes Caroline picked up a fellow on the highway. He was drinking, pulled a gun, forced her to turn down a dirt road, and shot her as she was running away. He then rummaged through her purse, but oddly enough didn't leave any prints on it.

Columbo asks Blair where he was at the time. Blair says he taped two shows—from 10 to 11:30 and from 3 to 5:30. He'd had a headache, so he shaved and took a nap in between tapings. Columbo mentions Raskin had told him the door was locked. Before leaving, Columbo puts upright the fallen picture on the desk, to see Caroline's smiling face behind the cracked glass.

The following morning, Columbo drives to the Blair estate, while listening to an instructional foreign language tape. He repeats after the instructor in butchered Spanish. Police, media and onlookers are gathered outside the iron gate, which is guarded by a young Hispanic patrolman, Zapata.

In the house, Columbo meets the Blairs' heavyset, no-nonsense maid, Elsa Hoffman, who's carrying a plate of sirloin steak. She calls for Otto. Columbo says the food looks very tasty. Elsa scoffs; tasty, perhaps, for the dog—it had been left out all day and night. Even Otto the puppy turns up his nose at it.

Elsa shares that Mrs. Blair kept a French chef who prepared a weekly menu especially for her. Mr. Blair was typically out. "Of course," she says, "I guess, in Mr. Blair's business, he's lucky to get a chance to eat at all." Columbo can sympathize.

Blair, working in the library, is interrupted by loud barking and vicious growling. He flings open the room's French doors to see Columbo crouched over, facing two ferocious-looking Dobermans. Blair commands, "Merlin! Mandrake! Down!"

But he quickly realizes Columbo is scratching their chests as they nuzzle his face.

Blair is shocked. He'd acquired and trained the dogs to protect his wife. He walks back into the library to call Lange. He tells the producer to fire the head cameraman, then slams down the receiver. Blair apologizes to Columbo. He knows he should be in mourning, but he's trying to cope by immersing himself in his show—and his show has a lot of problems.

Columbo says he stopped by to report that they have not been able to identify the fingerprints. He does wonder why his wife had her chef prepare Steak Bombay last night, if she thought he'd arranged for drinks and a buffet at the studio at 7:00. Blair says maybe she forgot. Columbo also ponders why someone who was so terrified of intruders that she needed guard dogs would pick up a hitchhiker on a lonely road. Maybe, Columbo shrugs, she forgot to be frightened.

A few days later, Columbo and Zapata go to Caroline's memorial service. As the maid and then the chef eulogize about their former boss, in the audience Blair tries to sweet-talk Mavis. He asks if he can join her in Palm Springs for the weekend. Disgusted, she stalks off. Columbo takes it all in.

After the service, a tipsy Raskin corners Blair. He wants to discuss his new show concept. "It's called *Perfect Alibi*," Raskin says. "Each week, the contestant who stages the most perfect murder wins a seven-day trip to Mexico City. Of course, the killing doesn't occur on camera."

Blair points toward the door. "You're drunk. Get out."

But Raskin continues. He describes the proposed first show, about a guy who pretends to be sleeping in his office, but he's really miles away, killing his wife. If he's someone famous, he'd have to wear a costume—say, Frankenstein. On a movie lot, who'd pay any attention to someone in a crazy getup? The murderer couldn't use his limo or driver. Better to use his beat-up old second car that never leaves the garage—perhaps a gray sedan with a scrape down the side.

Just then, Columbo approaches. Under his breath, Blair tells Raskin to drop by his office tomorrow morning at 10:00.

The next day, Columbo interrupts Blair and Lange while they are adding canned laughter to his programs. Columbo marvels at the trick. Blair excuses himself to take care of some paperwork at his bungalow. Columbo offers to tag along, so he can update him on the case. He shares that some joggers saw a car speeding from the area of the murder—driven by Frankenstein. Doesn't everyone in Mr. Blair's audience dress up in similarly outlandish outfits?

Blair acts confused: "Are you saying someone in my audience killed Caroline?"

Columbo says no, but maybe he noticed one of them acting strange. Blair says he sees hundreds at a time during an average taping. They could *all* be practicing psychos for all he knows. Columbo thinks his cigar may be causing Blair to cough so he tries to open the office window. He can't. Blair says it's been stuck for weeks, ever since the heavy rains. Columbo and Blair try together to open the window, but it's impossible. Columbo exits, just as a Makeup woman arrives, carrying a shaving kit.

Columbo and Zapata head to the police automobile pound to get a closer look at Caroline's Caddy. Columbo ponders why the derelict's prints were on the bottle, but not on the doorhandle—or anywhere else inside the car. He also demonstrates how the passenger would probably have had to place the bottle between the seats with his left hand—and the prints were of a right hand. They reconstruct the shooting to confirm that Caroline should have been able to run much farther before a passenger would have had time to get out of the car, cross to the other side, and shoot her.

That evening, Blair, Mavis and Raskin are dining at a hip Beverly Hills restaurant to toast Raskin's marvelous new idea for a show. They're unexpectedly joined by Columbo, who's brought along the entire Frankenstein disguise, right down to the boots with faint traces of mud. He'd borrowed the costume from the studio's wardrobe department.

Later, at his bungalow, Blair informs Lange that he will indeed pitch Raskin's lousy idea to the network. Blair then dictates a memo into his cassette recorder, demanding that Maintenance replace the stuck window immediately with an easy-sliding aluminum frame and sash, or else.

When Blair arrives home, he tells chauffeur Tommy to clean every inch of the gray sedan. He then goes upstairs to continue boxing up his late wife's belongings. Moments later, Columbo appears, surprised to see Blair packing up her things just days after her death. Blair explains it's too painful to see her clothes every time he opens a drawer or closet door. At the bottom of Caroline's garment drawer, Blair spies a manila envelope. He surreptitiously slides the contents out enough to read the top sheet scribbled in his wife's handwriting: "HERE ARE YOUR LETTERS BACK. DON'T BOTHER TO CALL ANYMORE. I WON'T BE HOME TO YOU. – C." Blair hurriedly closes the drawer and moves on to the next one.

Columbo has come to report that one of the joggers remembered Frankenstein was driving a small gray sedan—much like the one the chauffeur is currently cleaning. Blair can't believe Columbo would assume that, out of all of the hundreds of thousands of gray sedans in Southern California, they must be the same car.

"And you assumed that perhaps Tommy was Frankenstein?" Blair scowls, as he continues packing, as Columbo wanders into the bathroom to look at Blair's electric razor. "Or maybe Mrs. Hoffmann? Or possibly the French chef? I know! It was the Dobermans, Merlin and Mandrake! But not me, Lieutenant. I was in a locked office with a window that won't open and fresh shellac on the floor of the adjoining office, and my secretary in front of the door, and—"

And, yes, shaving with this razor, Columbo adds, as he clicks on the shaver. But why, since the girl from Makeup visits every day to shave him?

Blair says she didn't come that day. Columbo agrees, because he knows Blair had his secretary cancel his appointment.

Once Columbo leaves, Blair scurries to the dresser and pulls out the envelope. Inside is a stack of love letters to his wife. He looks down at the Romeo's signature and roars with laughter.

Blair heads to Raskin's house, carrying a bottle of champagne. He brings news that the network loved Raskin's idea for a new show and has given them a 13-week commitment. He pours champagne into two glasses, subtly slipping some white powder into Raskin's. They toast and drink.

Blair thanks Raskin—for telling him he recognized the gray car Frankenstein was driving. It gave him time to clean it before Columbo got to it. He also confesses he just poisoned his champagne.

Raskin staggers backwards and rushes into the bathroom, desperate to expel the contents from his stomach. Once he's enjoyed a good laugh, Blair admits he didn't really poison Raskin's drink. The sounds of retching stop. Blair says he didn't have to. He found Raskin's letters to Caroline and her letter breaking off their affair. "Racy stuff, Dave, great motive for murder—jilted lover and all that," Raskin smiles. "If Columbo got 'em… along with an anonymous tip that the murder weapon is one of the studio prop guns. Don't ever try blackmail if you can be blackmailed yourself."

Raskin doesn't understand. What about the new network deal? Blair says he was never going to take such an idiotic idea to the network. Oh, and he didn't lace the champagne with poison—just a powerful laxative.

The next morning, Columbo accompanies the costumed audience members as they file into the studio for the next taping. A page singles out Columbo. "You, in the hobo's outfit. Please, sir—over with the other derelicts, if you would."

Columbo finds Blair in the control room, berating Raskin, who looks like he hasn't slept. The dressing down makes Mavis uncomfortable, so she leaves to set up a trapeze stunt for a Bond-All Glue commercial.

Blair gets called to the stage, leaving Columbo alone with Raskin. The Lieutenant knows Raskin left the lot about a half-hour before Mrs. Blair was killed. Did he see anyone else leaving then? Raskin says no.

Columbo then goes to watch the commercial being filmed. A stuntman is supposed to drop from a trapeze, 20 stories above Wilshire Boulevard. He is suspended by a strap held by a rope which is affixed to wooden blocks using Bond-All Glue. The stuntman starts pulling himself up the rope. Columbo is impressed. But he's there to ask Mavis about what he'd overheard at the memorial service. Mavis says her discussion with Blair was private, but she concedes she did go to Palm Springs—alone. She also confirms that, at the time of the murder, she was in the bungalow… with Blair in his office napping and shaving.

Mavis heads over to Blair's dressing room, to let him know Columbo suspects him of murder. Blair scoffs. He's more interested in rekindling their romance. Mavis fears that getting back together with Blair could make her a suspect. Infuriated, Blair calls an old friend—the police chief—to complain about a certain pesky Lieutenant.

Columbo borrows the gray sedan and drives up near the scene of the murder, wearing the Frankenstein mask. He passes the same group of joggers who'd spotted Frankenstein driving away from the murder. They immediately recognize the car and its distinctive scrape along the side.

That evening, Columbo is bowling with his Smoking Guns team in the Police League. Suddenly, Blair storms into the bowling alley, furious. He demands to know what right Columbo had to go to his house and drive his car—against a direct order from his superior officer. Columbo produces a search warrant.

Columbo returns to the TV studio to find Mavis piecing together the Bond-All Glue commercial. He persuades her to unlock the bungalow. He finds the cassette recorder on the desk; that could explain the sound of the razor. But how did Blair get out and back in again? He couldn't have gone through the front, or Mavis would have seen him. He couldn't have gone through the side door, or he would have messed up the wet shellac. And he couldn't have gone through the window because it won't open.

A little while later, Blair's limo pulls up to the bungalow. He sees a light on in his office. He opens the door and looks inside. His electric razor is lying on his desk, buzzing.

The next day is Saturday, but Blair has spent all day at the console, working on his show. He hasn't seen Mavis, who earlier—Lange informs him—was on Stage 11, taping another commercial. Blair says someone broke into his bungalow last night, someone with a key. It must have been Mavis. Hours later, a security guard stops by the control room to hand Blair a package from Mavis. It's a video cassette, which he inserts into the player.

On the screen we see a mockup of a sash-type window in a frame set in a snowbank. Light snow is falling. There's a snowman in the background. Suddenly, Old Man Winter jumps in front of the camera and raps on the window frame. He says that you can try to keep him away, but he'll find his way through cracks and crevices, like through this window. He tries to open the window, but it doesn't budge. "Blast!" says Old Man Winter. "This window's been sealed shut with Bond-All Glue. My plans are foiled!"

The final lines repeat on loop, over and over. Ruffled, Blair phones Mavis. He gets her voicemail. He slams down the phone and hurries to his bungalow. As he opens the door, he can hear the buzzing razor. But inside his office, sitting on the desk is not his razor but the cassette player. He hits stop, just as Columbo appears in the doorway. He recounts how Blair carried out the murder, and how he can prove it once the police lab checks the bottom of his window frame for traces of Bond-All Glue. Blair chuckles, knowing that he had ordered Maintenance to replace the window two days ago.

Columbo pulls back the drapes to reveal not a lovely new window with an aluminum sash, but a gaping hole in the wall. Blair is astonished. Columbo had had the old window removed before Maintenance could get ahold of it.

The mystery was an especially clever one, with a new twist for *Columbo* viewers: letting them know *who* committed the murder, but not *how* they pulled it off. Yet the story faced two major obstacles—first, that Columbo had tangled with show business personalities before, including on *Requiem for a Falling Star*, *Fade In to Murder*, and the recently aired *Murder, Smoke and Shadows*. Peter Falk preferred a variety of settings for the mysteries and a range of occupations for the murderers. More importantly, Simmons and Kallis' replacements as lead producers—Jon Epstein and Penny Adams—were looking to do something a little hipper.

Link remained as executive producer for the wheel over one more season. Gores consented to crank out one final television script: a *B.L. Stryker*.

And, in later seasons, Fischer would contribute three more stories, as a favor to his old friend, Peter Falk. Fischer would use elements from *The Bride of Frankenstein* in these scripts. The memorial service—in which one character after another speaks about the dearly departed—is reminiscent of the funeral scene he'd write for *Rest in Peace, Mrs. Columbo*, and the scene where the joggers identify the car feels like the ending of *Butterfly in Shades of Grey*.

Double Vision

During the NBC era, the story editor on *Columbo* was credited as "executive story consultant." This tradition began the first year under Levinson and Link and was, perhaps, their way of delineating that they were, in fact, the true story editors. When Richard Alan Simmons took over during Season 6, he had no use for a story editor or consultant. Every word of every script would be going through him.

With the advent of the ABC years, Simmons was assigned an executive story consultant, though he truly would be a consultant—sitting in on story meetings, making suggestions on drafts, and offering ideas for clues. He was 72-year-old Jackson Gillis, hired as a concession to Link and Falk to ensure the show would be true to its roots.

Gillis had made a name for himself in the early 1950s with teleplays for half-hour detective series like *Front Page Detective, Racket Squad,* and *I'm the Law,* before latching on to *Adventures of Superman, Spin and Marty, The Hardy Boys,* and *Lassie.* Then came the show that would make him—*Perry Mason.* His ingenious plotting was perfect for tight hour-long mysteries with unpredictable twists. For *Perry Mason's* third season in 1959, Gillis cranked out eight scripts. He'd write hundreds of pages more over each of the next six years—31 scripts total, and in Season 4 served as the show's story editor.

Gillis first worked on *Columbo* during its inaugural summer. He submitted a spec script that became *Suitable for Framing,* then cranked out a quick-turnaround adaptation for *Short Fuse,* when the last-minute episode was added for Season 1.

When Steven Bochco left the show at the end of Season 1, Gillis was hired to take his place as executive story consultant, which meant not only polishing all eight scripts in year two, but also writing full scripts for half of them. Unable to work during the Writers Guild strike of 1973, Gillis was dropped from the series, two shows into Season 3. Thereafter, he'd strictly freelance—for shows like *Wonder Woman, Murder, She Wrote,* and even *Columbo* (*Troubled Waters, Last Salute to the Commodore*).

When Simmons left after Season 8, Gillis was again free to pitch ideas to the show that had employed him as a consultant. As the master of the switcheroo, Gillis had several doppelganger stories under his belt, including Season 2's *Double Shock* starring Martin Landau as murderous twins, and the *Perry Mason* episode *The Case of the Dead Ringer* in which the prime suspect looks exactly like Perry.

In June 1989, Gillis began brainstorming a new idea for *Columbo*: a

VETERAN *COLUMBO* scribe Jackson Gillis contributed as a writer or a story consultant to more than a dozen scripts... until Richard Alan Simmons joined the show in 1977. Gillis resumed submitting scripts and story ideas once Simmons left in 1990. *[Credit: Candida Gillis]*

mentally disturbed woman who kills her identical twin and takes her place, making it look like the work of a serial killer. He tentatively titled the story *The Twins*.

Bill Link thought no one crafted better clues than Gillis, particularly the gotcha in *Suitable for Framing*, in which Columbo plants his own fingerprints on a stolen painting to nail an art critic. Link thought he had an even better clue. What if the killer were identified by a *monkey's* fingerprints? Link checked with friends at the LAPD crime lab to make sure it would be possible. He then worked with Gillis to create a story that incorporated both his gotcha and the twins idea. Gillis spent the next six months turning it into a full teleplay, *Double Vision*, completed on December 8, 1989.

As the opening credits unfold, a young blonde waitress finishes up her late-night shift at the chili joint and heads home. As she nears her front porch, she's ambushed and shot in the forehead by a slight, shadowy figure, clad in black and wearing a ski mask. The assailant then kneels over the body, brushes her hair away from her gunshot wound, and, using a red marker, starts drawing red rays, creating a sunburst around the bullet hole. The killer steps back and takes a Polaroid photo of the corpse.

The next morning, gorgeous blonde model Alice Sanders returns home after a ride on her horse. Her maid, Carmelita, is reading about the "Mystery Slaying" in the local newspaper when the phone rings. It's Alice's twin sister, Meg. Alice dreads receiving the call. She assumes something must be wrong. Meg doesn't sound like she's calling from a hospital in Switzerland. Meg says, no, she's at Denver Airport, en route to Los Angeles. Alice is only going to be in town a couple more days, then is leaving to get married in South America. But she would be happy to pick her up when her flight arrives. Meg, however, is secretly calling from a local motel.

During the ride home, Alice asks Meg why she cut her hair so short. Meg says she has been wearing a wig, ever since being attacked by another patient at the hospital. She "was so upset because I can leave whenever I want and she can't, that she knocked me down and chopped it half off with a butcher knife."

At home, they reminisce and talk about Alice's fiancé, Ricardo, until Alice has to leave for a photo shoot with Cecil Whitney. The eccentric old Englishman lives with a menagerie, including a capuchin monkey that sits on his shoulder eating peanuts. Meg asks Alice to take along a tiny tape recorder so she can "hear what the old foof *really* says about me."

The moment Alice rides off, Meg hurries to Alice's bedroom and bathroom, to wipe down every object and surface—and then cover them with her own fingerprints. She then cuts the downstairs phone lines.

A bit later, Carmelita returns home from an errand to find the front door open. She steps inside and shrieks, seeing who she thinks is Alice lying on the floor with a bullet hole and red markings on her forehead. The maid grabs the phone, but the line is dead. Terrified that the killer might still be in the house, she flees. Meg rises. She's dressed in the same outfit that Alice wears. She wipes the markings off her forehead.

Not long after, Alice arrives, steps inside, and Meg shoots her in the forehead. Meg then positions her body just as hers was. She draws the red lines on Alice's forehead and cuts off half her hair. She then removes the wig from her own head, revealing a full, beautiful head of hair, and places it on Alice's head. Finally, Meg jumps on Alice's horse and gallops off.

Before too long, the police are on the scene, led by Columbo and Sgt. Baker. The sergeant is convinced that the slaying is the work of the killer who murdered the waitress, especially after discovering Polaroids of the victim that were outside the house—similar to the one taken of the first victim and mailed to the local paper.

Columbo gets distracted looking at all the photos on the wall. The pictures of the sisters date back to a hand lotion ad they posed for when they were little. Meg, now posing as Alice so we'll call her "MegAlice," tells him her sister hadn't done any modeling since her mid-teens and had been in Europe for the last 14 months. She's mortified to think that she may have been the killer's intended target. Just in case, the police will assign her a watchman while she's in town: strapping, young Officer Charlie.

Columbo's not totally convinced. It might be a copycat murder. He looks through Meg's purse, noticing there's no passport or return plane ticket. Don't people usually buy roundtrip airfare?

Columbo heads for the airport, to confirm Meg's flight from Denver… only to discover she didn't arrive that morning—but three days prior.

Charlie accompanies MegAlice to the bridal salon to be fitted for her wedding dress. The clerk asks her to step on the scale, just as Columbo walks in. MegAlice is relieved to find out that she weighs exactly the same as Alice did during her initial fitting. Columbo shares his airline discovery. MegAlice produces the passport, saying she found it in Meg's jeans while doing the wash. Columbo says he'd like to have recent photos of Meg that he can use to try to find people who saw her over the past few days. Perhaps he could show them new photos of Alice instead. So, MegAlice offers to take him to see Cecil.

Cecil hasn't developed any prints yet, so he gives Columbo a contact sheet with various poses. Cecil also apologizes to MegAlice for speaking poorly of her sister. MegAlice shrugs it off, even repeating some of his insults that she had heard on the tape recording. As Columbo peers at the contact sheet through a magnifying glass, he's jumped by the monkey, just as the primate had earlier greeted Alice.

Alice's house, meanwhile, has been overrun by forensics experts, searching every inch for the killer's fingerprints. MegAlice is miffed; wouldn't the killer wear gloves? But Columbo had ordered the search because serial killers frequently stalk their prey and may spend considerable time lying in wait. Her irritation turns to joy as she's handed the phone—it's a long-distance call from Ricardo. The search turns up lots of MegAlice's fingerprints, a few of her sister's and Carmelita's—but no one else's.

Columbo then takes MegAlice to a dingy motel, where the clerk had IDed Meg. MegAlice knows the place from Meg's past. "I think it's the same place she called me from for help once, because she couldn't pay the bill and the boy she was with had already skipped out." Meg had mentioned in her letters that this motel was where she lost her virginity and, after the man ran out on her, contemplated suicide. As they're leaving, Columbo asks if he could see some of Meg's letters.

Back at the house, MegAlice locates some of her old letters—and destroys a couple that were threatening. She hands Charlie a few others to pass on to Columbo. Columbo compares them to other writing samples and discovers that MegAlice's handwriting is identical to Alice's, but totally different from Meg's. He then heads to the morgue, to look at the victim's pendant. He learns that, when the girls were kids, they had filed their names off of their matching lockets, so they could play tricks on others. But what about her teeth? The coroner agrees to take X-rays.

Columbo brings the X-rays to Alice and Meg's dentist, to compare them to the girls' charts. The dentist just so happens to be performing dental work on MegAlice. When the dentist leaves to speak with Columbo, MegAlice switches the X-rays between her and her sister's files.

Wondering if the murders are the work of a known sex offender, Columbo has MegAlice join him at a police lineup of criminals, including Felix Ledbetter, a lowlife with priors—for stealing firearms, using drugs, and assaulting prostitutes. Ledbetter lives in a motel not far from where the waitress was murdered. Columbo informs MegAlice that the two victims were killed with the same type of bullet, but the police can't be sure the women were killed with the same gun without actually having the weapon.

Columbo visits Cecil to have him print enlargements from the contact sheet. Cecil mentions some of the trouble Meg used to get into—including forging checks with her sister's signature.

Columbo continues on to Alice's house, to update MegAlice. He notices that she has a mild sunburn, while her sister—who was supposed to have just arrived from Switzerland—had a nice tan. MegAlice explains that, as a model, she needs lily-white skin and she forgot to wear a hat during her last horse ride. And, although it got cold where Meg lived, it was also very bright and sunny.

After Columbo leaves, MegAlice bolts into action. She dresses in black, then slips into a hidden compartment behind the laundry chute. The passageway leads to a cavernous wine cellar where she has been hiding a wrapped bundle. She escapes out a back exit. She finds Ledbetter's motel room, sneaks in while he is inserting a needle into his arm, and whacks him on the side of the head. We see she's wearing a black ski mask. From the bundle, she removes a revolver, two red markers, and Polaroids of her victims, which she pins to the wall. She then pours lighter fluid over and around Ledbetter, drops a lit match, and runs out the door.

The next morning's headlines proclaim "Serial Killer Dies in Fire." Reporters converge on Alice's house. MegAlice is pleased to see Columbo show up, so she can say goodbye. Columbo has brought along a special guest—Ricardo, who's flown in from Argentina. Thrilled to see each other, the couple excuse themselves to the bedroom. Columbo decides he'll wait. He passes the time reviewing the enlargements—when one catches his eye.

The following day, as MegAlice and Ricardo are about to leave for the airport, Columbo returns just one more time. He shows an enlargement showing the monkey grabbing Alice's necklace. He had the morgue check the corpse's necklace and they found fingerprints—the monkey's. "I don't believe you," MegAlice retorts. "You're nothing but a policeman. You're not even my doctor."

"No, Meg," Columbo answers, gesturing toward a psychiatrist standing in the doorway, "but *he* can be, if you want him."

MegAlice grabs the photo out of his hand and moves toward a wall mirror. She looks at the photo, then at herself. "I'm Alice… You know I am," she says, softly. "I'm Alice… aren't I?"

Suddenly, in the lower corner of the mirror, the monkey fades into view. She watches in horror as her hallucination creeps closer to her reflection, then leaps onto her shoulder, and wraps its arms around her neck, reaching for her necklace. She grabs a lamp off a table and hurls it at the mirror. The mirror, along with the reflections of her and the monkey, shatters. Meg sinks to the floor, folding into a fetal position. Columbo looks down sadly on her.

The script was exciting, a return to form with an edgier feel, reminiscent of two of the series' grittiest entries, both by Peter Fischer (Season 3's *A Friend in Deed*, in which the murderer tries to frame a masked bandit, and the same year's *Publish or Perish*, in which the murderer kills the ex-con he'd set up).

Double Vision did need some work. For his second draft, dated February 1, 1990, Gillis built in some opportunities for Columbo character moments. When Columbo visits MegAlice to tell her about Meg's dental records from Switzerland, he has the maid serve Columbo a messy taco.

The script also needed a clearer point of inspiration for Columbo to crack the gotcha. Gillis had Columbo learn of Ledbetter's death while reading the newspaper as he ate chili at the beanery. An article notes the victim was found clutching his throat, since he died of smoke inhalation, and a photo shows Ledbetter wore a crucifix on a chain around his neck. Together, they make Columbo think of the girls' pendants.

It also received a more dramatic finish, showing that Meg now truly believes she is Alice. When Meg is presented with the evidence of the pendant, she snaps, telling Columbo that she thinks *he* is really a twin. "Because you're exactly like another one I knew, once. Obsessive, perpetually mixed up," she says. "So did your twin die in childbirth, too? Do you have nightmares sometimes? When you aren't sure who you are? Which one? The twin who lived, or the twin who died?"

Columbo tries to have Meg led away by people who can help her, but she thinks they want her autograph and will be taking her to her honeymoon in Argentina.

To finish out Columbo's second season on ABC, executive producer Jon Epstein opted to go with Gillis' other script, *Murder in Malibu*, and let *Double Vision* sit until the fall. At that time, the series switched from being part of a wheel to being a series of stand-alone specials. At the same time, the old guard—Link, Gillis and fellow story consultant Bill Driskill—were released. Howard Berk was commissioned with reviving *Double Vision*.

Rather than follow Gillis' lead in instituting minor tweaks, Berk reworked major elements of the story, so it better spelled out Meg's motivation and made more sense (especially in that MegAlice wasn't ready to run off with Alice's fiancé, whom she'd never met before). In place of a fiancé, Alice would have a manager, Richard, who has been carrying a torch for her for years. She, however, always kept their relationship professional, because she knew her sister had a crush on him.

Instead of riding in on her horse, which might have left detectable fibers or sweat, Alice would arrive in a red sportscar.

In Berk's version, Alice wouldn't be a model but a celebrated concert pianist, who got her start touring and recording with her similarly talented twin sister, until the pressure got to Meg and she was sent away to a sanitarium

MONKEY BUSINESS: Peter Falk scavenged Bill Link's primate-fingerprints clue from *Double Vision* to serve as the gotcha for 1991's *Death Hits the Jackpot*. *[Credit: NBCUniversal]*

in Switzerland.

Instead of dreading Meg's arrival, Alice would be thrilled to see her and would invite her to join her on tour. "No good," Meg would reply. "I've been competing with you all my life—from nursery games to boyfriends to music. Whatever we did, I always felt I had to catch up. I was lucky, Sis. Few more weeks back there, post-treatment, and I'm finished. And that means I'm finished competing with you ever again."

Berk submitted his draft on November 8, 1990, just after production wrapped on the second of the three episodes planned for the season.

Two weeks later, Epstein died. The show went on hiatus for about eight weeks, then returned to make *Columbo and the Murder of a Rock Star*, without naming an official replacement for Epstein.

Falk agreed to two specials for the next season, with himself as executive producer. He alone would select which scripts to film. And, since he was always uneasy with female murderers and, apparently, mental illness, Falk permanently shelved *Double Vision*. Yet he did love Link's gotcha clue. So he had the screenwriter of the very next episode, *Death Hits the Jackpot*, pair his victim with a chimp that could leave its fingerprints on the killer's pendant.

Stunt Girl

While working on initial revisions to *Double Vision*, Jackson Gillis also hammered out three-page-long treatments for two more *Columbos*, both dated January 29, 1990. One, after nearly three years, would become *A Bird in the Hand...*. The other, *Stunt Girl*, would never see the light of day.

— 📖 —

Bonnie Sue, "seemingly an innocent of little learning but gorgeous musculature," has been taking classes that teach recent widows how to face the world alone. She finishes up for the day, and leaves the Women's World School in a modest bus. A few stops away, she transfers to a limousine, which whisks her to the Beverly Hills mansion she shares with her loud, abusive husband, Sam. Just not for much longer.

Sam is facing so many indictments that his own lawyers are abandoning him. So he's hatched a plan to flee the country, with the help of his naïve wife and his wimpy financial advisor, Clarence. After Sam disappears, Bonnie Sue and Clarence will maintain the illusion that he's still in town, while methodically cashing out Sam's securities and wiring the funds to a secret overseas account. Once they've cleaned out his known accounts, they'll join him south of the border.

Sam thinks he has the perfect plan. He trusts them both, unconcerned that Clarence not-quite-secretly lusts for Bonnie Sue. Sam is confident that Clarence is too weak to act on his urges, that Bonnie Sue is too innocent to be anything but faithful, and that, if Clarence ever did try anything, Bonnie Sue could deck him with one punch. Plus, Sam plans to dump his wife as soon as they reunite.

So Sam merrily sneaks off for Mexico, flying his small private plane. It's not until he's well on his way that he realizes he has a stowaway—Bonnie Sue. Worse, she's wearing a parachute and pointing a gun.

A solitary Baja prospector is the only witness to a distant flash, a muffled explosion, and flames on the horizon.

A few days later, Bonnie Sue is summoned to Mexico to ID her dead husband. She arrives to find Columbo is already on the scene. Unfortunately for her, the prospector had a metal detector, which led him to find the bullet in Sam's charred chest. In combing through the wreckage, Columbo also discovers that the plane is missing one regulation-required parachute.

Back in California, Columbo figures out that, ever since Sam's departure, Clarence had been living with Bonnie Sue in her house. And now *he* has gone missing. Columbo notices that she does receive brief, reassuring phone calls from him, but evidently the coward has gone into hiding to leave Bonnie Sue to face the heat alone.

The Feds are equally alarmed that, since Sam's death, most of his securities have been liquidated and transferred abroad from his high-tech home office. Bonnie Sue admits that, as his legal wife, she signed a lot of paperwork under orders from Sam and Clarence, who'd explained that she would be helping them "escape this unfair prosecution by the government." Really, she had no idea what any of it was for.

Columbo has his hands full with Bonnie Sue. As Gillis described her, "She is such an exasperating mixture of seeming-bimbo ignorance and startling, homespun truth. In a way, it's almost like Columbo prying into his own female counterpart."

Columbo then learns that Bonnie Sue wasn't just taking introductory secretarial classes at Women's World—as she had told her husband—but Estate Management and Corporate Investment courses. Confronted with the truth, Bonnie Sue breaks down and confesses that the ruse was her lover Clarence's idea. All she had wanted to do was help Sam, not hurt him! She claims she has no idea how Sam was killed—and is confident no one can ever prove otherwise.

No one… except Clarence. He lives in a modest, stilted beach house, which Columbo has had under 24-hour surveillance ever since Sam turned up dead. Yet it's been dark for days. A nonstop manhunt and a stakeout at the airport have also proven fruitless. It appears that Clarence successfully skipped off to Europe to meet up with Sam's transferred bankroll.

Columbo's not so sure. He has dogs sniff near the beach house and then digs underneath it to turn up the rotting body of Clarence. "For, of course, it's

Bonnie Sue who created the illusion of Clarence's presence and laid his escape trail," Gillis concluded. "Everything could be blamed on him, and her story never contradicted—if she had simply killed Clarence first. She's not sorry, either. Both of them deserved what they got!"

Gillis, who wrote more scripts for *Perry Mason* than for any other show, was pitching something akin to a bad episode for that program. Not so coincidentally, a 1960 *Perry Mason* episode, *The Case of the Frantic Flyer*, has a similar setup: after apparently getting double-crossed by his lover, a scammer crashes his private plane in the desert, and the wreckage is discovered by a grizzled prospector. *Stunt Girl* lacks the clever clues and unforeseen twists of a typical Gillis thriller. The whole murder plot—with the villain incapacitating the spouse while airborne, then parachuting to safety to make the crash look like an accident—had already been done in Season 3 on the Johnny Cash-starrer *Swan Song*. Worse, there's no indication why Bonnie Sue would bury Clarence's body next to his beach house, or why Columbo would start digging there. There's no final gotcha—in fact, there's little evidence at all proving Bonnie Sue's guilt. And Gillis' contention that she would be in the clear if only she'd killed Clarence first makes little sense.

Wisely, *Columbo's* producers declined this pitch.

Shooting Star

While compiling story ideas for Season 9, Bill Link contacted Philip Gerson, who had just completed three years as a writer and story editor alongside Robert Van Scoyk on *Murder, She Wrote*. While batting around possible scenarios with Link, Gerson pitched a mystery with a twist—we see the murderer commit the crime in Act One, but we eventually learn the killer is acting at the behest of an inmate whom Columbo had put away 20 years earlier.

"So there were two antagonists, two villains, one of whom would seem to have the perfect alibi because he was in prison," Gerson recalled. "It was a somewhat nontraditional Columbo, and Peter was very interested in that. Peter said, 'Oh, yeah, let's try that.'"

After Gerson wrote a detailed treatment, Falk got cold feet. "He decided that he really just wanted to do regular *Columbos*," Gerson said. "He didn't want to do something that broke the formula, which I completely respect. It was just a little too different."

Gerson was paid for the work and, because Falk liked his writing, was invited to compose a full script—with a totally different plot. That meant lots of meetings with Falk to shape the story. Gerson recalled, "I remember lots of situations where you would think that the story meeting was over and it wasn't over. I'd be on my way out the door practically and it would be 'One more thing…' One day, I came out of one of these eternal meetings that Link had been in also. I turned to Link and said, 'I feel like I should just confess to him and get it over with.'

"He and Columbo were the same—you'd think you were done and instead of him leaving the room and coming back, it would be you leaving his office. It was like a reverse staging."

Through the 1980s, primetime soap operas like *Dynasty*, *Dallas*, *Knots Landing*, and *Falcon Crest* were all the rage. So Gerson modeled his murderer after the female leads on *Dynasty*—an actress who in real life was like Joan Collins' treacherous Alexis, but whose character on a nighttime soap was like Linda Evans' sweet, naïve Krystle ("butter wouldn't melt in her mouth").

Gerson completed his last draft of *Shooting Star* on October 22, 1990.

Glamorous actress Stella Reeves stars in a hit primetime soap opera, playing the kindhearted Clover Mannington. Behind the scenes, she's anything but. She had been a famous movie star, but now detests that she's growing older. Stella has a much younger boyfriend, who she has brought on to her TV show as a producer and writer. While promoting her new fragrance, Stella announces to the press that she and her beau are to be married. Soon after, she discovers that the cad has been having an affair with her much younger stuntwoman. Stella is both humiliated and incensed.

Stella has also been receiving sexually threatening letters from a superfan. She devises a scheme to solve both problems. Stella instructs her stuntwoman to stop by her house at 7:30 that night to try on the new dress she plans to wear for the next day's filming. She says she wants to make sure the gown won't hinder the stunt the stand-in is supposed to perform. Stella then contacts the stalker and invites him to her home at 8:00.

The stuntwoman arrives promptly at Stella's mansion. After the visitor changes into the dress, Stella shoots her in the back. Not long after, the superfan—who looks like a "greasy pervert"—shows up. Stella makes sure he closes the French door behind him, so his fingerprints will be on the handle. Then, using a different gun, she shoots him in the chest. She slips on rubber gloves, so she can restage and tidy up the crime scene. She then repositions the bodies and places the gun she killed her stand-in with in the dead fan's hand. From the outside, she smashes a glass mullion in her French doors, to make it look like a break-in. But while removing the gloves, Stella loses one of her press-on nails. Finally, she calls the police. She claims she heard a gunshot, ran down the stairs, and—realizing the intruder must have mistakenly shot her double from behind—was forced to kill him in self-defense.

The next morning, Stella must make an emergency trip to the manicurist to rebuild and repolish her nail.

Columbo, meanwhile, goes to search the dead man's apartment, where he is surprised by the man's roommate. Unbeknownst to Columbo, it was the roommate—not the murder victim—who had written the threatening letters. The flatmate, however, can tell what happened and attempts to blackmail Stella.

In time, Columbo catches on to the shakedown attempt and has an undercover cop call Stella, pretending to be the real blackmailer and demanding a meeting. When Stella arrives to meet him, Columbo's hiding in the shadows. She figures out Columbo's plan and thwarts him. Columbo needs more proof.

Throughout the investigation, Columbo can't get the doorhandle on his Peugeot to work right, so he keeps asking anyone he meets if they can fix it (for cheap). Now, as Columbo reaches in through the side window to open the car door from the inside and the handle breaks off, he realizes that the fingerprints on the French door handle are reversed. They were made from the inside of the house, not from someone who was reaching in from the outside.

Earlier, Columbo had also visited his wife's manicurist, where he'd learned that nail polish colors can be custom-mixed. The distinctive red Stella was wearing in her fragrance ads, which had been photographed a few hours before the murders, is different from the color she now wears.

Although Gerson didn't write the part of the murderer for anyone in particular, it was the time "when all of those soaps were on, so I guess the hope was that one of those women would have done it." Which shouldn't have been a problem, since so many of the lead guest stars on Columbo during its tenth season were soap opera regulars, including *Murder in Malibu's* Andrew Stevens (*Dallas*), *Rest in Peace, Mrs. Columbo's* Ian McShane (*Dallas*), *Columbo Goes to College's* Stephen Caffrey (*All My Children*), and *Columbo Cries Wolf's* Rebecca Staab (*Guiding Light*) and Ian Buchanan (*General Hospital*, and later

The Bold and the Beautiful, Days of Our Lives, and *All My Children*).

But, as fun as the setting was, the backdrop may have been the episode's undoing. According to Gerson, "I have to say, if I were to be critical of my script, it would be that it's a little too funny. There's a lot of somewhat campy humor in it, because it's *Dynasty*. I have no idea what it was that worked or didn't work about that for (the producers) but, if I had to guess, I think that might have been part of the reason."

It also couldn't have helped that, by the time Gerson submitted his final draft, Bill Link had left the show.

Gerson would go on to work with Link on an unproduced pilot, and then write for and co-executive produce *Dr. Quinn, Medicine Woman* and *Legacy*.

8
The First Specials (1990-1995)
A New Sheriff in Town

*C*olumbo continued in the fall of 1990 for a tenth season, but in the form of six standalone specials, rather than as part of multi-series wheel. From then on, ABC was open to as many as three *Columbos* a year, fully aware that far fewer would be produced, due to Falk's lack of time and his indecisiveness over scripts.

For Seasons 8 through 10, Falk held the title of co-executive producer and, in fact, had held unofficial veto power since the 1970s. But starting in 1992, he now had the title to go with it. He was named executive producer. He was officially running the show.

The problem was that, while Falk was fiendishly inventive, he wasn't a writer. He initially leaned on Patrick McGoohan as his co-executive producer and occasional director, for help in developing stories. Now he just had to find them. Upon learning from a friend that Ed McBain's *87th Precinct* novels were popular, Falk promptly purchased the rights to turn at least two of the books into *Columbos*.

McBain's novels, however, are police procedurals, not parlor-room mysteries. They're grittier, don't have many clues, and involve an entire squad of policemen. Falk figured he just needed to have them rewritten so they had fewer detectives and more clues. He had Robert Van Scoyk adapt the first one (*So Long as You Both Shall Live*) and Van Scoyk suggested one of his *Murder, She Wrote* writers, Chris Manheim, to work on another.

Killer's Choice

"They sent it to me. I read it, and it wasn't me at all," Manheim recalled. "So I thanked them, but said, 'I just don't feel called to this material in the least.' The story itself was just icky, involving a rape and all this stuff. I just thought I'm not the right writer for this one. I had always been told: writing is hard enough; never write something you don't have any kind of appeal for. If it's only for the money, don't do it. So I took that to heart, because I just knew after I read it, this isn't me.

"Then they sent me this other book (*Killer's Choice*), and I thought, 'Well, you know, yeah, this I could see how this might work,' although it was written in like 1957 or '58, and all the technology made most of their crime procedural stuff really dated. I mean, you'd go: 'Well, why didn't they just dust for fingerprints?' That kind of thing."

She first met with McGoohan, but he soon left the team due to health issues. From then on, all consultations were directly with Falk. He was frequently vague and indecisive, but he definitely wanted more clues, including a big gotcha. As screenwriter Philip Gerson noted, Falk "had a guy who came up with clues-absent stories. He just came up with cool clues, and they would be suggested to you. It was sort of like in the old days on sitcoms there was like a joke room and a story room, and it was like somebody from the joke room had come up with a joke that you had to put in the script. I always thought that was so interesting, coming up with a clue and, 'Okay, let's see if we can make this work.' He loved his clues."

Manheim said Falk compiled this backlog into a "clue book." Falk thought the gotcha clue in *Killer's Choice*—the murderer being outed by a postmark on an envelope—was weak. So, he pulled a stronger envelope clue from his clue book and had Manheim write it into her script.

Vivacious redhead Annie Boone lies dead on the liquor store's floor, covered in broken glass from all the shattered booze bottles. Proprietor Franklin Phelps has few details about his dead clerk; he's more concerned with his lost inventory. He sees one silver lining: there's no money missing from the till. Phelps can only tell Columbo that Miss Boone was 32, divorced, had a small kid, lived with her mother, and had been working for him for about a year.

The Lieutenant heads for Annie's apartment, where he meets her precious 5-year-old daughter, Monica, and Annie's mother, Mrs. Travail. The woman

MORE THAN 30 years before *Columbo* considered adapting Ed McBain's *Killer's Choice*, the novel served as the basis for a 1962 episode of NBC's *87th Precinct*, a series starring Robert Lansing. Weeks earlier, a young Peter Falk had guest-starred on the series.

relates that, seven years ago, Annie married a photographer, Theodore. Annie was attractive and fun-loving, but none too bright so, in time, Theodore outgrew her and asked for a divorce. She began seeing other men, such as gambler Frank Abelson, bank teller Arthur Cordis, and someone named Jamie. Mrs. Travail mentions that Annie had spoken kindly of her boss, a considerate man who had once sent her a dozen roses when she was sick.

Before the liquor store, she worked in sales for a furniture dealer.

The personnel manager at the furniture store recalled Annie as capable and well liked; he was disappointed when she quit. But he understood; she'd received a job offer at a much higher salary.

Columbo finds ex-husband Theodore Boone at his studio, photographing a sassy model in leopard skin. Theodore describes his marriage as the happiest five years, two months, and 11 days of his life. He still doesn't know why Annie wanted a divorce—only that he wasn't enough for her. With all her talent, he can't understand why she would sell furniture or liquor. He partially blames Annie's jealous mother for their breakup. Theodore wants his daughter back and thinks the court will grant his wish now that Annie's dead. The last he heard from Annie, she'd mentioned receiving a threatening letter in the mail. She had been frightened and wanted to talk about it, but they never got the chance.

Theodore's lawyer confirms that his client has been trying for the last year to get his daughter back. He officially filed papers the day after Annie was killed. They had earlier been trying to get Monica back by arguing that Annie was an unfit mother because she had become an alcoholic.

Columbo calls on one of Annie's girlfriends, who denies that Annie was a drunk. The woman reports that Annie was dating several men casually, but the one she was sleeping with was her boss, Mr. Phelps.

At Phelps' mansion, Columbo meets Mrs. Phelps, an attractive woman in her 40s. She admits knowing her husband was having an affair, but she didn't want to make a ruckus and risk losing him. This wasn't his first dalliance, so she was confident Franklin would soon tire of Annie. From several days before the murder until several days after, Mrs. Phelps says she was out of the state and—the evening of the killing—was at an all-night party, where she was seen by numerous other guests.

Columbo then speaks privately with her husband, who grudgingly confesses that he was in love with Annie. Phelps has an ironclad alibi for the time of the murder: he had spent the night with yet another woman.

The Lieutenant tracks down Frank Abelson at the pool hall. He describes Annie as lots of fun, and skilled at both shooting pool and distracting other patrons with her short skirts.

At the bank, the proper Arthur Cordis can't believe Annie ever shot pool. They'd spent their time together at the ballet. Cordis had recently broken off their relationship, because he felt he was getting far more serious about it than she was. In fact, Annie frequently spoke of hanging out at the apartment of a man named Jamie.

Columbo asks Monica about Jamie. The little girl says her mom would visit a Jamison Gray, whom she called "the nicest, saddest man she ever met." Monica also mentions that, earlier in the day, she received a phone call from a mysterious stranger. He was looking for a blue envelope addressed to her mommy.

Columbo locates Jamie Gray—who had hit it off with Annie at a bar a few months ago. She began visiting him about once a week, to talk. He's blind.

In the meantime, the police discover Annie's apartment has been ransacked. Columbo is certain the missing letter is vital. He has the apartment combed. The blue envelope is found, tucked between the pages of a department store brochure. Columbo notices the perforations on the stamp are torn slightly unevenly. The edge lines up perfectly with the jagged end of a roll of stamps sitting on the desk of Mrs. Phelps. The jealous wife had flown back into town just long enough to kill Annie and prevent her from stealing her man.

Killer's Choice was reminiscent of the film noir classic *Laura*, in that everyone the detective interviews knew the victim with a completely different personality. Manheim enjoyed working with Falk to shape the story.

"It wasn't like he was some actor giving you two bits of advice and didn't know what he was talking about. He really knew the character, so you were getting it straight from the horse's mouth," she said. "Part of the reason the meetings went so long is because he really liked telling stories and he was a great raconteur. He would tell stories on himself that were so charming and free of ego."

After about four meetings with Falk, the script fell by the wayside. To this day, Manheim is unsure why, but admits, "I didn't think it was a particularly strong episode. I didn't think there was a lot of heart to it. I don't recall there being an especially personal angle for Columbo in it, so I just figured they must develop two or three for every one they shoot."

It may have been for the best, considering the two McBain novels that Falk did make (1992's *No Time to Die* and 1994's *Undercover*) are among the worst *Columbos* ever made. As for Manheim, she soon found herself as a regular writer on *Xena: Warrior Princess*, contributing to 25 episodes over the series' first five seasons.

Critic's Choice: Murder

Intent on keeping the show fresh and contemporary, Falk began to tweak the successful format. To viewers, like Paul Robert Coyle, the series seemed to be drifting. Coyle had been a successful freelance writer for 20 years, earning credits on *Barnaby Jones, Simon & Simon, Jake and the Fatman*, and other series. He decided to write a spec *Columbo* script that would return to the familiar formula, while breaking some ground—with the series' first African American villain. To play a murderous movie critic, Coyle envisioned James Earl Jones, whom he had written for on the recent 13-episode *Pros and Cons*.

He submitted a 102-page script, *Critic's Choice: Murder*, dated January 21, 1994. Coyle recalled, "My longtime agent, Ivan Green, was about to retire. One of the last things he did was to get the script into the hands of the Universal Studios executive, Charlie Engel, who had worked with Peter Falk since *Columbo* first began in 1968. Mr. Engel warned Ivan; he had never passed a script on to Falk before. He recommended mine. Peter liked it, and next thing I knew I was on my way to meet with Lieutenant No-First-Name Columbo himself."

At 50, African American movie critic Arthur Paul Kincaid is imposing and authoritative. His opinions are his livelihood. He delivers his *Two Cents' Worth* on the national news and syndicated to 200 newspapers. Tonight, he's to present the Best Director Award at the West Coast Critics Association's annual dinner at the Beverly Hilton.

As he leaves the TV studio, Kincaid steps into his gleaming Rolls-Royce Corniche and calls his secretary from his car phone. She informs him that Ariane Watkins asked that he call her before he goes to the awards dinner. He can reach her at the home of hotshot filmmaker Jace Lundy. Ariane used to be Kincaid's girl, so she wants to warn him that she'll be attending the ceremony with Lundy. "Jace feels badly about this… estrangement, or whatever you'd call it between you two," she says. "You know how grateful he is to you. If not for your early encouragement—"

Kincaid interrupts her, but Ariane knows it will be uncomfortable for him, especially if Lundy wins, since Kincaid was about the only critic who didn't love his nominated film.

Lundy does, in fact, win and uses his acceptance speech to not only praise Kincaid for his early mentorship, but also to take a few jabs.

Kincaid returns to his house. It's dark and lonely, filled with framed mementoes and lots of photos of Ariane. One picture on his desk depicts the three of them—although in it Ariane is looking past Kincaid, at Jace. Seeing the picture sours Kincaid; he slams it down on the desk, smashing the glass.

The next afternoon, Kincaid is to meet Lundy at a trendy Beverly Hills eatery for lunch. When Kincaid arrives, Lundy is sitting at a booth, besieged by well-wishers. Kincaid wonders why he isn't displaying the award statuette at his table. Lundy explains it still has to be inscribed. Kincaid asks sarcastically if he wants him to personally deliver the prize when it's done. Lundy says Kincaid misunderstands him; everything he has is because of him. "Speaking of everything you have, it's a shame Ariane couldn't join us," Kincaid retorts.

Lundy says he feared that if he'd invited her, Kincaid wouldn't have shown. He wants to make a peace offering and give him a big scoop for his next column. His next film will be *Days of Rage*, made from a script about the Black Panthers that Kincaid gave him when he was a film student at USC. Kincaid is shocked; he showed him that screenplay only as an example of proper formatting.

"It was a great story then. It's a great story now," Lundy insists. "Only difference is, now I have the clout to get it made."

Kincaid's upset. He says the story is dated; nobody's interested in the '60s anymore. And he doesn't believe Lundy has a feel for the material. Jace has already made up his mind. The author died in prison two years ago, and Lundy purchased the rights. And, best of all, he's casting Ariane as the privileged student-turned-radical girlfriend. Kincaid has heard enough. He storms out.

The next night, the weekly poker game at Lundy's bungalow office is just getting underway, when a figure outside slips a folded sheet of paper under Jace's windshield wiper.

Soon after, Kincaid arrives at a studio screening room, a few hours before a big preview. He walks to the front of the deserted theater and opens a door, to the right of the screen, marked "EXIT." Through the door is a short corridor, illuminated by a single overhead bulb. Kincaid wraps a handkerchief around his hand, reaches up, and carefully unscrews the hot, burning bulb. He leaves the darkened bulb hanging loosely in the socket, and disappears into the alley.

Later that night, Kincaid returns to the screening room shortly before the preview starts. He goes out of his way to greet several other famous critics in the lobby, then enters the theater just as the houselights dim, allowing him to slip out in darkness, just before the screen lights up. Once inside the corridor, Kincaid reaches up and screws the lightbulb back in, then departs through the alley door.

Meanwhile, Lundy's poker game is winding down. As he walks his guests out to their cars, he notices the note under his wiper. He reads it and is bummed. He jumps in his car and drives off. On his car phone, he calls Ariane to say he'll be home shortly, after a quick stop. He explains that he found a note from a studio employee about a projection problem last night at the Sunset 5 theater during a showing of his award-winning movie. "The theater's close by—won't take 10 minutes," he says.

At the theater, Lundy talks to the manager and the projectionist, but they insist they haven't had any problems or complaints with his movie. Confused, Lundy is making his way down a back stairwell from the projection booth when Kincaid emerges from an alcove—wearing a jogging suit, hood and gloves. He cracks Lundy over the head with a tire iron. After confirming Lundy is dead, Kincaid searches his victim's pockets, rips off his Rolex, and snatches his jewelry, wallet and keyring. He checks inside Lundy's jacket pocket and finds the folded letter. He drops Lundy's keys and flees.

Back at the screening, Kincaid emerges from the men's room just as the film ends. He spots another critic and tells her he just about made it through the movie, recounting several plot points "in vivid detail of a movie we know he didn't sit through."

Later that same night, the police are called to investigate Lundy's murder. They find his wallet two blocks away, emptied of cash and credit cards. There are no prints on the weapon. The theater manager tells Columbo about Lundy's note, but no one can find it. Ariane arrives at the scene, distraught over the apparent fatal robbery of her lover.

The next morning, Kincaid arrives at Lundy's house to deliver the award. He tries to console Ariane, reiterating he's still there for her, whatever she needs. He then notices Columbo is present. Since Columbo had dropped off Lundy's car, he asks Kincaid for a ride back to the theater.

The next day, Columbo catches up with Kincaid just as the critic is finishing up a lecture at UCLA's Royce Hall. The Lieutenant suspects that, since Lundy was last seen by his poker buddies and then called Ariane, the note must have been left on his windshield during the card game. Lundy undoubtedly was lured to that particular theater under false pretenses. Columbo also reports that a security camera at the record store across from the theater caught part of the murder. The tape didn't capture the killer's face, but it does show him taking the note and discarding the car keys. Kincaid says that during the attack he was at an advance screening, where he was seen by numerous colleagues.

Columbo calls on another critic—a Liz Smith-type gossip columnist, who mistakes him as trying to sell a hot tip. She confirms that Kincaid recapped the

THE VOICE of Darth Vader, James Earl Jones, would have made the perfect killer in *Critic's Choice: Murder*. A few years earlier, he had starred in the TV series *Gabriel's Fire* (*above*), which was retooled into *Pros and Cons*. *[Credit: ABC]*

movie afterwards—which was unusual, since he typically saved his opinions for his reviews. She didn't see where he sat; he disappeared into the darkness toward the front of the theater. Columbo's surprised, since he personally hates sitting close to the screen. The critic confirms Kincaid usually does sit in the middle.

Columbo then visits a memorial gathering at Jace's house. He asks Ariane if he can read the script for Lundy's planned next movie, *Days of Rage*, a fictionalized account of incidents from a black screenwriter's life, fighting—

sometimes violently—for civil rights. Kincaid is disturbed to see Columbo get a copy of the script. Kincaid then goes to the bar to see if Ariane will need a ride home later, since she left her car at the funeral parlor. Annoyed at his persistence, she rejects him forcefully and walks off. He smiles… because he got what he wanted—in her haste, she inadvertently left her purse behind. He opens it, slips out her car keys, finishes his glass of wine, and exits.

Kincaid goes to Ariane's car, wearing gloves and carrying a small paper bag. He opens the trunk and from the bag dumps out Lundy's Rolex and jewelry. Leaving the trunk open, he gets into the car, starts the engine, and backs out slowly—right into the side of another car. He shifts Ariane's car into neutral, removes the key, and heads back to the party, to redeposit the keys into her purse.

That evening, Kincaid settles into his theater seat for another screening when, just as the lights go down, Columbo appears. He tries to question Kincaid, but is repeatedly shushed by others in the audience. Columbo and Kincaid head to the lobby, so the Lieutenant can share his findings. It appears that Ariane's car was left in neutral, rolled backwards, and struck another car. The impact popped open her trunk, exposing the stolen goods. Columbo is confused since, by all accounts, Ariane loved Lundy and was about to star in his next movie. No, Kincaid says. Lundy told him at lunch that he was having second thoughts about giving her the part.

But Columbo had heard that, without Lundy, the movie would never get made. "Seems like a funny time to want to kill him—months before the movie went into production," Columbo ponders. "Plenty of time for him to change his mind again…" Kincaid says Ariane always acted impulsively.

The critic presumes she's been arrested; however, Columbo thinks she's innocent. He suspects someone at the memorial service swiped her car keys and planted the valuables. Plus, the tire iron was still in her trunk. If Ariane had murdered impulsively, why would she use someone else's tire iron? And luring Jace to the theater with a note certainly wasn't impulsive. Columbo asks to read Kincaid's review of the movie from the night of the screening.

The next day at police headquarters, Columbo is engrossed in reading the script for *Days of Rage*. Seeing the film script, another officer mentions he recently attended a sneak preview of another movie. The anecdote gets Columbo thinking.

He visits an ex-con, the cellmate to the screenwriter of *Days of Rage*. Columbo wants to know more about such a talented writer. The parolee laughs.

The next evening, as Kincaid drives to another screening, his car phone rings. His secretary alerts him that the location of tonight's preview has been changed... to the screening room he'd said he was at the night of Lundy's murder. When Kincaid arrives, he sees no cars. The theater looks deserted. He asks a custodian sweeping the carpet where the screening is. She shrugs. Columbo appears, claiming, "I know how you did it, sir. And I can prove it."

Columbo has figured out that the deceased inmate didn't write *Days of Rage*; he had a third-grade education. He could barely read or write. He must have been paid to be a front for the real author... Kincaid, hiding his violent past. Kincaid reluctantly admits he indeed wrote the script, but notes the statute of limitations on crimes he committed in his youth expired a long time ago. And that's no proof of murder.

But Columbo can prove Kincaid left the theater on the night of the murder. He notes that a scene he described in his review wasn't in the film shown that night. It was deleted after an earlier sneak preview that Kincaid must have attended. Plus, he found Kincaid's fingerprints on the lightbulb beyond the EXIT. Kincaid had handled the bulb with a handkerchief when loosening it, but not when retightening it.

Coyle's script was certainly a return to the traditional *Columbo* format, with an unexpected twist. We assume Kincaid killed out of jealousy, to get his old girlfriend back, only to learn that he's all too happy to frame her to hide his past. Several scenes even echo previous episodes (the tire iron killing in a parking garage from *A Stitch in Crime*, the projection booth murder in *Double Exposure*, and the pompous, villainous critic of *Murder Under Glass*).

Falk was anxious to discuss the script. He asked Coyle to meet him at his home in Beverly Hills, but—as Coyle pointed out—"not in the house, but in a side cottage that he used as an artist's studio. His hobby was sketching the human form, and we were surrounded by easels and charcoal or pen-and-ink drawings of his favorite subject, the nude female form. It was like kicking it with Hef at the Playboy Mansion. Peter didn't dress sloppily like his TV character; he always wore expensive shirts and slacks. His mannerisms, though, were familiar. Columbo was endearingly chummy and rambling (but his ramblings always disguised a sharp detective's mind). Peter was charming and amusing, and my impression was that as a writer and executive producer he was... a very good actor."

Falk would say, "This is good, Paul... I really like this... there are, I don't know, a few problems... I can't quite put my finger on what they are... let's talk it through. I really want to do this... I'm wide open. Let's put our heads together and we'll figure something out..."

Falk liked Coyle's idea of casting James Earl Jones as the critic, though they had no idea if he would say yes.

Falk and Coyle's first meeting rambled on for several hours. So did the next one. They also had a series of phone calls, each lasting about an hour. "Just call the office whenever you have a thought," Falk urged. "My assistant will put you through to me, wherever I am."

During their meetings, Falk always had a copy of Mark Dawidziak's book *The Columbo Phile* close at hand, so he could easily reference what the show had done before.

Coyle kept reworking the story to try to solve Falk's vague concerns. According to Coyle, "He couldn't quite articulate what problems he had. Just that, after all these years, he was looking to tweak the familiar formula. Exactly how, he couldn't put his finger on. I made many suggestions and, in fact, rewrote the whole thing in outline form. Peter kept promising to call the studio and authorize a deal, but it never happened."

After several weeks of consultations and rewrites, Coyle still hadn't been offered a contract. His agent had retired, so he couldn't ask him to call Business Affairs. Each time he brought up the issue, Falk would reply, "Oh, that's right. I'll take care of it. About the script, just one more thing…"

The Writers Guild has a two-meeting rule, and a phone call can constitute a "meeting." After that, if work continues, a writer is due payment. Falk held the title of executive producer, but he wasn't acting in a professional manner. His predecessors all knew how to analyze a script, isolate problem areas, and suggest solutions. He did not.

"I was beginning to feel like one of *Columbo*'s murderers—this guy was slowly driving me nuts!" Coyle recalled. "I liked Peter personally, but enough was enough. I wasn't doing anymore free rewrites. I could have gotten the Guild involved, and demanded payment. I *should* have. But I let it go."

9
The Final Specials (1997-2003)
Petering Out

Résumés didn't impress Peter Falk. If he trusted someone and liked their work, he didn't care what they'd done before. And as executive producer, Falk was in charge of compiling his own team. Jack Horger had been a longtime editor on the Universal lot, where he worked on three straight series with Peter Fischer. Horger recalled, "I was getting a little bored with hour episodic and I heard a rumor that Peter Falk was going to start another two-hour *Columbo*. I wandered over to his office, knocked on his door, went in, and said, 'You don't know me, but I'd like to put my hat in the ring for cutting it.' He said, 'I'm sorry. I got an editor. He's done the last eight years with me.' 'I totally understand. Thank you for your time.' That's how I got my jobs.

"As I was heading out the door, he said, 'One more thing…' I turned around. '…would you like to produce it?' This doesn't happen. I just stared at him in disbelief. He could read it on my face. He continued, 'I've got an editor, but I don't got a producer.' 'You know I've never done that before.' 'That don't matter to me. We'll learn together.' I could not believe it."

The same attitude extended to scripts. Falk didn't care who wrote it, if he liked it. A few years earlier, he'd personally greenlit a spec script by three unknowns, among them his personal assistant, April Raynell. It became *Caution: Murder Can Be Hazardous to Your Health* (1991).

Murder by Suicide

Meanwhile, another neophyte in Boston, Frank D'Angeli, called the *Columbo* Production Office seeking to submit his own script. Raynell "read him the riot act." Under no circumstances would the show look at a script from the outside. Crestfallen, D'Angeli put the script in a drawer.

Four years later, as a Christmas gift, D'Angeli's wife gave him a book called *How to Sell Your Screenplay in Hollywood*. The book encouraged writers to find a "champion" for their script. D'Angeli contacted Ted Kerin and Stephen Burns at The Ultimate *Columbo* Site. These webmasters said that, if D'Angeli sent them his script, they'd read it and, if they liked it, they'd forward it to a contact at the *Columbo* Production Office.

Sometime later, D'Angeli received a call from Francesca Redwine, former script reader for Season 8 producer Stanley Kallis and Raynell's successor as aide to Falk. Redwine loved his script and said she would forward it to Rob Levine, one of two executives brought in to help Falk identify and develop stories. Levine liked it, too, but thought D'Angeli was "overplaying the Columbo schtick." However, Levine gave it to Falk, who considered the clues solid and the story to have "integrity, consistency and holds together." Falk began going through the script, page by page, word by word, making notes in bullet points on a yellow legal pad. He was primarily concerned with the plausibility of clues—like how many pills would someone swallow if they were trying to kill themselves?

Redwine kept D'Angeli in the loop with regular emails. Falk felt the script was about 20 pages too long, a sentiment Redwine passed along to D'Angeli. Impulsively, D'Angeli trimmed 20 pages and FedExed his revised screenplay to Falk. The next morning, Falk opened the package and became furious. He wanted to know why there was a new version. Redwine explained, "Oh, the writer shortened the script for you." Falk threw the stack of pages against the wall. "Things are moving too fast!"

Nonetheless, about six months later, on December 17, 1998, Falk gave the go-ahead for the studio to purchase *Murder by Suicide*—now trimmed to 94 pages—for $15,000.

Beverly Hills socialite Victoria Ludman is suffering from a terminal disease. Her gold-digging, philandering husband, Walter Jansen, has assumed the reins of the investment group that bears her name, but he has wielded that power for personal gain, spending lavishly and doctoring the books. As a well-known philanthropist, Victoria is heartsick that Walter is tarnishing her company's reputation. With only a short time to live, she is determined that Walter will not profit from her passing.

Walter arrives home to discover his wife has ingested an overdose of pain pills. Victoria tells him he is a beaten man. She has willed her assets to charity, and the mega-million-dollar insurance policy Walter took out on her life will not be paid in the case of suicide. Victoria then collapses. Walter ponders how he can mask the cause of Victoria's death. He grabs her medication bottle, counts the pills inside, and checks the label. There are only three pills missing from the bottle. Hmm, his plan might work.

Walter loads Victoria's body into one of his five automobiles, after carefully planting her fingerprints on the doorhandle and the seatbelt latch. He then drives down a deserted stretch of road and intentionally slams into a tree, triggering the airbags. Once the airbags deflate, Walter lowers Victoria's headrest and forcefully snaps her neck backwards. He then uses a cellphone to call for help.

At the behest of the Commissioner, Columbo visits the scene of the accident. Walter states that he and Victoria were headed for the hospital; she was in extreme pain, and additional painkillers didn't help. Walter chose a remote route to avoid traffic. He saw a green light ahead, so he sped up the car. Suddenly, Victoria screamed that a small animal darted onto the road. He swerved into a tree and caused the death of his wife.

Columbo expresses his condolences. Yet the Lieutenant is immediately suspicious. Why did Walter change cars? Walter explains that his BMW was low on gas; he selected the Lexus because Victoria had never ridden in it before and thought she might enjoy it.

At first glance, the medical examiner suspects Victoria may have taken a whole lot more than three pills. So, Columbo visits a drugstore and asks the clerk if he can speak with the pharmacist. The clerk offers to help, but Columbo explains, "It's of a sensitive nature and I think that I would really like to talk to—"

"Laxatives are down that aisle right there, sir," she interjects.

Columbo finally is directed to the elderly druggist, who shares that he filled Ms. Ludman's prescription two days ago. Her habit was to refill it when she had about two weeks of pills remaining.

Later, Columbo goes to the car dealership where Walter purchased the Lexus. News of the accident surprises the salesman, since that model is one of the safest cars on the road. He points out the vehicle's myriad safety features, such as ABS brakes, a mobile phone in case of emergency, adjustable headrests to prevent whiplash, and both driver- and passenger-side airbags. The clerk deduces that if the airbag gave her whiplash, her headrest must have been set too low.

The salesman explains how airbags work: if you hit something while traveling faster than eight miles per hour, sensors in the car trigger an explosive powder inside the bags. The bags will inflate almost instantly to hopefully prevent serious injury. They remain inflated for a few seconds in case of another impact, then the gas dissipates and the bag deflates.

Columbo now confronts Walter to tell him his wife's neck wasn't broken in the accident. He thinks Walter did it, and he can prove it. They drive to the scene of the crash. Columbo points out the streetlight, which is controlled by computers to keep the cross traffic moving. There are pressure-sensitive plates under the road just before the intersection. "You told me last night that you had a green light as you approached this spot," Columbo recounts. "You said that is why you were going so fast just a few feet after the intersection. I knew you were lying, sir. I knew that the only way you would've had a green light was if another car had been in front of you, and you told me yourself that there were no other cars in the area."

Walter scoffs. He says he'd lied about a green light to avoid a traffic ticket. "If your proof of me committing some kind of crime rested on this, then you should be committed for impersonating an officer," he retorts.

But Columbo has more. Victoria couldn't have seen an animal dart in front of the car; she'd left her glasses at home. The medical examiner confirmed she'd taken *40* extra pills. No one who took 40-plus painkillers would be able to walk to a car, let alone buckle themselves in. Her fingerprints were on the doorhandle and seatbelt buckle but, if she had latched them herself, her prints would have been smudged. "The prints we found were pristine."

Walter switched to the only car he owned with an adjustable headrest. He must have broken his wife's neck, because police discovered a clump of Victoria's hair on the rear passenger seat and floor, hair with fresh follicles still attached—hair that must have been forcibly pulled from her head. They also found hair *under* the headrest, so the rest must have been lowered after she was seated.

Columbo admits that, because Victoria took so many pills, it's possible she was dead by the time Walter broke her neck. There is a slight chance she was alive, but all the tests have been inconclusive. "If she was, then that's murder, sir."

Walter realizes that if Victoria was dead when he found her, the only charges

MURDER BY SUICIDE screenwriter Frank D'Angeli envisioned *Star Trek: The Next Generation's* second-in-command officer, Jonathan Frakes, as the murderous husband. Frakes had recently completed *Star Trek: First Contact* (1996). *[Credit: Paramount]*

he could conceivably face were reckless driving and, perhaps, mutilation of a corpse. "And with the right lawyer," he smiles, "that person would have the charges tossed out before you even had a chance to finish the paperwork."

Walter has a sudden epiphany. He remembers that, yes, Victoria was dead when he put her in the car.

Back at police headquarters, Columbo is exasperated that the medical examiner cannot prove whether Victoria died from the pills or the broken neck. He dejectedly arrives in the squad room in time for his 40-years-of-service party. He lights up a congratulatory cigar, to the dismay of several colleagues. Just then, the key to solving the crime hits him.

The next morning, Columbo, Walter and two policemen visit an auto repair shop. A technician is preparing to set off the airbags of a car that is going to be junked. Columbo instructs everyone to pay special attention as the bags fill with explosive powder. He explains that when he was smoking in the precinct, others in the room couldn't help but breathe his smoke. If Victoria was alive after the accident but before Walter broke her neck, she would have inhaled the airbag's powder. Columbo pulls out the results of a test he'd requested from the coroner. "High levels of potassium nitrate and sodium azide. She was alive."

Columbo has beaten the man who mocked him mercilessly. An officer approaches Walter to handcuff him. "Hold on a second, officer," says Columbo, pulling out his own pair of cuffs. "This one, I'll do myself."

Sensing the series was nearing its end, D'Angeli suggested that, if Falk chose to make *Murder by Suicide* his swan song, the 40-year-anniversary party could easily be changed to a retirement party. Then the closing image of Columbo uncharacteristically requesting to cuff his last arrest would add a touch of finality to the show and the character.

For the part of the murderer, D'Angeli envisioned Jonathan Frakes (Commander Riker of *Star Trek: The Next Generation*), convinced that the actor could play "a cold-blooded SOB who busted Columbo's chops the whole episode." D'Angeli had patterned the character after the villain in one of his favorite episodes, *An Exercise in Fatality*'s Milo Janus, the ruthless narcissist played by Robert Conrad and one of the few adversaries Columbo genuinely abhorred. Similarly, D'Angeli said, "Walter and Columbo are going to hate each other. And that's why, at the end, Columbo wants to put the cuffs on him himself."

Once D'Angeli sold the script, he immediately went to work on a second *Columbo*—a follow-up to *Now You See Him*. His sequel, called *Now You See Him, Now You Don't*, was to have David Cassidy play the Great Santini's son, who's seeking revenge for Columbo years earlier having put away his father, who had been played by David's real-life father, Jack Cassidy.

D'Angeli also co-authored a science fiction screenplay called *Stranded*. Levine invited D'Angeli to the studio for a private tour and to discuss his new script. During his visit, the group stopped to take a photo next to Columbo's Peugeot. "It was here," D'Angeli recalled, "he gave me the bad news. Though Peter was executive producer, ABC was mad he paid a nobody for a script, and they refused to let him produce it. I was crushed. I like Rob Levine a lot,

COINCIDENTALLY, screenwriter Frank D'Angeli got up close and personal with Columbo's Peugeot, on display at Universal Studios, just before learning his script would not be used. Note the backup Peugeot in the background. *[Credit: Frank D'Angeli]*

so I figured that was exactly what happened, or he was softening the blow for me, regarding why it wouldn't be produced."

It probably didn't help that ABC was beginning to sour on *Columbo*. Right before purchasing *Murder by Suicide*, Falk had them buy another script by a neophyte, *Murder with Too Many Notes*, which was filmed but sat on the shelf for over two years before it aired.

D'Angeli's screenwriting career was also put on the shelf. *Stranded* was optioned by three producers, but never made. Instead, D'Angeli adapted it into a novel (under the pseudonym Douglas Wentworth), and the book won the IPPY Gold Medal in Science Fiction.

Hear No Evil/ Columbo's Last Case

Working again with Patrick McGoohan in 1998 on *Ashes to Ashes* and *Murder with Too Many Notes* reinvigorated Falk. He was excited to get going on the next one.

Nancy Meyer, Falk's other development executive alongside Rob Levine, brought in Barry Glasser, a one-time studio marketing executive who had created several animated series, and Mark Bruce Rosin, a former magazine editor, studio story editor and author (including of 1987's bestseller *Stepfathering*). The two writers delivered a powerhouse pitch for a "classic *Columbo*" and received an immediate green light to develop it into a full script. They submitted *Hear No Evil* on August 19, 1998.

Celebrity exposé author Nina St. Clair is keynoting the annual Penelope Ambrose Memorial Writers Conference, held at the spacious Santa Barbara compound of the late queen of historical romance novels. Nina got her start as Penelope's research assistant. During the event, Nina brushes off Lauren Chesley, a young journalist who wears hearing aids and seems overly sensitive to sound.

Nina's publisher, Geoff, is also her ex-husband. He reports that Lauren has been asking uncomfortable questions about Nina's past. So Nina lifts Lauren's notebook from her purse, just long enough for a peek inside.

The next morning, Nina stakes out Lauren's house while the cleaning woman is finishing up. Nina phones and, disguising her voice as Lauren's, instructs the maid to leave a key under the doormat for the cableman. Nina then lets herself in, where she discovers that Lauren is writing a tell-all book about her. She also notices vial after vial of medication, a telephone equipped with an amplifier, and a copy of the novel *De Montesquieu's Revenge* by Ambrose and St. Clair. Nina promptly visits an electronics shop to purchase an audio generator, a tiny device for testing sound equipment.

That night, using an 800 phonecard, Nina calls Lauren, pretending to be a publisher interested in hiring her. She promises to call back the following evening between 6 and 7. During that hour, Nina is in Washington, D.C., being interviewed by Larry King. During a commercial break, Nina rushes down the hall, past a vending machine, to a payphone. Before Lauren can pick up, her answering machine begins recording. Nina hangs up. She calls back seconds later and whispers, so Lauren will turn up the volume on her phone's amplifier. Nina then holds the audio generator and a mini speaker against the mouthpiece of the receiver, and cranks it up. The piercing noise shocks Lauren, who slumps to the floor, clutching the phone.

Nina returns to Larry King. After the interview, she realizes she had left an earring near the payphone. Nina returns to Los Angeles by private charter and heads straight for Lauren's house, where her victim lies dead on the floor. Nina removes the phone from her hand, wipes off the blood, and instead slides a hairbrush into her stiffened fingers. Nina rewinds the answering machine, deletes any mention of her from the computer, and snatches Lauren's notes and copy of *De Montesquieu's Revenge*.

Investigating the next morning, Columbo is perplexed. Why was Lauren clutching her dog's brush? Why would a deaf woman have the volume so low on her TV? Why would she leave a key for the cable guy, when she had a satellite dish? And what happened to the romance novel the maid remembers seeing on the desk?

Lauren's appointment book leads Columbo to Geoff, who volunteers that last night was the first he'd spent with Nina since their divorce. She suggested the sleepover, in exchange for flying to and from D.C. on his company's jet.

The clues pile up. The coroner determines Lauren died from a stroke, possibly triggered by a stress reaction to something she'd heard or seen. The recording of Nina's hang-up call was found to contain a split-second metallic thud. Forensics finds traces of Lauren's blood on her phone receiver. Columbo is introduced to audio generators at a counterspy shop. In reviewing the tape of what Lauren was watching when she died—*Larry King Live* with guest Nina St. Clair—Columbo notices Nina's earring disappears after a commercial break.

So, the Lieutenant heads to Washington, D.C., to ask Larry about Nina and her earring. Seated on the talk show's iconic set, Columbo's questioning of Larry soon turns into Larry's interview of Columbo—asking about his raincoat and all the famous people he's met. Afterwards, walking to the payphone, Columbo passes the vending machine, just as a soda drops with a metallic thud.

A receipt found at Lauren's house leads Columbo to an antique bookshop in Laguna Beach. The bookseller remembers Lauren hoped to purchase his 200-year-old French encyclopedia of crime. Rebuffed, she instead sat at his desk taking notes from the tome. Twelve years ago, the bookseller had owned a second copy, but his records show it was bought by a "Penelope Ambrose" and picked up by one "Nina St. Clair."

Columbo visits Penelope's longtime caretaker and confidante. Mrs. Anderson shares that Nina spent 10 years as Penelope's researcher, but longed to be a writer. She finally got the chance. After her mentor passed, Nina completed her final novel. Mrs. Anderson never saw any French encyclopedia. Columbo takes note of Penelope's expansive perfume collection and her apiary where a beekeeper cultivates "Ambrose Private Label Honey."

Columbo has Geoff persuade Nina to visit the Ambrose house. Before Nina can escape, Mrs. Anderson insists she take a jar of honey. Walking to the apiary, the woman recalls how, on the day she was stung to death by bees, Penelope was wearing perfume that had been given to her by Nina. Mrs. Anderson has brought along the original atomizer and furiously begins spraying Nina. Nina freaks out, as the hooded beekeeper walks closer and closer, surrounded by a massive swarm.

The beekeeper removes his hood—it's Columbo. The French encyclopedia supplied Nina with not just material to use in the novel, but also a method with which to murder Penelope. Madame de Montesquieu killed a rival by doctoring her perfume with a tropical oil that incited bees—similar to the substance Columbo detected in Penelope's atomizer… and since replaced with colored water.

Hear No Evil was simply one of the strongest scripts the team had ever seen. Briskly paced and intricately plotted, it was a perfect mixture of new (fresh ingenious clues, a one-of-a-kind murder) and old (Columbo is accompanied by Sgt. Degarmo and notes Mrs. Columbo is a big fan of Nina's books). The story even feels like an early-years *Columbo* without being repetitive (the opening recalls Abigail Mitchell's writers conference in *Try and Catch Me,* video capturing the missing earring evokes the disappearing carnation in *Étude in Black,* and the murderer's freakout finale is reminiscent of Roddy McDowall's crackup in the aerial tram at the end of *Short Fuse*). There are even direct callbacks to *Ashes to Ashes* (Columbo telling Larry King he recently nabbed the Mortician of the Year) and *Columbo Goes to College* (Nina praising the Lieutenant's solving of the similarly high-tech crime).

Screenwriter Glasser was expecting a request for changes, but none came. "They were very high on it," he said. "That's one thing I heard that I'd never heard before in my entire career as a writer: we were told they had no notes on that script and were ready to go on it."

Falk absolutely adored the script, particularly the exchange with Larry King, and began playing with the dialogue in that scene to get the tone just right. Meyer did have Glasser and Rosin slightly "prune" the script, condensing it from 105 to 103 pages. They also wrote an alternate "last speech" for Nina, to give Falk options. In the original ending, Nina tells Columbo he would have made a great subject for a book, and Columbo—while cuffing her himself—says so would she. It's a shame Lauren Chesley won't get the chance to write it. In ending number two, a defiant Nina vows that her next book—about her own case—will be her biggest seller yet.

Falk wanted to make sure that the script's treatment of hives and bee swarms was plausible, so Meyer showed him a recent Fox made-for-TV movie about deadly bee invasions. She also researched bee-rental companies and emailed Kim Flottum, the longtime editor of *Bee Culture* magazine to estimate how many bees she'd need to simulate a sufficiently menacing swarm.

Flottum responded: "A swarm can be huge in volume, but not very dense in bees. Conversely, it can be small in size and very dense in bees. You would probably do better with closeups. Older 'killer bee' movies did some very unnatural biological stunts (throwing buckets of bees) into a scene to simulate scary parts, but they looked fake. I suggest you get a good beekeeper (bee wrangler) to set up a situation wherein a large artificial swarm is located in a spot. Then, move the queen in a small cage from the swarm to a location 20 to 30 yards away. The bees in the swarm will locate her by scent, and begin flying toward her. A dark background (trees, a dark building) and proper lighting would show the bees well—and scare hell out of most people watching (and probably most people acting).

"You can make the artificial swarm fairly large (10 pounds of bees is about enough to fill a bushel basket) with little problem in control, so you will have lots and lots of bees in the air when you need them."

Just in case, production made sure to budget an extra $15,000 to add computer-generated bees.

It was expected that the same behind-the-scenes crew as *Murder with Too Many Notes*, then in the middle of post-production, would return. Falk would remain executive producer, with Chris Seiter as line producer, Jack Horger as co-producer, Bruce Gorman as associate producer, and Patrick McGoohan as co-executive producer. But after wrapping *Too Many Notes*, McGoohan bowed out. Falk quickly found a worthy replacement. Series co-creator Bill Link agreed to return to the show as co-executive producer. *Hear No Evil*'s $4.5-million budget allotted $732,050 for Falk the actor, $100,000 for Falk the producer, $50,000 for Link, and $200,000 for the guest murderer. If the guest star demanded more, ABC would have to kick in the difference.

Larry King was interested in playing himself, but since he taped half of his shows in Washington, D.C., and the rest in Los Angeles and New York, his scenes would have to be scheduled for when he was in California. He'd be paid $30,000.

The team had originally hoped to film in the spring of 1999, during King's next visit to the West Coast. As planning and negotiations dragged, filming was delayed until the summer after Falk completed a special for Showtime. This would allow *Hear No Evil* to be completed in time to air during

THE TOP CHOICE to play *Hear No Evil's* murderer, Nina St. Clair, was *Murphy Brown* star Candice Bergen *(left)*. When the opportunity to do Columbo stalled, Bergen signed on to play the villain in *Miss Congeniality* (2000) with Sandra Bullock. *[Credit: Warner Bros.]*

November sweeps week.

The production team, studio and network all wanted Candice Bergen to play Nina St. Clair. Bergen had just finished her tenth and presumably final season of *Murphy Brown*. Everyone was on board to make her an offer—everyone, that is, except for Falk. He wanted the role to go to his wife, Shera Danese. Shera had already appeared in six *Columbos*, rising from a small role in 1976's *Fade In to Murder* to co-murderer in 1997's *A Trace of Murder*. ABC was adamant they secure a higher-profile actress. Falk dug in his heels. The project began to drift.

Urgency to shoot the episode picked back up in November of 1999. Assuming the casting stalemate would be resolved, ABC was anxious to

PETER FALK campaigned for his wife, Shera Danese, to play *Hear No Evil*'s murderer. She was about four years younger than Candice Bergen and had appeared in six *Columbos*, most recently 1997's *A Trace of Murder*. [Credit: NBCUniversal]

proceed. Susan Fudderman at ABC Broadcast Standards & Practices had just two areas of concern. First, after being convinced that a substance resembling bee pheromone could incite bees to sting, she wanted assurance that no one could duplicate bee pheromone based on the "formula" in the script.

Second, Fudderman expressed concern over the detailed description of Lauren's murder. In particular, she wanted to avoid giving "instructions on how to torment the hearing impaired" in describing the use of the audio generator. Two scenes contained details on the use of the device (when Nina buys one at an electronics shop, and when Columbo learns how noise can kill at the counterspy store). Falk suggested having the shop owners explain the way an audio generator works in a different, less scientific way, likening it to how when the right voice attains the right pitch, it can shatter glass. Meyer suggested substituting a made-up word for "audio generator" such as "cybernetic oscillator auricular dynamo" or "electronic oscillator."

ABC and Falk, however, still could not agree on the guest star. "They had their ideas, he had his. It was absolutely a casting impasse," said Glasser, who was surprised to later learn of Falk's hardball tactics with the network. "Peter loved (the script). That's the irony of this. Peter was completely unlike anything Mark and I would have expected. When we walked in there, he was very likable, very low-key, very congenial. He was not a superstar; that was not his persona. He was very comfortable with himself. And he liked our work, so he was comfortable with us. So we had a wonderful working relationship with him; there were no affectations. None. And so the person we worked with was not the person who presented himself to ABC. That's when the superstar showed up, when he dealt with ABC."

Rosin agreed: "I don't know that Peter acted in a way that was arrogant toward ABC, but his attitude of intransigence just stopped (the project). It was heartbreaking for us, because we loved the script. Barry and I are mystery fanatics, and we were both so proud to write a great *Columbo* and to have the network love it so much. It was a dream come true."

Glasser and Rosin would continue writing plays and screenplays as a team and on their own (Rosin writing and producing 2017's *55 Steps*, starring Helena Bonham Carter and Hilary Swank). Glasser later became a teacher and Rosin now devotes much of his time to writing books.

After gathering dust for two-plus years, *Murder with Too Many Notes* finally premiered in 2001, to decent ratings. ABC was receptive to another *Columbo*—but it would have to feature a modern setting and younger characters to appeal to a younger demographic. Set amid the rave music scene, *Columbo Likes the Nightlife* turned out fine, if a bit awkward. The ratings were poor. ABC had little interest in continuing the show.

Yet Falk was determined to go out on his own terms, to give his beloved character a proper send-off. *Hear No Evil* was the best script he had, and it presented a perfect opportunity to present a retrospective of Columbo's career.

First, there are all the callbacks to earlier episodes. In addition, throughout the story, Nina encourages Columbo to write a book about his own adventures. Falk realized the device could tie a perfect bow around 35 years of mysteries. He personally rewrote portions of *Hear No Evil* to stress that the case would be the Lieutenant's last—and even titled his version *Columbo's Last Case*. But no network was interested. Falk was getting up in years and *Columbo* mania had peaked—or so it seemed.

In recent years, *Columbo* has enjoyed a resurgence in popularity. A reboot seems inevitable. The trick would be retaining enough of the format and especially the character to preserve what made the show work. And what better place to start than dusting off the wonderful original scripts that *almost* got made?

Index

55 Steps, 194
7th Voyage of Sinbad, The, 118
A Bird in the Hand..., 163
Adams, Penny, 154
Adventures of Superman, 156
All My Children, 167-168
Amazing Randi, The, 136
Anderson, Bob, 86
Any Old Port in a Storm, 11, 33, 117, 142
Arnold, Danny, 59
Ashes to Ashes, 187, 190
Aykroyd, Dan, 129
B.L. Stryker, 130, 154
Banacek, 48, 131
Banyon, 48
Barnaby Jones, 174
Barney Miller, 59
Benton, Doug, 9-10, 33
Bergen, Candice, 192-193
Berk, Howard, 74, 81, 86, 161-162
Blacke's Magic, 117
Blees, Bob, 102
Blow Out, 47
Bochco, Steven, 9, 19, 74, 156
Bold and the Beautiful, The, 168
Brady Bunch, The, 59
Bride of Frankenstein, The, 143-154
Brooks, Albert, 46
Buchanan, Ian, 167
Burns, Stephen, 182
Butterfly in Shades of Grey, 117, 154
By Dawn's Early Light, 72, 74
Caffrey, Stephen, 167
Cahn, Sammy, 19
Candidate for Crime, 11, 73
Capote, Truman, 34, 44
Carlito's Way, 47
Carrie, 47
Carson, Johnny, 34, 36
Cash, Johnny, 20, 165
Cassidy, David, 186
Cassidy, Jack, 186
Castle Keep, 59
Casualties of War, 47
Caution: Murder Can Be Hazardous to Your Health, 181

Chambers, Everett, 72, 74, 86, 88-89, 102, 117, 129
Chapman, Michael, 46
Chekhov, Anton, 36, 42
Cocks, Jay, 34, 47
Cohen, Larry, 11-14, 18-20, 32-33
Collins, Joan, 166
Columbo and the Murder of a Rock Star, 31-32, 163
Columbo Cries Wolf, 167
Columbo Goes to College, 47, 167, 190
Columbo Goes to the Guillotine, 136
Columbo Likes the Nightlife, 141, 194
Columbo Phile, The, 180
Columbo's Last Case, 187, 195
Conrad, Robert, 91, 186
Conspirators, The, 86
Cool Million, 11
Couch Trip, The, 118, 129
Coyle, Paul Robert, 174, 179-180
Critic's Choice: Murder, 174-180
Culp, Robert, 19
Curtis, Tony, 73
D'Angeli, Frank, 182, 186-187
Dagger of the Mind, 72, 102, 117
Dallas, 166-167
Danese, Shera, 192
Dawidziak, Mark, 180
Days of Our Lives, 168
De Niro, Robert, 34
De Palma, Brian, 33-34, 44, 46-47
De Paul, Gene, 19
Dead as a Duck, 48-59
Dead Weight, 46, 57
Deadly State of Mind, A., 103, 129, 141
Death Do Us Part, 20-32
Death Hits the Jackpot, 136, 162-163
Death Lends a Hand, 141
Dishy, Bob, 72-73
Dostoevsky, Fyodor, 34
Double Exposure, 47, 179
Double Shock, 156
Double Vision, 86, 154-163
Dr. Quinn, Medicine Woman, 168
Dragnet, 118
Dressed to Kill, 47
Driskill, Bill, 71-72, 74, 88, 161

Duel, 34
Dynasty, 166-167
Eddie Capra Mysteries, The, 117
Ellery Queen, 74, 88, 103, 131
Engel, Charlie, 7, 174
Epstein, Jon, 154, 161, 163
Étude in Black, 190
Evans, Linda, 166
Exercise in Fatality, An, 11, 90, 103, 186
Fade In to Murder, 46, 89, 154, 192
Falcon Crest, 166
Falk, Peter, 7-9, 11, 31, 33, 47, 59, 71-73, 81, 86-89, 91, 102-103, 116-117, 128-131, 136, 154-155, 162, 165, 169-170, 173-174, 179-182, 186-188, 190-195
Family Affair, 59
Fiebleman, Peter, 117, 129
Fischer, Peter S., 8, 71-72, 74, 87-88, 103-104, 117, 131, 143-144, 154, 160, 181
Flicker, Theodore J., 48-50, 59
Flottum, Kim, 191
Forgotten Lady, 70-71
Frakes, Jonathan, 185-186
Friend in Deed, A, 103, 160
Fudderman, Susan, 193-194
Gable, Clark, 87
Gabriel's Fire, 177
Gangs of New York, 47
Geller, Uri, 136
General Hospital, 167
Gerson, Philip, 165-168, 170
Get Christie Love!, 74
Gideon Oliver, 130
Gilligan's Island, 59
Gillis, Jackson, 9, 18, 32-33, 74, 131, 155-157, 161, 163-165
Glasser, Barry, 188, 190, 194
Gores, Joe, 143, 145, 154
Gorman, Bruce, 191
Gossett Jr., Lou, 130
Gould, Elliott, 118
Green, Ivan, 174
Greenhouse Jungle, The, 71, 73
Greetings, 34
Griff, 103
Guiding Light, 167
Hackman, Gene, 48
Hamilton, George, 129
Hammett, 143
Hardy Boys, The, 156
Hargrove, Dean, 8-9, 18, 20, 33-34, 46-48, 73
Harryhausen, Ray, 118
Hart, Moss, 117

Have Gun – Will Travel, 118
Hear No Evil, 187-195
Hec Ramsey, 59
Henry, Buck, 48
Hi, Mom!, 34
Horger, Jack, 8, 181, 191
I Dream of Jeannie, 48
In Cold Blood, 34
In Deadly Hate, 104-117
Irving, Richard, 87, 89, 102
It's Alive, 33
Jake and the Fatman, 174
Jeremiah Johnson, 59
Jones, James Earl, 174, 177, 180
Kallis, Stanley, 137, 142, 154, 182
Kaufman, George S., 117
Kaufman, Millard, 137, 141-142
Kerin, Ted, 182
Kibbee, Roland, 9, 18-20, 33-34, 48, 72-73
Killer's Choice, 170-173
King, Larry, 188-191
Klugman, Jack, 102
Knots Landing, 166
Kojak, 143
Kolb, Ken, 86, 117-118, 128-129
Kowalski, Bernie, 86, 89, 137
Lady's Set for Death, The, 144-145
Landau, Martin, 156
Larry King Live, 189
Lassie, 156
Last of the Redcoats, 136-142
Last Salute to the Commodore, 58, 86, 88, 156
Law & Harry McGraw, The, 117
Lesser of Two Evils, The, 117-129
Let's Make a Deal, 141, 146
Levine, Rob, 182, 186, 188
Levinson, Richard, 9-11, 74, 88, 103, 117, 130-131, 143, 155
Link, William, 9-11, 74, 88, 103, 117, 130-131, 143-144, 155-157, 161, 163, 165, 168, 191
Lion in Season, A (see *Roar of the Crowd*)
Little House on the Prairie, 102
Lovely But Lethal, 142
Madigan, 18
Magician, The, 74
Magnum, P.I., 143
Make Me a Perfect Murder, 141
Manheim, Chris, 169-170, 173
Mason, Paul, 49
Matter of Honor, A, 33, 71
Matthau, Walter, 129
May, Elaine, 48, 117
McBain, Ed, 136, 169, 173

McCloud, 74
McCoy, 73
McDowall, Roddy, 190
McGoohan, Patrick, 88, 169-170, 187, 191
McMillan & Wife, 48-49, 59, 74
McShane, Ian, 167
Metzler, Bob, 87-89, 102
Meyer, Nancy, 180, 188, 190-191, 194
Mind Over Mayhem, 19
Miss Congeniality, 192
Mission: Impossible (film), 47
Mission: Impossible (series), 59, 74
Mod Squad, The, 48
Most Crucial Game, The, 19
Mrs. Columbo, 86, 117, 130, 143-144, 154, 167
Mulgrew, Kate, 130
Murder, a Self Portrait, 142
Murder by Suicide, 182-187
Murder by the Book, 11, 20, 116
Murder in Malibu, 32, 161, 167
Murder Network, The, 143-144
Murder Out of Tune, 12-20
Murder Under Glass, 131, 135, 179
Murder with Too Many Notes, 187, 191, 194
Murder, Inc., 11
Murder, She Wrote, 117, 131, 156, 165, 169
Murder, Smoke and Shadows, 136, 154
Murphy Brown, 192
Name of the Game, The, 34
Negative Reaction, 103
Night Gallery, 48
No Time to Die, 136, 173
Now You See Him, 73, 186
Now You See Him, Now You Don't, 186
Old Fashioned Murder, 116-117
Perry Mason, 47, 156, 164-165
Phantom of the Paradise, 44, 47
Philadelphia Story, The, 87
Pine, Les and Tina, 86
Police Story, 137
Prescription: Murder, 87
President's Analyst, The, 48
Presley, Elvis, 48
Pros and Cons, 174, 177
Publish or Perish, 103, 161
Quincy, M.E., 102
Radnitz, Brad, 33, 59, 71
Ransom for a Dead Man, 32
Rayfiel, David, 59
Raynell, April, 181-182
Redwine, Francesca, 8, 182
Remington Steele, 143
Requiem for a Falling Star, 142, 154

Rest in Peace, Mrs. Columbo, 117, 154, 167
Reynolds, Burt, 130
Richard III, 104-105, 108
Rifleman, The, 118
Roar of the Crowd, 74-86, 89, 117
Rockford Files, The, 74
Rogers, Fred, 49-50
Rogers, Will, 50
Rosin, Mark Bruce, 188, 190, 194
Ross, Stanley Ralph, 59
Scarface, 47
Scorsese, Martin, 46-47
Segal, George, 48
Seiter, Chris, 191
Sex and the Married Detective, 32, 136
Shakespeare, William, 36, 104, 117
Shatner, William, 46
Shooting Script, 33-47
Shooting Star, 165-168
Short Fuse, 9, 86, 156, 190
Simmons, Richard Alan, 86, 102, 129-130, 136-137, 141-143, 154-156
Simon & Simon, 174
So Long as You Both Shall Live, 136, 169
Spielberg, Steven, 33, 46, 136
Spin and Marty, 156
Staab, Rebecca, 167
Star Trek: The Next Generation, 185-186
Stevens, Andrew, 167
Stitch in Crime, A, 179
Strange Bedfellows, 117
Streets of San Francisco, The, 48
Stunt Girl, 163-165
Sugar and Spice and Everything Nice, 59-71
Suitable for Framing, 156
Sunset Boulevard, 25, 34
Swan Song, 20, 59, 165
T.J. Hooker, 143
Trace of Murder, A, 192-193
Trials of O'Brien, The, 131
Troubled Waters, 72, 156
Try and Catch Me, 142, 190
Twilight Zone: The Movie, 136
Undercover, 173
Untouchables, The, 47
Van Scoyk, Robert, 131, 135-136, 165, 169
Walters, Barbara, 137
Way We Were, The, 59
Westheimer, Dr. Ruth, 136
Wild Wild West, The, 118
Williams, Paul, 44, 46-47
Wonder Woman, 156
Xena: Warrior Princess, 173

www.ingramcontent.com/pod-product-compliance
Lightning Source LLC
Chambersburg PA
CBHW060523080526
44586CB00012B/594